Treating Chronic Depression with Disciplined Personal Involvement

James P. McCullough, Jr.

Treating Chronic Depression with Disciplined Personal Involvement

Cognitive Behavioral Analysis System
of Psychotherapy (CBASP)

 Springer

James P. McCullough, Jr.
Department of Psychology
Virginia Commonwealth University
Richmond, VA 23284-2018
USA
jmccull@mail2.vcu.edu

Library of Congress Control Number: 2005938502

ISBN-10: 0-387-31065-7   e-ISBN 0-387-31066-5
ISBN-13: 978-0387-31065-7

Printed on acid-free paper.

Printed in the United States of America.   (TB/MUY)

9 8 7 6 5 4 3 2 1

springer.com

To Mike, John, and Kristin—
... through the years, our three children have personally enriched
my life.

Foreword

Chronic depression has only been recognized as a significant clinical problem within the past 10-15 years. It has been neglected in large part because clinicians and researchers tend to focus on acute depressive episodes at the expense of more chronic, low-grade symptoms, and because it has frequently been misdiagnosed (and often dismissed) as a personality disorder.

However, chronic depression is a significant clinical and public health problem. In the recent National Comorbidity Survey Replication, the lifetime prevalence of dysthymic disorder, just one of the several forms that chronic depression can take, was 3.4% in a nationally representative community sample (Kessler et al., 2005). Approximately 30–40% of depressions seen in clinical settings are chronic, and chronic depression is associated with significant impairment in functioning, high health care expenditures, and untold personal suffering (Klein & Santiago, 2003).

Importantly, chronic depressions differ from more classical, episodic major depression in a number of ways. Chronic depressions are more likely to emerge from a background of childhood adversity and abuse, are associated with higher rates of mood disorders in first-degree relatives, and are coupled with greater personality dysfunction and psychiatric comorbidity (Klein & Santiago, 2003). Perhaps most importantly, chronic depression is less likely to respond to antidepressant medications and traditional antidepressant psychotherapies than non-chronic major depression (Stewart et al., 1989; Thase et al., 1994).

In the mid-1970s, Jim McCullough was one of a small group of clinical researchers who recognized the importance of chronic depression and the unmet needs of those suffering from it. He conducted several important studies documenting the course and psychosocial consequences of chronic depression (e.g., McCullough et al., 1988). At the same time, he devoted his clinical practice to patients with chronic depression, and developed a new treatment approach, the Cognitive Behavioral Analysis System of Psychotherapy, or CBASP (McCullough, 1984).

CBASP was the first, and remains the only, approach to psychotherapy that was specifically developed for chronic depression. Jim recognized that the emotional dysregulation, history of adversity and interpersonal difficulties, self-focused rumination, lack of self-efficacy, and pessimism regarding the possibility of change posed significant problems for existing therapies, and called for a more highly structured, skills-oriented and interpersonal approach. The core of CBASP involves teaching patients an approach to social problem-solving that provides them with concrete skills to address the seemingly overwhelming interpersonal problems in their lives. CBASP is a highly structured approach that is grounded in specific problematic interpersonal situations and focuses on achieving tangible, attainable goals (McCullough, 2000).

Jim has demonstrated a remarkable commitment to testing CBASP empirically in methodologically rigorous clinical trials. After developing and refining his approach through a series of careful single subject studies (McCullough, 1991), he and Dr. Martin Keller spearheaded an influential multi-site clinical trial that demonstrated that CBASP was as efficacious as antidepressant medication. Moreover, the combination of CBASP and pharmacotherapy was remarkably effective, producing response rates substantially higher than in any previous study of chronic depression (Keller et al., 2000).

Jim has continued to refine and test CBASP and to disseminate it to the practice community. The present volume comes out of Jim's collaboration with a dedicated group of CBASP therapists at multiple academic medical centers and psychology departments across the country who are currently participating in a National Institute of Mental Health-sponsored study examining the efficacy of CBASP in chronically depressed persons who have not responded to an initial series of medication trials.

One of the aspects of CBASP that has made it unique among cognitive-behavioral therapies is its interpersonal focus, and particularly its emphasis on using the patient-therapist relationship as a therapeutic tool. The present volume further develops this theme, presenting Jim's current thinking on the psychotherapist's disciplined personal involvement role in the therapy. Jim thoughtfully explores the ways in which therapists' contingent personal responses that make their reactions explicit to patients can be used to provide feedback, validate patients' experiences, and foster change. As Jim details, this topic has been neglected in the contemporary psychotherapy literature, but there is a small research literature supporting the utility of careful therapist self-disclosure.

Jim is a skilled and experienced clinician, a respected scientist, a dedicated teacher, a generous colleague, and a champion of persons suffering from chronic depression. His warm and supportive, but straightforward and direct style comes across clearly in his writing. This volume will introduce readers to the latest developments in the CBASP approach, and stimulate thinking about the nature of the therapeutic relationship, and the optimal role and appropriate limits of therapists' personal involvement and self-disclosure in psychotherapy.

References

Keller, M.B., McCullough, J.P., Klein, D.N., Arnow, B., Dunner, D.L., Gelenberg, A.J., Markowitz, J., Nemeroff, C.B., Russell, J.M., Thase, M.E., Trivedi, M.H., & Zajecka, J. (2000). A comparison of Nefazodone, the Cognitive Behavioral Analysis System of

Psychotherapy, and their combination for the treatment of chronic depression. *New England Journal of Medicine, 342,* 1462–1470.

Kessler, R.C., Berglund, P., Demler, O., Jin, R., Merikangas, K.R., & Walters, E. E. (2005). Lifetime prevalence and age-of-onset distributions of DSM-IV disorders in the National Comorbidity Survey Replication. *Archives of General Psychiatry, 62,* 593–602.

Klein, D.N., & Santiago, N. J. (2003). Dysthymia and chronic depression: Introduction, classification, risk factors, and course. *Journal of Clinical Psychology/In Session, 59,* 807–816.

McCullough, J.P. (1984). Cognitive-behavioral analysis system of psychotherapy: An interactional treatment approach for dysthymic disorder. *Psychiatry, 47,* 234–250.

McCullough, J.P. (1991). Psychotherapy for dysthymia: Naturalistic study of ten cases. *Journal of Nervous and Mental Disease, 179,* 734–740.

McCullough, J.P. (2000). *Treatment for chronic depression: Cognitive Behavioral Analysis System of Psychotherapy.* New York: Guilford.

McCullough, J.P., Kasnetz, M.D., Braith, J.A., Carr, K.F., Cones, J.H., Fielo, J., & Martelli, J.F. (1988). A longitudinal study of an untreated sample of predominantly late onset characterological dysthymia. *Journal of Nervous and Mental Disease, 176,* 658–667.

Stewart, J.W., McGrath, P.J., Quitkin, F.M., Harrison, W., Markowitz, J., Wager, S., & Liebowitz, M.R. (1989). Relevance of DSM-III depressive subtype and chronicity of antidepressant efficacy in atypical depression: Differential response to phenelzine, imimpramine, and placebo. *Archives of General Psychiatry, 46,* 1080–1087.

Thase, M.E., Reynolds, C.F., Frank, E., Simons, A.D., Garamoni, G.D., & McGeary, J. (1994). Response to cognitive-behavioral therapy in chronic depression. *Journal of Psychotherapy Practice and Research, 3,* 204–214.

Daniel N. Klein, PhD
Professor of Psychology
SUNY at Stony Brook

Preface

This book, like its earlier companion, *Treatment for Chronic Depression: Cognitive Behavioral Analysis System of Psychotherapy* (McCullough, 2000), was written during a national multisite study of chronically depressed outpatients (Kocsis, 2002). I functioned as the "CBASP" psychotherapy coordinator on both projects, supervising clinicians who regularly sent me videotapes of their clinical work and who participated in four teleconference calls a month. The subject matter of the earlier book was repeatedly discussed and debated on teleconference calls and through email exchanges.

I wrote this book for several reasons. One, our CBASP psychotherapists had pioneered a unique type of therapist intervention called *disciplined personal involvement* (McCullough, 2000), and it had become increasingly obvious to me that a formal description of the intervention was needed. One aspect of this intervention involves contingent personal reactions that are delivered for inappropriate in-session behavior; this technique is called *contingent personal responsivity* (CPR). A second technique, the *Interpersonal Discrimination Exercise* (IDE), is used salubriously to heal early trauma.

The second reason I wrote this book is because several of our CBASP psychotherapists have been questioned by colleagues concerning the ethicality of disciplined personal involvement; thus, a justification for this intervention was clearly warranted.

I also wrote the book to encourage empirical investigation of the personal involvement techniques. As long as a proscription against any personal involvement predominates in the field—and this practice taboo has existed for more than a century—any scientific study of nonneutral techniques is precluded. I have included a section in the appendix detailing several ways that the personal involvement techniques can be operationalized and assessed for efficacy. In addition, I also suggest ways to dismantle the CBASP model in future randomized clinical trials to determine if disciplined personal involvement adds significant change variance over and above the major CBASP change technique, Situational Analysis.

And finally, the book was written so that potential CBASP trainees will understand what CBASP training entails. I've had extensive experience training veteran psychotherapists to administer CBASP. A few individuals feel comfortable with the general contingency motif of CBASP but reject the strongly endorsed non-neutrality role for therapists. There is nothing wrong with this reaction; however, knowing ahead of time what is involved in the training content will save predictable difficulties later on.

Why does CBASP advocate a nonneutral role for the psychotherapist? There are two reasons: (1) the psychological needs of the chronically depressed patient dictate that the clinician move beyond the traditional neutral role and engage the patient in a direct and personal manner—for many patients, a safe and authentic human encounter with his or her therapist will be a first-time experience; and (2) CBASP is an acquisition learning model of treatment. Good teaching mandates that therapists *model* (Bandura, 1977; Bandura & Walters, 1964) appropriate interpersonal behavior, "*consequate*" patients' maladaptive in-session behavior with contingent personal responsivity, and, finally, *personally heal* early trauma experiences received at the hands of maltreating significant others. The latter goal is accomplished when patients are able to discriminate successfully the person of the therapist from maltreating significant others.

As always, I am deeply indebted to a number of persons who have contributed both directly and indirectly to the writing process. The first individual is Dr. Kent G. Bailey, professor emeritus of the Department of Psychology, Virginia Commonwealth University. Kent's strong encouragement 3 years ago helped me undertake the task of putting the book together. He read some of my early chapters and made helpful comments—and always with robust words of encouragement. I review some of his cutting-edge work and research in the latter portions of Chapter 2. I hope I've done justice to his views. Professor Bailey is a *pioneer* of therapeutic nonneutrality when it comes to his use of disciplined personal involvement with psychotherapy patients.

Another colleague to whom I owe much is Dr. Marilyn L. Spiro. Marilyn has worked with me for 5 years. She is a certified CBASP therapist and trainer and an exceptional psychotherapist who has conducted a successful private practice in Richmond, Virginia for over 25 years. She has also helped me for several years in the NIMH study (Kocsis, 2002) as a psychologist on the project. Marilyn and I have engaged in numerous discussions about disciplined personal involvement, and her feedback and wise counsel have been very helpful.

Another strong source of personal support has been Dr. J. Kim Penberthy, assistant professor of psychiatry at the University of Virginia Department of Psychiatry. A certified CBASP therapist and trainer, Kim continues to contribute significant personal support and encouragement to me as well as sing the praises of CBASP to audiences around Virginia. Much of Kim's academic work has involved training and supervising psychiatric residents at UVA as they administer the CBASP model.

I cannot say enough about Barbara L. Baker, who is the best "organizer" I know. I am usually a very disorganized individual when it comes to administration and management. Over the past few years, Barbara has somehow been able to neutralize the negative consequences stemming from my lack of management skills and indirectly given me time to write and complete the text.

Many of Virginia Commonwealth University's PhD clinical graduate students have contributed significantly to my writing efforts. Duane P. Gray, Patrick J. Jehle, Joanna S. Kinnaman, Carla A. Mazefsky, Mary Kathleen McDonald, Bridget L. "Pixie" Perry, Katherine L. Schaefer, and G. Todd Vance all took the time to answer questions about their reactions to my practicum training and supervision, wherein I taught them to administer disciplined personal involvement. Their questionnaire data, along with the responses of others, are described in Chapter 4. Carla A. Mazefsky, one of my practicum trainees, treated a 16-year-old chronically depressed female and published the first successful CBASP single-case study with an adolescent patient (DiSalvo & McCullough, 2002). During this same period, another single-case study was published by a second practicum student, who administered CBASP successfully to an adult male (Jehle & McCullough, 2002). Further contributions of the above clinical students, many of whom have completed their training and earned the PhD degree, were also realized while I observed their therapy videotapes and conducted individual and team supervision. From them, for example, I learned the importance of verbally "preparing" patients for the personal involvement role of the therapist before it is administered in the session. Lengthy discussions during individual practicum supervision as well as during team meetings further clarified this and other personal involvement issues. Additional contributions came from G. Todd Vance and Katherine L. Schaefer. Their individual answers to my question about disciplined personal involvement on the VCU clinical program's doctoral preliminary examination during the spring 2005 exam gave me substantive ideas about how to write the appendix research section. Another clinical graduate student with whom I have worked, Jennifer J. Runnals, helped significantly by contributing her computer graphic skills to draw most of the figures contained in the text. Jen has also served under my practicum tutelage and implements the personal involvement techniques smoothly and effectively.

Once again, to my CBASP psychotherapist colleagues who have labored "in the trenches" with chronically depressed outpatients in yet another large national study, I extend great respect and my deepest-felt gratitude and appreciation. They have taught me that no matter how refined my therapy model becomes, there will always be *outliers* who present problems that none of us has anticipated. They have also informed me of the many ramifications of personal involvement by reacting honestly to my proposals and then trying them out—sometimes with success, other times, with failure; regardless, we subsequently talk and attempt to make sense of the patient's response or lack thereof. This book, in part, has taken form during these endless conversations. I don't know what it's like to write a book without constant feedback throughout the writing process and without a supportive and collaborative company of friends constantly discussing the material.

My CBASP colleagues in the current study are Barbara E. Pritchard and Lucy E. Wilson from the University of Arizona; Stephen Bishop and D. Matthew Evans from Brown University; Baruch Fishman, Susan Evans, and Patty E. Matz from Weill Cornell Medical College; G. Gregory Eaves and Welby L. Pinney from the University of Texas, Southwestern Medical Center at Dallas; Barbara O. Rothbaum and Jill D. Rosenberg from Emory University; Sander J. Kornblith and Elizabeth

M. Pacoe from the University of Pittsburgh; Bruce A. Arnow and Lisa I. Post from Stanford University; and Dina Vivian and Darla J. Broberg from the State University of New York at Stony Brook.

Last, but certainly not least, is Janice A. Blalock, who continues to administer CBASP to chronically depressed patients in numerous smoking cessation studies at M.D. Anderson Cancer Center in Houston, Texas.

I also want to extend special appreciation to two colleagues, Bruce A. Arnow of Stanford University and Daniel N. Klein of SUNY at Stony Brook (a principal investigator in our current NIMH study and a close personal friend and colleague), both of whom reviewed the research material in the appendix and provided many helpful and insightful suggestions. I want to make it clear, however, that the contents in the appendix are mine alone, and I bear total responsibility for whatever limitations are present in these research proposals.

Finally, I mention with gratitude the person who has taught me many things about writing—Margaret O. Ryan. Margaret is a freelance editor who lives in Los Angeles; she has been a significant contributor on this as well as on other projects. As I've said before, Margaret knows the CBASP model better than I do, so when she provides feedback, I listen closely. When I become too verbose, she trims; when I don't say enough, she asks for more elaboration; when I understate my case, she underlines and uses exclamation marks; and when the text wanders or is discontinuous, she calls me back to the task at hand. She remains for me an editor *par excellence*.

James P. McCullough, Jr.
Richmond, Virginia

Treating the chronically depressed adult—dislodging the refractory cognitive-emotional and behavior armor that is the disorder—is analogous to breaking through a granite wall using a 10-pound sledgehammer. One hits the wall repeatedly in the same area with little or no effect until, almost imperceptibly, a slight hairline crack appears. Under continuous pounding, the crack gradually enlarges until, finally, the wall breaks and crumbles.

Contents

Foreword   vii

Preface   xi

1   **Disciplined Personal Involvement**   **1**
Disciplined Personal Involvement Scenarios   1
Disciplined Personal Involvement for the Chronically Depressed
    Patient   3
Use of the Word "Patient"   5
Self-Disclosure Research Literature   6
Aims of the Book   8

**Part I   Personal Involvement Taboo and the Needs of the Chronically
     Depressed Patient**

2   **History of the Personal Involvement Taboo**   **11**
Sigmund Freud (1856–1939)   12
Carl R. Rogers (1902–1987)   13
Therapeutic Alliance Research Tradition (1936–present)   20
Kiesler's Interpersonal Psychotherapy   23
Personal Involvement Pioneers: Garry Prouty and Kent G. Bailey   30
Summary   36

3   **Treating the Chronically Depressed Patient**   **38**
Overestimating the Capability of the Chronically Depressed Patient   38
Psychopathology of the Chronically Depressed Patient   40
Interpersonal Isolation of the Chronically Depressed Patient   45
Case History: Sara   47
Summary   53

Part II   Pedagogy of CBASP Training

4 Disciplined Personal Involvement Training   **57**
    Rationale and Pedagogy for CBASP Training   58
    Personal Issues and Questions of CBASP Trainees   61
    CBASP Therapist Responses to Personal Involvement Training   68
    Conclusions   76

Part III   Pedagogy of CBASP Treatment

**5 Creating Contingent Environments Using Contingent Personal
    Responsivity**   **81**
    Therapist Role Characteristics   82
    Situational Examples of Contingent Personal Responsivity   85
    Conclusions   122

**6 Healing Interpersonal Trauma Using the Interpersonal
    Discrimination Exercise**   **123**
    Normal and Preoperational Models of
        Cognitive–Emotional Functioning   124
    Sessions 1 and 2 of CBASP Therapy   129
    CBASP Transference Hypothesis Construct   131
    The IDE: Discriminating Malevolent Affective Experiences from
        Healing Ones   133
    IDE Verbatim Scenarios: Demonstration of the Method   134
    Conclusions   158
    Afterword   159

**Appendix   Research Investigations to Determine How
              CBASP Works**   **160**
    Two Types of Dependent Variables   161
    Needed Stage II CBASP Research   162
    Performance Measures Reflecting In-Session Acquisition Learning   163
    GTE Measures That Can Be Used in Future Stage II Trials   173
    Summary of Remaining Stage II Research Questions   174

References   **176**

Index   **188**

1
Disciplined Personal Involvement

Principle A: Beneficence and Nonmaleficence. Psychologists strive to benefit those with whom they work and take care to do no harm .... Because psychologists' scientific and professional judgments and actions may affect the lives of others, they are alert to and guard against personal, financial, social, organizational, or political factors that might lead to misuse of their influence. Psychologists strive to be aware of the possible effect of their own physical and mental health on their ability to help those with whom they work.
—American Psychological Association, *Ethical Principles of Psychologists and Code of Conduct* (2002, p. 3)

Disciplined Personal Involvement Scenarios

During the fall of 2003 I was lecturing to a group of Finnish psychotherapists about the treatment of the chronically depressed adult. While discussing the Cognitive Behavioral Analysis System of Psychotherapy (CBASP; McCullough, 1984a,b,c, 2000, 2001, 2003a) and how disciplined personal involvement is administered, one member of the audience asked me to role-play a situation in which she would be the chronically depressed patient and I would be the therapist. Here is what happened:

Patient: Dr. McCullough, we always talk about my personal life. I know nothing about yours.

Dr. McCullough: That's true. What do you want to know about me?

Patient: I do know you've been married for a long time. Have you ever had an affair? [The audience exploded in riotous laughter; I never took my eyes off my partner.]

Dr. McCullough: (*after a long pause*) I'm really uncomfortable answering your question, and I don't want to.

Patient: I thought you asked me what I wanted to know.

Dr. McCullough: I did, but I still have the right, as you do, to decide what I will disclose about my personal life and what I won't.

Patient: Okay then, have you ever had difficulties in your marriage?

Dr. McCullough: Yes, I have. Do you want to spend some time talking about this?

Another incident occurred with a male patient who was diagnosed with double depression. He became confused about our relationship.

Patient: I guess we have sort of a quasi-friendship. I mean, we don't hang out and smoke cigars like real friends do.

Dr. McCullough: No, we don't. I've said "no" several times to your requests to hang out in bars. Do you have any idea why I've turned down your invitations?

Patient: I'm not sure.

Dr. McCullough: What would have happened to our work had we started frequenting bars together?

Patient: I guess we would become just like me and the rest of my buddies—shooting the bull and not talking about anything really important.

Dr. McCullough: My sentiments also. Our work would have gone down the tube. I didn't want that to happen. In terms of our friendship, I'm not sure how it could be any closer. I know you pretty well, probably better than many of your buddies; and I must say you know me pretty well. But we don't hang out, smoke cigars, and shoot the bull in a bar.

Here is another common occurrence for CBASP therapists who attempt to deepen the relationship with chronically depressed patients.

Dr. Scott: I've felt really close to you today. We've addressed some difficult problems you've had at work.

Patient: Therapists are not supposed to feel close to patients. Besides, I'm paying *you* to help *me*.

Dr. Scott: You must think of me as a machine—no feelings—just someone who gives you technical assistance.

Patient: You've been trained not to have personal feelings for patients.

Dr. Scott: How do you know so much about me?

Patient: I really don't, but that's what I've always heard about psychotherapists.

Dr. Scott: What's missing in your conclusions about me?

Patient: I don't know.

Dr. Scott: Let me ask it this way. What do you usually do when you want to find out something about someone?

Patient: I'm not sure. I've never been close to anyone.

Dr. Scott: Let me make a suggestion. Why don't you ask me what I meant earlier when I said that I felt close to you.

Patient: I don't know where to start.

Dr. Scott: It doesn't matter where you start, ask anything you want about us. [This dialogue took quite some time. Finding out that Dr. S was a real human being offered the patient new interpersonal possibilities.]

The final example occurred several years ago while I was working with a patient diagnosed with chronic major depression.

Patient: I've never let myself trust anyone before. How could I possibly trust you? You're a psychotherapist who is trained to do the things you do. You would be this way, no matter who I was.

Dr. McCullough: You're right. I try to be direct and honest, regardless of whom I'm with.

Patient: No, I don't mean that. I mean you're a professional.

Dr. McCullough: You didn't hear what I just said.

Patient: What do you mean?

Dr. McCullough: I'm going to say it again. I would always try to be honest with you as well as try to be myself, period.

Patient: What do you mean, you would be yourself?

Dr. McCullough: Good question. Now, we'll get to the real me and not some impression you've had about psychotherapists, in general. I was never trained to be myself as a psychotherapist. I had to learn that on my own.

Patient: You mean, they don't teach you such things in school?

Dr. McCullough: That's right. In fact, my mentors taught me *not* to be my true self with patients. I was taught to keep personal opinions to myself, not to let you know my true feelings, not to show you how you affect me personally, and especially not to become personally involved with you—the last was the big taboo. However, I found such teaching too constrictive. So, I try to be myself with you and others.

Patient: Somehow I've felt that. I had that feeling when you disclosed that you had had difficulties with depression when you were younger. Do you remember? It was several weeks ago. But I couldn't let myself believe you weren't just playing a role or using some technique on me.

Dr. McCullough: Believe it! And if you find you can trust me as you get to know me, please let me know.

Disciplined Personal Involvement for the Chronically Depressed Patient

Rethinking the Personal Involvement Issue

The personal involvement issue between therapists and patients needs to be rethought when treating the chronically depressed adult. Clinical trainers, researchers, and practitioners have traditionally reacted too quickly in rejecting this therapeutic role. The time has come for the personal involvement issue in psychotherapy to be placed on the table, discussed openly, and empirically investigated.

Disciplined personal involvement does not mean that therapists and patients become drinking buddies, business partners, date, sleep together, contact each other when there is nothing else to do, share gossip, meet for coffee after hours, or become chat room pals. Rather, personal involvement in this context denotes a particular type of *therapist role enactment* that is based upon, first, the well-established learning principles of B.F. Skinner (1953, 1968), whereby therapists choreograph personal reaction contingencies in the session so that patients learn new associations, and Albert Bandura's concepts of imitation learning and modeling (1976, 1977; Bandura & Walters, 1964; Meichenbaum, 1971). Bandura notes that in many languages "the word for 'teach' is the same as the word 'show,' and the synonymity is literal" (Reichard, 1938, p. 471). The second type of therapist role enactment using disciplined personal involvement heals trauma experiences arising from early encounters with significant others. The first type of personal involvement role enactment is discussed in Chapter 5, and the second type is described in Chapter 6.

CBASP therapists are trained to be themselves with patients to achieve specific ends. Adding personal responsivity (emotions, thoughts, and behaviors) to the therapist's repertoire accomplishes four in-session goals: It (1) "consequates" in-session behavior (i.e., uses personal responses as a behavioral consequence); (2) teaches adaptive behavior after showing patients how their negative behavior throws obstacles in the way of obtaining interpersonal goals; (3) teaches and models empathic behavior; and (4) differentiates the therapist, in a salubrious way, from significant others who have maltreated the patient. Personal involvement never implies a license to run roughshod over the patient or to flaunt feelings and attitudes for self-aggrandizement. It must be used judiciously, with the above goals always in mind (McCullough, 2000, 2003b, 2003c). Chapter 4 describes the CBASP personal involvement training procedures, the personal and professional issues individuals face during training, and the problems they encounter when administering the techniques for the first time.

From a psychoanalytic point of view, personally responding to patients denotes an "objective" type of countertransference. Some analytic theorists (e.g., Epstein & Feiner, 1979) distinguish between "subjective" and "objective" countertransference. *Subjective countertransference* (Spotnitz, 1969) describes the irrational and defensive reactions a therapist experiences with a particular patient at a particular time. These anxiety and conflict reactions of clinicians arise from the problematical residue of earlier unresolved developmental issues. *Objective countertransference* (Winnicott, 1949), on the other hand, arises from the immediate impact patients exert upon therapists. Therapists *respond* (versus *react*) personally to what patients do and say. These responses are evoked when a patient, for example, is frequently late or forgets session appointments, changes the subject whenever sensitive topics are broached, makes hostile comments about the therapist's competency or mind-reads the therapist's capabilities with statements such as "You could never care about me" or "I know you think I'm stupid and crazy." These examples represent behavioral patterns that characterize many chronically depressed adults. The patterns can be modified when therapists feel free to respond to patients as human beings and make explicit how they are affected by patients' behavior.

Such response-related strategies immediately engage therapists and patients in a personal relationship; neutrality is not present because the patient is personally confronting the consequences he or she just produced—that is, the therapist's response.

Disciplined personal involvement requires (1) *maturity* that reflects a stable psychological identity; (2) the therapist's awareness of his or her interpersonal "stimulus value" for the patient (McCullough, 2000); and (3), a constant reevaluation of therapist responses to ensure that they are given with the sole aim of increasing the individual's well-being.

Is Personal Involvement Universally Recommended?

The diagnosis of the disorder, the needs of the patient, the technique being used, the outcome goals of a particular therapy model, and the interpersonal capabilities of the clinician dictate whether or not disciplined personal involvement should be administered. Regarding treatment goals, in classical Freudian psychoanalysis (Levy, 2000) personal involvement of therapists with patients is discouraged to avoid interfering with the goal of analysis, which is the interpretation of patient transference. Thus, neutralizing (through personal analysis) and inhibiting personal responses toward patients (countertransference) are bedrock requirements for the analytic trainee. In contrast, as noted above, CBASP outcome goals are quite different from those of classical psychoanalysis; the goals of consequating in-session behavior, modeling empathic behavior, and choreographing interpersonal healing experiences to neutralize early trauma dictate the need for disciplined personal involvement.

The Personal Involvement Taboo

Chapter 2 traces the history of the century-old proscription against becoming personally involved with patients. Psychotherapy training, research, and practice in the United States since the early 20th century have accepted, almost without question, the severe limitations this taboo places on therapist behavior. Another contributing factor to the maintenance of the taboo stems from the fact that, with one exception, psychotherapy training, research, and practice have almost totally overlooked the factor of *patient learning*. One would think that since behavior change is a core issue for therapists, patient learning would also be a central concern. Such has not been the case. Outside of the behavior therapy movement during the 1960s and 1970s (e.g., Ayllon & Azrin, 1968; Bandura, 1961, 1969, 1977; Browning & Stover, 1971; Herson & Barlow, 1976; Ullman & Krasner, 1965), patient learning has been a nonissue in psychotherapy circles. Therapists rarely ask how they might facilitate in-session learning as well as improve treatment response *by using themselves personally as choreographers of a learning environment.* Instead of highlighting in-session learning, I've watched practicum trainers and other psychotherapy supervisors place severe restrictions on the therapist–patient relationship and continue to disengage learning from psychotherapy.

Use of the Word "Patient"

I must explain why I use the term *patient* and not *client* to designate the individual receiving psychotherapy. First, although *client* is the commonly used label for helpees in applied psychology, I adhere strongly to a biopsychosocial model of health and illness (Akiskal & McKinney, 1973, 1975; Barlow & Durand, 1999; Blanchard, 1977; Engel, 1977; Gentry, 1984; Kiesler, 1999) that makes the *patient label* more appropriate. Not surprisingly, I rely on the multiaxial system of

DSM classification (DSM-IV: American Psychiatric Association, 1994) to diagnose and assess the psychosocial functioning of the people who come to me for help. Second, the word *patient* (Latin: *patiens*) appropriately describes one who endures pain, suffers, or who receives some kind of treatment to resolve the pain. The label *client* (Latin: *cliens*) *implies a different type of professional relationship that I find nondescript of individuals participating in psychotherapy. To me, the client* moniker suggests a nonsuffering customer involved in a professional relationship with a lawyer, accountant, broker, architect, banker, or real estate agent. Interpersonal intimacy, although it may occur in professional–client relationships, is the exception and not the rule; in addition, reciprocal collaborative participation to resolve intrapersonal suffering is not a goal of the professional–client liaison. Third, I use the term *patient* to provide continuity in the text.

Self-Disclosure Research Literature

A large psychological and psychoanalytic research literature exists under the general rubric "self-disclosure." To avoid the misperception that the main aim of this book is to comment and elaborate on this existing body of literature, a brief overview of self-disclosure research is presented below; then I summarize the research conclusions and show how my definition of disciplined personal involvement, as well as the role personal involvement plays in CBASP psychotherapy, differs significantly from the self-disclosure construct.

Hill and Knox, in a recent review of self-disclosure research, define *therapist self-disclosure* "as therapist statements that reveal something about the therapist" (2002, p. 255). These authors describe two types of disclosure: (1) *self-disclosing disclosure* (general information about the therapist that does not involve the patient); and (2) disclosure by the therapist that does implicate the patient as well as the dyadic relationship. Hill and O'Brien (1999) label the second type, *immediate self-disclosure.*

There are several points to note after reviewing the self-disclosure literature: (1) One major research conclusion is that self-disclosure positively affects the *quality* of the dyadic relationship (e.g., Bridges, 2001; Hill & Knox, 2002; Knox, Hess, Petersen, & Hill, 1997; Safran & Muran, 2000; Teyber, 1992; Wachtel, 1993). (2) Self-disclosure research studies are reported with very little attention given to patient diagnosis or the type of therapy technique administered. Norcross describes the absence of patient diagnosis and therapy definition as problems for psychotherapy relationship research, saying that researchers pay scant attention to the "disorder-specific and therapy-specific nature of the therapy relationship" (2001, p. 351). Norcross continues:

The therapeutic relationship probably exhibits more causal impact in some disorders and in some therapies than in others. As with research on specific treatments, it may no longer suffice to ask "Does this relationship work?" but "How does the relationship work for this disorder and this therapy?" (p. 352)

(3) The predominant orientation of self-disclosure researchers is usually psychodynamic (e.g., Bridges, 2001; Greenberg, 1995b; Hill & Knox, 2002; Manning, 2005; Maroda, 1999a, 1999b; Safran & Muran, 2000; Tansey & Burke, 1991). (4) Most self-disclosure research represents a subcategory within the larger therapeutic alliance research tradition—a longstanding psychotherapy research program that is discussed in Chapter 2.

Researchers draw several general conclusions about the effects of self-disclosure on therapy patients. Knox et al. (1997) report that patients often perceived therapist self-disclosures as beneficial and helpful and as leading to insights as well as to new perspectives (i.e., learned something new about themselves); in some instances, it appeared that self-disclosure had a "modeling effect" on patient behavior, whereas other patients felt reassured that their behavior was "normal" and that they were not alone in their struggles (i.e., achieved a *sense of universality*: Robitschek & McCarthy, 1991; Yalom, 1975). Bridges (2001) concludes that self-disclosure deepens the therapeutic encounter and enhances patients' emotional experience and connection with clinicians. Manning (2005) points out that self-disclosure confirms the patient's sense of him or herself, teaches empathy, demonstrates how his or her behavior affects others, encourages collaborative behavior and humanizes the therapist. Barret and Berman (2001) note that patients who were exposed to therapist self-disclosure reported lower symptom distress levels and liked their therapists more. The researchers suggest that self-disclosure may improve the quality of the therapist–patient dyad and lead to better treatment outcomes. Finally, Hill and Knox (2002), reviewing the state of self-disclosure research, conclude that self-disclosure is generally more helpful than harmful and that therapists self-disclose for multiple reasons (e.g., to model behavior, to teach empathy, to normalize the patient's situation, to impart a sense of universality).

The distinguishing characteristics of CBASP disciplined personal involvement, when compared to therapeutic self-disclosures are the following:

1. Personal involvement techniques are linked to the goals of CBASP therapy. The goals of personal involvement are (a) to connect the patient perceptually with his or her environment; (b) to modify maladaptive interpersonal behavior; and (c) to address and ultimately heal developmental trauma arising from negative experiences with maltreating significant others.
2. The presentation of disciplined personal involvement in this book is limited to patients with chronic depression, and no broader claims of its utility for other patients are made.
3. The rationale for disciplined personal involvement is based on the intrapersonal and interpersonal *needs* of the chronic patient (see Chapter 3).
4. The implementation of disciplined personal involvement is based on learning theory principles (Chapters 1, 5, 6) developed by Skinner (1968) and Bandura (1977), with behavioral contingencies and modeling as central components.

5. There are instances in which the CBASP therapist intentionally interrupts the focus on the patient to direct the patient's attention to the therapist in order to penetrate and modify refractory perceptual patterns. These tactics contradict those of self-disclosure researchers who strongly advocate a sustained focus on the patient (e.g., Hill & Knox, 2002). This maneuver, as well as other novel personal strategies, is described in Chapter 3 and further illustrated in Chapters 5 and 6.

In conclusion, self-disclosure research is a welcome beginning in a field that has placed excessive restrictions on therapist behavior for too long. As Norcross (2002) states, we need to know more about which type of therapy model works for which type of patient and what techniques within the model affect the target behavior most effectively. Hopefully, the current attempt will move us closer to this goal.

Aims of the Book

This book will demonstrate why I feel that disciplined personal involvement is necessary in the treatment of the chronically depressed adult; my aim is to open the door to a general discussion of disciplined personal involvement so that this psychotherapy construct can be empirically investigated. I realized early that in training CBASP therapists to become personally involved with patients, I had to address the stringent proscriptions against personal involvement which all of us have known since our academic and medical training days. In Chapter 2 I broadly address the issue of how we have maintained the personal involvement taboo for 100 years, up to and including the present day.

We turn now to a discussion of the historical origins of the personal involvement taboo by looking at several major psychotherapy traditions in psychiatry and psychology.

Part I
Personal Involvement Taboo and the Needs of the Chronically Depressed Patient

2
History of the Personal Involvement Taboo

The analyst's role is one for which there is no model in real life.

—A. Hoffer (2000)

For 100 years psychotherapy has been taught in clinical academies and medical schools, administered to patients, and subjected to extensive research, it has generated myriad therapy permutations, been vigorously attacked and arduously defended, changed the life of millions, damaged some, and left still others unaffected. Today, psychotherapy is generally considered by patients to be beneficial and to improve the quality of their lives, particularly if they stay in treatment long enough (Seligman, 1995). Various interpersonal styles are used by therapists, who may be sensitive or callous, gentle or aggressive, empathic or interpersonally detached, humorous or dour, obsessive or hysterical, dominant or submissive, friendly or hostile, conforming or maverick, quiet or boisterous, collaborative or adversarial, and directive or nondirective. Or, therapists may exhibit an admixture of several of these styles or possess attributes that characterize one or both of these polar opposites.

Regardless of the therapist or the type of therapy administered, there is one fixed and inviolate rule for practitioners today; therapists generally inhibit their personal responses to patients because personal involvement with patients is strictly taboo. For years I've listened to clinical graduate students tell me what their supervisors instruct them regarding personal involvement: *Do not become personally involved with your patients!* This proscription is almost always articulated by someone in the audience when I describe the CBASP personal involvement construct and how it is used. This has been true of audiences in the United States as well as abroad.

The history of the personal involvement taboo includes a discussion of several prominent psychotherapy traditions. We begin with Sigmund Freud's psychoanalysis, look at Carl Rogers' person-centered psychotherapy, briefly review more than 50 years of research on the therapeutic alliance, discuss the Kieslerian interpersonal movement in psychotherapy to show how interpersonal research has moved us closer to personal involvement with patients, and, finally, review the work of two personal involvement pioneers who have transcended the taboo and utilized the therapist role in novel ways.

Sigmund Freud (1856–1939)

Sigmund Freud's "talking cure," an innovative technique he developed in the early 1900s (Freud, 1938, 1956; Jones, 1953), was created to resolve the psychological problems of his neurological patients. The psychoanalytic method emerged from the physician's strong belief in the deterministic nature of all mental life. Freud viewed the idiosyncrasies of mental life as causally linked to real past events, which begin to exert their influence upon the patient from birth. During psychoanalysis, patients are guided to make associations between long-forgotten memories and current affective processes. The newly associated connections result in two patient outcomes: (1) released psychic energy, which was now freed for utilization in the present ("to enable him [the patient] to save his mental energy which he is expending upon internal conflicts", Freud, 1963, p. 248); and (2) a positive, empowering impact on psychosocial functioning ("to make the best of him [the patient] that his inherited capacities will allow and so to make him as efficient and as capable of enjoyment as is possible", Freud, 1963, p. 248). Freud viewed treatment success as contingent upon a meticulously crafted relationship with each patient. Psychoanalysis required analysts and patients to adhere to stringent guidelines that Freud lucidly prescribed. The patient was taught to do the following:

... treatment is begun by the patient being required to put himself in the position of an attentive and dispassionate self-observer, merely to read off all the time the surface of his consciousness, and on the other hand to make a duty of the most complete candor while on the other not holding back any idea from communication, even if (1) he feels that it is too disagreeable or if (2) he judges that it is nonsensical or (3) too unimportant or (4) irrelevant to what is being looked for. (Freud, 1963, p. 234)

Freud described the analyst's role using an equally exact prescription. The analyst must regard

... the material produced by the patient's associations as though it hinted at a hidden meaning and of discovering that meaning from it. Experience soon showed that the attitude which the analytical physician could most advantageously adopt was to surrender himself to his own unconscious mental activity, in a state of *easy and impartial attention*, to avoid so far as possible reflection and the construction of conscious expectations, not to try to fix anything that he heard particularly in his memory, and by these means to catch the drift of the patient's unconscious with his own unconscious. (1963, p. 235)

Because the goals of psychoanalytic treatment required uninterrupted access to the unconscious life of the patient, the analyst's role necessarily receded into the background. Thus, an early therapist role prescription required analysts to provide a *blank screen* persona. Freud strongly believed that if physicians interacted directly with patients, the pristine unconscious processes would be corrupted and remain inaccessible, thereby compromising the success of the analysis.

Today, many classical psychoanalysts continue to adhere to these rigid, separatist guidelines (Levy, 2000). The most extreme description of a disengaged therapist role comes from Axel Hoffer (2000), who reiterates Freud's view by saying that "(1) the analyst's responsibility is to enhance the patient's capacity for conscious and unconscious conflict elucidation while, (2) conflict resolution remains both the prerogative and responsibility of the analysand" (p. 37). When it comes to wishing or hoping for salubrious change in the patient, Hoffer warns that such wishes or needs signal only countertransference intrusion. He readily admits that the analyst's role "is one for which there is no model in real life" (p. 38). By this he means that clinicians must maintain a strict facade of *anonymity* (i.e., neutrality in regard to having power and influence over the patient's life) and *abstinence* (i.e., prevention of countertransference intrusions in the patient's life: viz. suggestions, encouragement, even hope that the patient will improve). The classical analytic tradition provides us with the ultimate separatist model of the therapist–patient relationship. Overt interpersonal interaction has been, and remains, *verboten.* Interactions between the players in the session are addressed in this one-person therapy model (Aron, 1996; Balint, 1968) only through the transference interpretations of the analyst.

I once knew an analyst whose waiting room resembled an isolation chamber. The room contained one leather sofa, a large plant, and a dull brown carpet. Two nondescript pictures hung on the walls. The receptionist sat behind a Venetian blind enclosure, containing a small open slit that allowed her to see when patients arrived. She did not speak with patients. The analyst explained that he maintained this environment to prevent interference with patients' transferences.

One interesting aspect of classical psychoanalysis is seen in its heavy-handed proscriptive approach to the therapist role. Because Freudian theory was never informed by psychology's century-old experimental learning tradition (e.g., constructs such as *shaping, transfer of learning, generalization, counterconditioning,* and *classical conditioning of emotionality),* Freud's views of psychopathology as well as those of his followers are based on a 19th-century view of the irrational man and woman who must be "fixed" by the triumphant infusion of rational knowledge. The source of the knowledge is the analyst. Classical psychoanalysis conceptualizes the change task as requiring the patient to remain perceptually and behaviorally disengaged from his or her immediate environment (i.e., disengaged from the direct moment-to-moment responses of the therapist). The analyst keeps the individual's attention focused solely on his or her inner world—a world devoid of direct environmental influences. The personal involvement taboo between therapists and patients began at the beginning of the 20th century in Freud's practice of neurology. Time has not changed this proscription.

Carl R. Rogers (1902–1987)

Several years ago, while supervising a second-year clinical psychology graduate student who was having interpersonal difficulties with a chronically depressed adult, the following crisis arose. The patient repeatedly made sarcastic comments about the therapist's inexperience, calling into question his competence and credibility. These hurtful utterances congealed into an interpersonal roadblock, and the student candidly admitted that he wanted to transfer the case. I suggested that instead he tell the patient how hurtful the comments were and inquire why the person wanted to hurt him. The student demurred, saying that he could never do this. Explaining himself, he said: "I've always heard that psychotherapists must never disclose personal feelings. The only emotion we are allowed to express is unconditional positive regard." What my trainee unknowingly implicated was Carl Rogers' stand on the personal involvement taboo. We'll briefly discuss how the taboo has been maintained by applied psychology.

Sixty years earlier, Carl Rogers introduced his unique treatment approach to psychology in a paper entitled "Newer Concepts of Psychotherapy" (Rogers, 1940). He presented the paper to the University of Minnesota Chapter of Psi Chi. Psychoanalysis had dominated the mental health field between World Wars I and II. The demands for psychological assessment and psychotherapy for hundreds of thousands of soldiers became enormous during and after World War II (Todd & Bohart, 1999). Applied psychology was ripe for a paradigm shift. Rogers provided the direction and impetus for the shift with his nondirective psychotherapy model. His 1942 book Counseling and Psychotherapy offered the first viable psychological theory and treatment alternative to nonanalytic practitioners. Over the next few years, his perspective influenced the field in another way: It moved clinical psychology from an assessment-dominated profession to a treatment-research-oriented profession (Todd & Bohart, 1999).

When I read Counseling and Psychotherapy (Rogers, 1942), decades ago, I realized that I was witnessing the beginning of a revolution. The innovations Rogers initiated were sweeping and pervasive in the nascent field of applied psychology. He proposed radically new roles for the psychotherapist in a unique treatment approach first known as "nondirective," then "client-centered," and ultimately "person-centered" psychotherapy (Rogers, 1942, 1951, 1959, 1978). During the remainder of this section, his work is referred to as *person-centered psychotherapy*. The major assumptions for the model were derived from his strongly held individual-humanistic social philosophy. An important source of influence was American philosopher and educationalist John Dewey (1916/1997: Democracy and Education). Dewey was an ardent proponent of progressive evolutionary thought that extended back to Darwin. Dewey's evolutionary thought and optimistic view of the human organism characterized the philosophical mood in the United States during the early 20th century. He wrote that under the proper educational conditions, individuals could actualize the innate propensities of life, namely, *individual and societal–collective growth* (Dewey, 1916/1997). Consistent with Dewey's social-philosophical optimism, Rogers argued that psychotherapy "clients" have the innate capacity for self-directed phenomenological change and self-actualization within a therapeutic environment in which the counselor's "vantage point is from the internal frame of reference of the patient himself" (Rogers, 1951, p. 494). A person-centered role requires the therapist to maintain a nonjudgmental, accepting, and empathic attitude toward the patient. This role enactment, he argued, creates an in-session atmosphere that frees the innate growth process of the individual (Prouty, 1994). Rogers' concept of *self-structure* comprises the major treatment focus for person-centered psychotherapy.

The Self

Self-structure (the sense of "I" or "me") arises from a person's interactions with his or her environment. Development of the self emerges out of one of the basic needs of all people: to be accepted by others (Rogers, 1951). The evaluations of others, combined with the self-values that accrue, lead directly to the construction of consistent patterns of perceptions that constitute the "I" or "me" (self-structure). Children find pleasure doing many things, and they may be either rewarded or punished by parents for their pleasure-seeking behavior. Punishment received for engaging in pleasurable activities results in an internal conflict between the desire to obtain pleasure and the desire to avoid pain. When the individual is negatively evaluated/rejected by significant others for engaging in certain behaviors, expressing particular emotions, or embracing certain attitudes, these valuations are introjected into the self and become perceived as essential parts of the self. Said another way, parts of my self-system and the associated self-values that result mirror the experiential components that have been negatively evaluated by significant others.

Thus, *interpersonal rejection* is the etiological source for maladjustment in Rogerian theory. If the "true" value (innate worth) of the person is eclipsed by the negative introjected values of significant others, the self becomes a house divided. Psychological maladjustment exists when the person denies awareness of certain negatively valued parts of the self; this denial, in turn, prevents their integration into the self-system. Tension, anxiety, and lowered self-esteem are the prominent signs of maladjustment. The goal of psychotherapy is to enable the client to relinquish the introjected values of others that prevent the individual from becoming his or her real self. As noted above, this goal is accomplished in an environment of prescribed acceptance, wherein the patient progressively discovers that *all* parts of his or her conscious and unconscious self are acceptable to the therapist.

The goal of person-centered therapy is psychological adjustment, defined as a process whereby "the individual perceives and accepts into his self-structure more of his organic experiences, he finds that he is replacing his present value system— based so largely upon introjections which have been distortedly symbolized—with a continuing valuing process" (Rogers, 1951, p. 522). In summary, Rogerian theory is

> ... basically phenomenological in character and relies heavily upon the concept of the self as an explanatory concept. It pictures the endpoint of personality development as being a basic congruence between the phenomenal field of experience and the conceptual structure of the self—a situation which, if achieved, would represent freedom from internal strain and anxiety, and freedom from potential strain; which would represent the maximum in realistically oriented adaptation; which would mean the establishment of an individualized value system having considerable identity with the value system of any other equally welladjusted member of the human race. (Rogers, 1951, p. 532)

In Rogers' (1942) view there were two different kinds of psychotherapy: his *nondirective approach,* which put a high premium on the right of every individual to be psychologically independent and to maintain his or her psychological integrity (without interference from others); and *directive approaches,* which he described as valuing social conformity and the right of the able to direct and influence the lives of weaker souls.

Taking a moment to describe some of Rogers' unique therapist role prescriptions will further clarify the nature of the person-centered approach. His recommendations for the role may seem strange to some of us who live in a different mental health environment where *directive therapy models* predominate (e.g., Beck, Rush, Shaw, & Emery, 1979; Klerman,Weissman, Rounsaville, & Chevron, 1984; Linehan, 1993; McCullough, 2000; Nay, 2004).

The Rogerian Therapist: A Warm Blank Slate

The major goal of the therapist is to help the patient relinquish his or her defensiveness concerning any feelings, thoughts, behaviors, memories, or attitudes of privacy that lead the person to assume that certain matters should not be openly discussed (Rogers, 1942). The relinquishment occurs when the patient concludes that his or her therapist will not criticize, suggest alternative strategies, or try to order or arrange the flow of the discussion. Such a state of affairs comes about only when the practitioner is completely willing to listen to the patient express any attitude or feeling. Rogers' ultimate goal for the patient is similar to that of the classical analyst who teaches the patient to free associate without fear of censure or evasive intrusion by the doctor. Rogers (1951) writes repeatedly that the person-centered role demands the utmost restraint and discipline on the part of the clinician.

Successful actualization of the person-centered role necessarily flows from Rogers' particular set of humanistic philosophical attitudes, which he encouraged his therapists to embrace (Rogers, 1951); thus, he conjoins a philosophy of life with the therapeutic role. Rogers' philosophy embraces the right of every individual to be psychologically independent and eschews all attitudes that view the clinician as superior to the patient in any way. The clinician must completely accept the patient, unequivocally respect the intrinsic worth of the individual, and trust completely in his or her capacity to achieve insight and constructive self-direction. Complete confidence in the patient's ability to move the flow of treatment in salubrious directions leads Rogers to make the following statement: "The skillful counselor refrains from intruding his own wishes, his own reactions, or biases, into the therapeutic situations" (1942, p. 89). The assumption here is that individual growth occurs autonomously, without any form of guidance input. The person-centered role also requires the clinician to put aside all concerns about diagnosis and personality assessment and instead focus complete attention on perceiving and understanding the patient as he or she understands him- or herself'. "Notice how the significant theme of the relationship is, 'we were mostly *me* working together on my situation as I found it.' The two selves have somehow become one while remaining two—'we were me' "(Rogers, 1951, p. 38).

Rogers also warns that the clinician must not be passive or indifferent. A detached interpersonal stance will be perceived as rejection. Rather, the clinician should function in an active and engaging manner, repeatedly clarifying feeling statements that should be delivered in a mirroring way, offered empathically and with a modicum of hesitancy. The clarification statement always contains an implicit question, "Am I right here?" (Rogers, 1951). Crisis moments, when the patient expresses desperate emotions, must not pull the therapist off the empathic–reflective baseline. The *internal anchor* during these crisis moments is always a basic confidence in the forward-moving growth tendencies of the patient. Again, the therapist must have absolute trust in the capacity of the individual to resolve his or her problems and to grow productively in a relationship where unconditional positive regard and acceptance are continually extended.

The treatment task and corresponding therapist role require that therapists endeavor to understand the patient, who is seen as unable to face certain memories and experiences because to admit them would be inconsistent or threatening to the current self-structure. Perceiving the patient's attitudes, confusions, ambivalences, and emotions with an accepting and safe demeanor paves the way for self-acceptance, whereby the disjointed components of the self can be integrated. When the therapist accepts the patient's contradictory behaviors as if they were an integral part of the individual, the result is that the person can accept these components as part and parcel of him- or herself.

The core therapist attitudes facilitating self-actualization and self-formative growth within the individual are unconditional positive regard for the patient, extended empathy, and verbal and nonverbal congruence that communicates genuineness on the part of the helper (Rogers, 1959).

Rogers' Continuing Legacy in Clinical Psychology.

Before discussing the Rogerian legacy in applied psychology, I want to express my deep respect for the life and work of Carl Rogers. In writing this section, I have read or reread most of his books, journal articles, and chapters. Rogers, like all of us, is a product of his age. I examine his contributions to our field by looking back, which is unfair in some ways; however, I take Rogers' momentous legacy and stamp on contemporary training, research, and practice in clinical psychology very seriously. The conclusions I draw may seem somewhat negative, but my respect for his life and work must never be doubted.

For over 50 years, Rogerian theory has continued to exert significant influence on clinical training, research, and practice. Not all of this influence has been positive. By discussing two negative aspects of his legacy, my intent is to show (1) how practicum supervisors, researchers, and practitioners still define the therapist role in a narrow-band way that results in unrealistic perceptions and behavior; and (2) how psychotherapy training, research, and practice continue to ignore the factor of *patient learning* and, in so doing, preclude experimentation with different didactic approaches that might enhance that learning. Next, I provide a historical review of each negative legacy and then offer personal observations to illustrate how each legacy continues to influence clinical psychology.

1. *Narrow-band definition of therapist role.* The first negative influence Rogers has had on clinical psychology is seen in the unrealistic ways many practitioners

view their role. Rogers argued strongly that therapists and patients must share equal status in the therapeutic dyad. He unwittingly created a role that mimics Hoffer's description of the classical analyst as "one for which there is no model in real life" (2000, p. 38). By neutralizing any perceived power differential between therapists and patients to prevent psychologists from viewing themselves as *stronger*, he created a role for which there is no real-life model. Ironically, and in order to maintain in-session equality, his therapist role can aptly be described as "larger than life." Person-centered therapists were trained to be caring, warm, empathic individuals who offered only unconditional positive regard and acceptance and asked for nothing in return. Rules guided the conduct of person-centered therapists (Rogers, 1942). Interviewers must only *listen*, not display *authority*, not give *advice*, not *argue* or *talk* or *ask questions,* except under certain extenuating circumstances. "It will be very evident that these rules, with their stress on the absence of advice, persuasion, and argument and with their clear emphasis on the fact that the interview is the client's, providing him with an opportunity to talk freely, are in harmony with the non-directive approach" (Rogers, 1942, p. 125). As I try to envision the sort of person who could successfully adhere to these rules, I conclude that the number must be small. It would require Herculean efforts to suppress and ignore any and all feelings, thoughts, and behaviors that might otherwise interfere with the total attention one extends to patients.

Patients, at the outset of treatment, do *not* share equal status with therapists. Role inequality (which has nothing to do with socioeconomic, gender, ethnic, religious, or professional status) stems from the *treatment expertise* and *experience* of the therapist as well as from the seriousness of the patient's *psychological problems.*

The clinical practicum student whom I described at the outset thought he had to match the prototype of the all-accepting practitioner, regardless of the negative behavior displayed by his chronically depressed patient. Because he could not do so, his frustration resulted in a request to transfer the case. There is a more realistic role alternative for clinical practicum trainees as well as for veteran practitioners who treat chronically depressed patients. Disciplined personal involvement (McCullough, 2000) provides therapists with the means to utilize their personal responses to patients as a major change vehicle. (These strategies are discussed in Chapter 5 and 6.)

2. *Absence of patient learning factor.* The second negative Rogerian legacy stems from the fact that patient learning was never an important consideration of person-centered psychotherapy. Consistent with the Rogerian tradition, contemporary psychotherapy as well as practicum training in our academies evince little interest in the patient learning variable. When patient learning is not of major concern to the clinician, psychotherapy becomes simply an "exposure" activity in which patients are exposed to either the person of the therapist or to one or more techniques. The irony is that regardless of the fact that learning issues have been neglected, most patients in psychotherapy actually engage in acquisition-like learning tasks (McCullough, 1984a, 1991, 2000, 2002; McCullough & Carr, 1987). That is, (1) patients are introduced to novel skills they did not have before therapy began (acquisition), (2) they are encouraged to practice these skills (practice to strengthen

novel learning), or (3) they learn new ways to experience themselves (acquisition), their therapists, and others, and (4) are once more encouraged to transfer (practice to strengthen the new learning) this new-found cognitive–emotive-behavioral learning to relationships on the outside. *The crucial question concerning how much of what is taught in psychotherapy is actually learned is rarely addressed.*

I feel that the amount of learning acquired is related to positive treatment outcomes as well as to the maintenance of those positive outcomes during the post-treatment period. We are beginning to obtain in-session and follow-up data that support these assumptions (Manber & McCullough, 2000; Manber et al., 2003; Klein et al., 2003). I always ask the patients I treat what they have learned from previous therapy experiences. Most do not have any idea what I am asking. Going further and inquiring what they did during their previous sessions with other therapists, a few would say only that they talked a lot or that their therapist was nice. Our neglect of learning in the contemporary delivery of psychotherapy aids and abets the notorious enemy of learning: *forgetting.*

I never thought about patient learning until the early 1980s. Participating enthusiastically in the behavior therapy movement during the late 1960s and 1970s (e.g., McCullough, Cornell, McDaniel, & Mueller, 1974; McCullough & Southard, 1972), I made a theoretical shift during 1980 by adding the cognitive variable to my single-case studies with chronically depressed adults. My work was no longer acceptable to the behavior journals, many of which were under the editorship of operant researchers. Cognitive data did not meet the requirements of the operant design space. It was then that I began to ask myself, "What *are* my patients learning?"

It seemed to me that one thing they were acquiring was problem-solving skills, so I began to consider the possibility that acquisition learning was taking place. I knew that acquiring cognitive learning, such as the kind involved in a problem-solving algorithm, was a slow process and required practice to strengthen the fledgling habits (McCullough, 1984c). I wrote two papers describing an acquisition learning proposal for psychotherapy research (McCullough, 1984b, 1984c). What I realized was that I was teaching patients cognitive skills, that they, in turn, acquired, to one degree or another. I also observed that patients who acquired the skills scored better on my outcome measures than those who did not. I began to include the acquisition learning–performance data along with other process and outcome scores when I submitted articles for publication (e.g., McCullough, 1984c; McCullough & Carr, 1987).

I also added one more descriptive component to the acquisition learning proposal. The idea came from Don Kiesler, who suggested that I had described a design that contained two levels of dependent variables. One level reflected the learning acquired over therapy sessions (e.g., McCullough, 1984a, 1984b: learned in-session performance scores were graphed over sessions), and the second level denoted the *generalized treatment effect variables* (i.e., the usual process and outcome dependent variables presented in traditional psychotherapy research) that were informed by the in-session learning. At the time, I argued that an acquisition learning design requires the clinician to operationalize the learning goals, measure the extent of patient learning, and measure the generalized treatment effects of learning (McCullough, 2000, 2002). The culmination of this research project was reported at an Association for the Advancement of Behavior Therapy (AABT) convention in New Orleans in 2000, when data were presented from the largest clinical trial ever conducted with chronically depressed outpatients ($n = 681$ S; Keller et al., 2000). Manber and McCullough (2000) reviewed the learning data and suggested that among 431 chronically depressed outpatients who received psychotherapy, those who achieved the highest performance scores on the problem-solving algorithm taught during the sessions were the patients who reported significantly better therapeutic outcomes. Additional analyses revealed that proficiency in the use of the problem-solving algorithm predicted treatment outcome independently of medication status and baseline depressive severity (Manber et al., 2003).

The general absence of a learning emphasis in psychotherapy training, research, and practice since Rogers' day has had enormous consequences in our profession. When therapists overlook the factor of patient learning, all that remains on the research playing field are the attitudes therapists hold toward patients, the phenomenological experiences of patients, and the therapist–patient relationship; in short, therapy becomes predominantly an *experiential activity* in which patient phenomenology (or the therapeutic relationship, more than likely) takes center stage. This outcome is exactly what has happened in clinical psychology.

Facilitating a therapeutic relationship is not synonymous with the provision of didactic activity and learning goals. Therapist instruction, skills training, repeated practice of skills in the session and beyond, performance-based feedback, acquisition learning across sessions, transfer of learning from the session to the outside, all taken together, constitute didactic activity. Such activity may be directed toward modifying emotionality, discriminating between those who can help versus hinder the patient, or imparting other verbal and nonverbal skills. Therapist use of personal responses to administer consequences to patients to modify their behavior also falls under the umbrella of didactic activity.

Conclusions. The two ways Rogers has negatively influenced clinical psychology are evident in how we continue to define the therapist role in sterile and unrealistic terms, and in how patient learning continues to be ignored in our training, research, and practice. Both legacies have strengthened and maintained the tradition of the unilateral delivery of psychotherapy, with the direction of in-session flow always running from therapist to patient. Because Rogers' theory precluded the expression of direct and honest therapist responses to patients, bidirectional action was inhibited; hence, the personal involvement taboo was effectively maintained.

Before I discuss ways to overcome these two legacies, another important empirical tradition in clinical psychology that fosters them—the therapeutic alliance research tradition—must be discussed.

Therapeutic Alliance Research Tradition (1936–present)

Recently a colleague and I were discussing the specificity–nonspecificity psychotherapy debate presented in the 2002 spring issue of <u>Clinical Psychology:</u>

Science and Practice. My friend remarked that "everyone knows it's the therapeutic relationship that really matters, not techniques." I tried to steer the conversation back to specific disorders and then discuss what techniques might or might not work. My colleague would not budge: for this colleague, the relationship is prepotent regardless of the technique used or the type of disorder treated. I find this view of psychotherapy widespread in our field today, and it is frankly distressing (McCullough, 2002). Taken literally, this approach to therapy suggests that if clinicians are accepting, caring, and empathic, it really doesn't matter what they do. I have not found this to be true in my practice, nor do I endorse such a view—nor am I alone in this view (e.g., Chambless, 2002).

These widely held beliefs about psychotherapy stem from the therapeutic alliance research tradition that has, for over 50 years, scientifically investigated the helping/working relationship (Zetzel, 1956) existing between therapist and patient. This tradition, following Rogers' lead, focuses mainly on the experiential dimension of the therapist–patient relationship and the phenomenological status of patients. Alliance researchers have drawn several conclusions about psychotherapy, all of which my colleague above espouses: (1) psychotherapy appears to be more effective than placebo control groups; (2) no one therapy technique has been shown to be more effective than another; and (3) the client variable seems to be the biggest contributor to successful outcome (40% of outcome variance), with the dyadic relationship ranking second (30% of the variance), and specific techniques accounting for only 15% of the variance (Lambert, 1992).

Many researchers in this tradition assume that nonspecific and common factors will always eclipse (in importance) specificity concerns such as technique and psychopathology variables (Lambert, 1992; Lambert & Bergin, 1994; Luborsky, Singer, & Luborsky, 1975; Luborsky et al., 2002; Martin, Garske, & Davis, 2000; Messer & Wampold, 2002; Rosenzweig, 1936; Smith & Glass, 1977). These assumptions and generalizations have led to oversimplified conclusions about alliance effects on treatment outcome (Horvath, 1995; Lambert, 1992; Luborsky, McLellan, & Woody, 1985) and to efficacy studies that compare relatively similar models, such as psychoanalytic and humanistic psychotherapies (Constantino, Castonguay, & Schut, 2002; Horvath, 1994). In contrast to these conclusions, recent studies focusing on specific disorder groups suggest that alliance effects may vary depending on the psychopathology of the disorder (e.g., Barber et al., 1999; Klein et al., 2003).

Briefly sampling some of the therapeutic alliance variables that have been found to contribute to therapeutic outcomes, we find the following: (1) the degree to which the therapist extends unconditional affirmation to the patient (Greenberg, Rice, & Elliott, 1993; Orlinsky & Howard, 1986); (2) various phenomenological characteristics of patients, such as negative attitudes, their degree of passivity versus involvement in the therapeutic process, as well as their ability to bond with therapists (Bordin, 1979, 1994; Safran 1993a, 1993b; Zetzel, 1956, 1966); (3) a correspondence in level of affective intensity and empathic resonance between therapist and patient (or, put another way, a "sense of being on the same wavelength . . . of being fully heard by, and fully hearing, the other person"—Orlinsky & Howard,

1986, p. 344); and (4) several interactional–structural domains involving how therapists and patients approach the therapeutic undertaking: (a) the reciprocal role investment of the dyad, including the quality of the relational *bond* (Goldfried & Davison, 1974, 1994; Greenberg, et al., 1993; Greenson, 1967, 1971; Horvath & Greenberg, 1994; Horvath & Luborsky, 1993; Safran, 1998; Safran & Segal, 1996; Safran & Muran, 2000); (b) the extent to which both therapist and patient agree on the *goals* of therapy (Bordin, 1979; Greenson, 1967, 1971; Safran & Muran, 2000); and (c) dyadic agreement concerning the specific *tasks*(i.e., what the patient will actually be doing) necessary to achieve the therapeutic goals (Bordin, 1979; Safran & Muran, 2000; Sterba, 1934, 1940). Revising Rogers' earlier view that the alliance is something the therapist alone establishes (i.e., one-person psychology), contemporary alliance investigators define the alliance as a two-person psychology (Balint, 1968; Ghent, 1989; Mitchell, 1988) or the collaborative product of the therapist-by-patient interaction.

Not surprisingly, the alliance tradition, with its focus on the therapeutic relationship and deemphasis of technique, has proposed few novel systems of psychotherapy. One exception is Sheldon Cashdan's (1973) interactional psychotherapy model. Methodologically, Cashdan's proposal was a *stage-process model of treatment* that delineated stage rules for therapist behavior as well as setting patient performance goals for each treatment stage. Interestingly, the CBASP model uses a Cashdan-like methodological stage–process structure in prescribing its own therapist rules and patient performance goals (McCullough, 1984a, 1984b, 1984c, 2000: Chapters 6 and 7). However, Cashdan, in keeping with other alliance researchers, paid no attention to patient learning. Traditional emphases on the importance of the dyadic relationship are currently seen in two recent therapeutic alliance texts receiving outstanding reviews and wide distribution (viz., Norcross, 2002; Safran & Muran, 2000) and in Guest Editor John C. Norcross's (2002) winter 2001 special issue of <u>Psychotherapy: Theory/ Research/ Practice/ Training</u>. Terms such as *teaching* and *learning* are not found in these texts or cited in the indexes, nor do such terms play a significant role in the therapeutic relationship literature discussed in the winter 2001 issue of <u>Psychotherapy</u>.

What can we conclude about this august research tradition? (1) The alliance tradition, like the work of Carl Rogers, has emphasized the patient–therapist relationship to such a degree that concerns for patient diagnosis are eclipsed. (2) Because the personal involvement taboo is clearly present in this research tradition, the Freudian–Rogerian rule of maintaining *therapeutic neutrality* characterizes the role of alliance clinicians. (3) Alliance researchers, by concentrating solely on the *quality of the patient–therapist relationship,* have simply replaced Rogers' emphasis on the *role of the therapist* with the *alliance variable,* which also prescribes therapist neutrality. One possible exception to neutrality occurs in instances of *therapeutic rupture* (Safran & Muran, 1995, 1996, 2000; Safran, Muran, & Samstag, 1994). When conflicts or alliance ruptures arise, clinicians are not required to expose their own personal involvement issues; however, they must be willing to focus on the maladaptive schemas of patients that contribute to relational breakage, remain sensitive to past trauma experiences of the individual that might be activated in the current relationship, assist patients to recognize their oppositional behaviors, metacommunicate to patients in order to expose their negative interpersonal impacts on the clinician (Kiesler, 1988), and, when therapist behavior has contributed to the rupture, admit and be willing to discuss their sins of commission or omission. However, reading case descriptions illustrating the employment of these reparation strategies (e.g., Safran & Muran, 2000) still leaves one with the impression that the heavy relational focus as well as therapist neutrality are maintained throughout. And surprisingly, (4) in reviewing the alliance research literature, I find it difficult to identify the person of the patient and therapist. Alliance emphases occlude the essential individuality of both participants.

(5) No learning emphases exist in this body of research. Patients are exposed to clinicians who are well trained in constructing and maintaining therapeutic relationships and repairing them when necessary; what patients learn during the process of treatment is neither measured nor discussed. Lastly, (6) there is no question that the therapeutic alliance is a crucial and multifaceted variable in all psychotherapy endeavors, nor can there be any doubt that the quality of the dyadic relationship contributes significant variance to treatment outcome (e.g., Klein et al., 2003). However, the personal neutrality relationship these therapists extend to patients makes Hoffer's (2000) comment about classical psychoanalysis highly applicable to the therapeutic alliance research tradition. This type of psychotherapy can aptly be described as a type of relationship "for which there is no model in real life" (Hoffer, 2000, p. 38).

Nevertheless, this longstanding psychotherapy tradition—which, as noted above, steadfastly maintains the Rogerian legacies in clinical psychology—sets the stage for us to move beyond the personal involvement taboo. The research and writings of interpersonal psychotherapist Donald J. Kiesler, whose work clearly places him within the alliance research tradition, have paved the way toward greater personal involvement and less neutrality on the part of psychotherapists.

Kiesler's Interpersonal Psychotherapy

Kiesler's interpersonal psychotherapy research (Anchin & Kiesler, 1982; Kiesler, 1983, 1988, 1996; Kiesler & Schmidt, 1993; Kiesler & Watkins, 1989) stands solidly within the alliance tradition. His work has added substance to the study of the therapeutic alliance by providing robust empirical support for a two-person psychology (Balint, 1968). Furthermore, he has addressed the patient psychopathology variable (Kiesler, 1986a, 1986b, 1996, 1999; Kiesler, Van Denburg, Sikes-Nova, Larus, & Goldston, 1990) to a greater extent than any other alliance researcher.

Kiesler's interpersonal theory derives from Harry Stack Sullivan's (1954) assumption that observational neutrality in regard to one's own therapeutic administrations is unattainable. Kiesler's theory and subsequent research seriously challenge the one-person psychology of Rogers as well as that of classical psychoanalysis. As noted above, his research focus and behavior modification strategies clearly position him in the *two-person psychology camp* (e.g., Balint, 1968; Safran and Muran, 2000). Therapists and patients are seen as cocreators (Kiesler, 1983, 1988, 1996) of the therapeutic relationship. By focusing attention on the parameters of the dyadic interaction, Kiesler makes clear that constructs such as *transference* (patient learned expectancies) and *countertransference* (therapist learned expectancies) can only be understood when they are seen as inherent properties of what Greenberg (1995a) terms the "interactive matrix".

From this perspective, Kiesler shows that the expectancies both interactants bring to, and ultimately act out (verbally and nonverbally), in any therapeutic moment directly inform what happens in that moment. For example, if a therapist is comfortable during moments of intimacy whereas his or her patient is frightened by them, then intimacy, whenever it occurs, becomes a serious interpersonal issue that directly influences what happens during such occasions. The concepts of transference and countertransference are integrated within an interpersonal perspective (Kiesler, 1988, 1996) in a technique called "therapist metacommunication"— which comes close to advocating disciplined personal involvement, as opposed to the unilateral delivery of techniques so characteristic of alliance psychotherapy. In the metacommunication technique, Kiesler (1988, 1996) suggests that the therapist's personal responses to the patient become the central focus of the session. We turn now to a description of the theory underlying metacommunication, the corresponding notion of complementarity, and a description of the technique itself. Metacommunication is a novel way to respond to patients' in-session behavior as well as a strategy that takes us closer to personal involvement with patients.

Theory Underlying Metacommunication

For Kiesler, metacommunication occurs when an interaction between therapist and patient becomes the topic of the conversation: "Therapeutic metacommunication or metacommunicative feedback refers to any instance in which the therapist provides to the patient verbal feedback that targets the central, recurrent, and thematic relationship issues occurring between them in their therapy sessions" (Kiesler, 1988, p. 39). With this definition, Kiesler moves us away from Hoffer's (2000) description of the therapist's role as having no precedent in daily living. Kiesler's technique looks more like a real-world interaction and less like the blank-slate persona so descriptive of the Rogerian tradition. He explains further: "The rock-bottom assumption of contemporary interpersonal psychotherapy is that the client–therapist interaction, despite its unique characteristics, is similar in major ways to any other human interaction" (Kiesler, 1996, p. 282).

Building upon the work of Sullivan (1953) and Leary (1957), Kiesler argues that the essential unit of behavior is the *interpersonal act*. Both Sullivan and Leary "assert that any interpersonal act is designed to elicit from a respondent reactions that confirm, reinforce, or validate a person's self-presentation and that cause that person to repeat similar interpersonal acts" (Kiesler, 1988, p. 8). In the interpersonal act, two parties conjointly behave in the above fashion; therefore, understanding the outcome of the act is contingent on the interaction of two individuals. Reciprocal or bidirectional influence is seen as always present in any therapist–patient encounter. Therapists are constantly bombarded—emotionally, cognitively and behaviorally—by patient behavior, and the impact evokes both covert and overt reactions from therapists (Kiesler, 1988, 1996): *Covert* reactions remain unspoken, whereas *overt* ones are verbalized or nonverbally communicated. Patients experience similar impacts as well as "pulls" for personal reactions from therapists. In summary, the behavior of each participant continually produces and receives behavioral consequences from the other in an ongoing and reciprocal interactive process (Bandura, 1977).

The interpersonal act (Kiesler 1983, 1988, 1996) couples or blends together two dimensions or motivations: One dimension denotes a *power* stance in relation to the other, whereas the second implicates an *affiliation* position. These motivational properties derive from interpersonal theory, which assumes that the need for control (power, dominance) and the need for affiliation (love, friendliness) underlie all human interaction (Kiesler, 1983, 1996; Leary, 1957). Kiesler (1983, 1985) conceptually and empirically describes the varieties of interpersonal acts in his 1982 formulation of the interpersonal circle, a circumplex design that positions the power control dimension (dominant–submissive) on a vertical axis and the affiliation dimension (friendly–hostile) on the horizontal axis. The interpersonal effects one individual has on another can then be plotted on the circumplex (e.g., Kiesler & Schmidt, 1993) by assigning to each dimension so many units of control and so many units of affiliation. Continued research on the interpersonal circle resulted in an instrument called the Impact Message Inventory (IMI) (Kiesler & Schmidt, 1993). The original four quadrants of the 1982 circle, derived from the intersection of the power and affiliation axes, were divided; the IMI circle now contains eight octants, each representing an interpersonal emotive–cognitive "action tendency" or pull on the recipient of the act (i.e. the *decoder:* receiver of the interpersonal message). The action tendency or pull for feeling a certain way toward the other, thinking a certain way about the other, or wanting to behave in a particular manner with the other results from the behavior of the actor (i.e., the *encoder:* sender of the interpersonal message). Actors are the *encoders,* or perpetrators, of interpersonal impacts. As noted, encoders act in ways to obtain confirmation, reinforcement, and validation of their self-presentation. Another way to say the same thing is to say that we behave interpersonally in ways that tend to validate our self-view. Encoding strategies often represent tacit knowledge (Nisbett & Wilson, 1977; Polanyi, 1968, 1976) that arises from sources lying beyond immediate awareness.

Kiesler's Notion of Complementarity

Recipients (decoders) of interpersonal acts tend to behave in *complementary ways* toward the actors (encoders; Kiesler, 1983, 1988, 1996). Kiesler explains that "our interpersonal actions are designed to invite, pull, elicit, draw, entice, or evoke 'restricted classes' of reactions from persons with whom we interact, especially from significant others" (Kiesler, 1983, p. 198). These "restricted classes" of reactions fall under the rubric of *complementary behavior*—that is, reactions we pull from others are predictable and familiar. When patients enter treatment, they behave in ways that are interpersonally similar to behaviors they enact on the outside. Thus, a patient's expectancies of the therapist's reactions will naturally mirror those reactions which the patient has consistently received, as well as come to expect, from significant others. This phenomenon is essentially a *transference expectancy:* Relational response patterns are transferred to the person of the therapist (Hilgard & Bower, 1966). By closely observing the covert interpersonal pulls for complementary reactions from the patient, even though we inhibit any overt reactivity, we can begin to discern and articulate the interpersonal style of the patient. Using the IMI (Kiesler & Schmidt, 1993) to make explicit the interpersonal "stimulus value" of patients (i.e., the salient emotive, cognitive, and behavioral pulls/action tendencies *we* experience when we are with patients) also has definite therapist role implications that are discussed in later chapters. Elaborating Kiesler's concept of complementarity will further demonstrate the utility of the IMI in clarifying the patient's stimulus value for the clinician.

Interpersonal complementarity, which is "operationalized" in graphic terms by the two-dimensional interpersonal circle (Kiesler, 1983), "occurs on the basis of (a) reciprocity in respect to the control dimension (dominance pulls submission, submission pulls dominance) and (b) correspondence in regard to the affiliation dimension (hostility pulls hostility, friendliness pulls friendliness)" (Kiesler, 1988, p. 14). The octant version of the interpersonal circle is shown in Figure 2.1. Moving counterclockwise around the circle, we leave the dominnant (D) octant and come to the hostile–dominant (H-D) octant, then the hostile (H) octant, and the hostile–submisive (H-S), submissive (S), friendly–submissive (F-S), friendly (F), and friendly–dominant (F-D) octants. Complementarity is actualized when an individual, for example, behaving in a F-D manner, pulls the partner to react from the F-S octant. The reverse is also true: F-S behavior pulls for F-D reactions. On the hostile side of the circle, H-D pulls for H-S behavior, and the reverse. An individual behaving in an H-S manner will evoke reactions from the H-D octant. Interpersonal complementarity does *not* mean that decoders (receivers of the message) will automatically behave in an overt manner toward encoders (senders). The action tendency may remain covert. Regardless of whether the complementary reaction is overtly or covertly expressed, it will be experienced by the decoder (recipient) as a pull or tendency to emote, think, or behave in predictable ways. Kiesler provides prototypical examples of octant behaviors and their complementary action tendency pulls in Figure 2.2. Connotative verbal descriptors adjacent to each octant denote prototypical "characterizations" for that octant. The arrows in Figure 2.2 show the directions of the complementary pulls, indicating how clinicians are naturally inclined to behave. The reader can look at each octant, taking into account its complementary pull, think about one patient he or she has treated recently, and then determine if the complementary descriptor is congruent with the reactions he or she actually experienced with that patient.

Profile Summary Sheet
IMPACT MESSAGE INVENTORY: FORM IIA OCTANT VERSION
Donald J. Kiesler and James A. Schmidt

Patient _____
Therapist _____
Session/Date _____ /_____

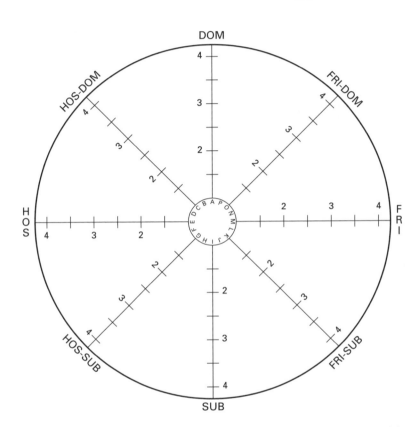

FIGURE 2.1. The octant version of the interpersonal circle. Reproduced by special permission of the publisher, Mind Garden, Inc., 1690Woodside Road, Suite #202, Redwood City, CA 94061: (650) 261-3500: from the *Impact Message Inventory: Form IIA Octant Scale Version* by Donald J. Kiesler, PhD. Copyright 1993 by Dr. Donald J. Kiesler. All rights reserved. Further reproduction is prohibited without the distributor's written consent.

The Metacommunication Technique

Administration of the metacommunication technique includes several steps. The first step begins when a therapist makes an objective countertransference decision (Epstein & Feiner, 1979) about the patient's prominent interpersonal impact. Said

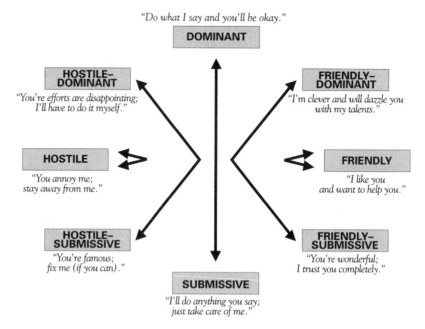

FIGURE 2.2. Octant complementary "pulls" of Kiesler's interpersonal circle. Reproduced by special permission of the publisher, Mind Garden, Inc., 1690 Woodside Road, Suite #202, Redwood City, CA 94061: (650) 261-3500: from the *Impact Message Inventory: Form IIA Octant Scale Version* by Donald J. Kiesler, PhD. Copyright 1993 by Dr. Donald J. Kiesler. All rights reserved. Further reproduction is prohibited without the distributor's written consent.

another way, the therapist identifies the evoking style (or pull) of the patient, which was exposed during an interaction. The patient may be duplicitously asking the therapist to tell him or her what to do by enacting submissive behavior (submission pulls for dominance). For example, submissive behavior may be communicated *verbally* in this manner: "I don't know what to do. You do, so please help me out and tell me." A *nonverbal* interpersonal act would include breaking into sobs or gazing at the therapist with a helpless expression. Either way, the strong pull is for assistance. Another illustration involves patients who disengage interpersonally or distance themselves (i.e., behave in a hostile–submissive manner, which pulls for a hostile-dominance reaction from the clinician) from some topic or subject whenever they become anxious. Patient avoidance strategies are often frustrating to clinicians, and clinicians might feel like saying something to this effect: "Dammit, if you're not going to deal with this problem, then why the hell are you sitting here!" This is a hostile-dominance reaction, which would represent a knee-jerk reaction to a hostile–submissive act.

These two examples illustrate how, in step 1, therapists must identify the evoking style of the patient. Both examples denote self-defeating and duplicitous styles.

Kiesler notes that in "assessing the patient, the therapist constantly decodes his or her linguistic and nonverbal messages" (1988, p. 22). The assessment data are derived from the patient's verbal and nonverbal behavior, the syntactic style of the patient's speech, and, as illustrated above, from his or her evoking style (Kiesler, 1988). Wisely, Kiesler adds a caveat to the assessment process, warning that objective countertransference assessment is valid only to the degree that the clinician is not threatened (made anxious) by the evoking message, such that he or she has difficulty disengaging from the impact or discussing the impact without distorting it. Noted earlier, problems disengaging from evoking messages arise from unresolved *subjective countertransference* issues.

During step 2, the therapist deliberately disengages from the evoking impact and decides what he or she will do. By not reacting in a complementary way, the therapist breaks into the patient's maladaptive cycle of interacting with others and offers an *asocial* response (Kiesler, 1988).

Step 3 is taken when the therapist actually responds in an asocial or noncomplementary manner: "The therapist responds to the patient in an asocial or disengaged way whenever the therapist withholds the customary, preferred, or expected complementary response" (Kiesler, 1988, p. 24). By being pulled into unfamiliar (and unexpected) interpersonal territory by an asocial reaction from the therapist, most patients experience a sort of "beneficial uncertainty" (Beier, 1966; Kiesler, 1988)—in short, they are thrown off guard. Making a noncomplementary response in the first case, above, means not acting in a dominant way and telling the patient what to do. In the second example, the therapist does not respond in a hostile-dominant fashion; instead, he or she would metacommunicate something to this effect: "Whenever we encounter something that makes you unsure about what to do, you cry and look longingly toward me. It makes me feel like I ought to provide you with answers." In a similar vein, metacommunicating to this patient could be done in this way: "It seems like every time we talk about something that makes you nervous or uncomfortable, you withdraw and pull back—you leave the conversation. It makes me feel alone, frustrated, and a little bit silly, wondering why I'm even talking about this stuff."

The goal of metacommunicative feedback is to reduce the extremes of behaving submissively (in the first case) and disengaging in the face of stress (in the second). By offering these individuals an asocial response, the clinician is attempting to pull both patients toward the "center" of the response circle, away from the extremes. This goal is accomplished by refusing to react with dominance when faced with submission or with a hostile-dominance response in the face of hostile–submissive behavior. Remaining on the friendly side of the circle and assuming a task-focused stance (see McCullough, 2000, Chapter 8) usually constitutes an asocial position on the circle for self-defeating behaviors. A task-focused stance helps patients discuss self-defeating interactive behavior and possible alternative strategies. Kiesler argues that metacommunicative feedback is "one of the most powerful asocial responses in the therapist's repertoire" (1988, p. 27).

Conclusions

Kiesler is the first alliance psychotherapist in over 50 years to offer a prescribed methodology that moves the therapist beyond the *blank-slate* facade of anonymity and toward more personal disclosure. From the field's inception, psychotherapists have asked patients to be direct, genuine, and honest when they would not and could not reciprocate. Substantive avenues for reciprocal behavior open up in Kieslerian psychotherapy, in which therapists are encouraged to behave like real human beings. Over the years, many patients have seen through our unilateral facade and protested in various ways.

For example, shortly after I had completed my clinical training, one of my patients made a very kind observation late one afternoon when she said, "Dr. McCullough, you look like you're tired." She offered a genuine empathic reaction to an obvious (though unintended) display of fatigue on my part. What I said in return was what I had learned in training: "We're not here to talk about me, we're here to focus on you" (I responded in a hostile–submissive manner). Her reply was almost inaudible but very instructive. She said, "Shit" (she reacted in a hostile-dominant way). I'd pushed her away, acted like a robot, and her reaction was appropriate. I wish she had metacommunicated with me then and there and said something like this: "When I try to be sensitive, you push me away. It makes me feel like you're not a real human being, like you're playing out a role." Kiesler has taken our psychotherapy tradition one step closer to personal involvement with patients. Next, we explore the work of two pioneers in the personal involvement arena, who have broken new ground by successfully transcending the personal involvement taboo.

Personal Involvement Pioneers: Garry Prouty and Kent G. Bailey

Garry Prouty's Pretherapy Method

Prouty (1994) stands within the Rogerian person-centered tradition. Rogers (1942) assumed that the patient's ability to make *psychological contact* was the sine qua non of the therapeutic relationship. Unfortunately, he provided no definition of psychological contact nor offered a description of how it could be learned, if the skill were absent, or restored if lost (Prouty, 1994). Eugene Gendlin, a Rogerian clinical psychologist, mentored Prouty during the latter's clinical training days. Prouty was particularly influenced by Gendlin, who felt that Rogers had overlooked a crucial change variable because of his exclusive focus on therapist attitudes. For Gendlin, the patient's perceptual experience of the therapist's attitudes (i.e., unconditional positive regard, empathy, and congruence), which he called the "experiencing gap," lies between the attitudes and the individual's reception (his or her experience) of them. He shifted the focus of therapeutic change from the therapist to the experiential processes in the patient. The experiential domain, according to Gendlin, was the critical psychological change variable in person-centered therapy (Van Balen, 1991). In adding the experiencing construct to Rogers' method, he initiated the Rogerian person-centered/experiential movement (Gendlin, 1964, 1968, 1974, 1979; Gendlin & Berlin, 1961).

There was one subject on which Rogers and Gendlin agreed: Both felt that the person-centered method would not work with schizophrenic or retarded psychotic patients. Rogers argued that retarded individuals lacked the necessary introspective skills, and that schizophrenic patients could not generate psychological contact because of their social withdrawal and isolation (Rogers, 1942; Rogers, Gendlin, Kiesler, & Truax, 1967). In a similar vein, Gendlin (1970) reasoned that because schizophrenic patients were perceptually disconnected from the world, they could not sustain social interaction or experience feelings.

Prouty's pretherapy model begins where Rogers and Gendlin stop. The method is designed *to prepare* schizophrenic and retarded psychotic individuals for individual psychotherapy. The pretherapy method concentrates on developing the psychological functions necessary for psychotherapy: reality, affective, and communicational contact (Prouty, 1994). He describes these three contact functions: (1) *reality contact* is the ability to be aware of one's perceptual environment and the people who inhabit it; it is operationalized by the ability to name people, places, and events; (2) *affective contact* is the ability to be aware of one's moods and the changes that occur in feeling shifts; it is operationalized as an expression of bodily or facial affect; (3) *communication contact* is the ability to communicate one's experienced reality with another; it is operationalized as the ability to form socially related words or sentences.

His work is significant for several reasons: (1) his focus on two specific patient populations (regressed schizophrenic and retarded psychotic patients) has enabled us to identify what works for whom; (2) he conducts intensive, single-case research to determine ways to teach contact and experiencing skills to both groups; the intensive study of the single patient provides one of the most effective design procedures with which to develop new therapeutic techniques (McCullough, 1984b); (3) patient learning and measurement of the generalized treatment effects of learning constitute essentials parts of his program; (4) his work with these two patient groups indicates that personal involvement (behavioral, emotional, and physical availability to patients) is necessary to administer the methodology. Reading about his methodology reminds me of the work of Eugene Bleuler. He quotes Bleuler, who writes that his "main endeavor was to be close to his patients; working with them, playing and walking with them, even organizing dancing parties with them . . . . It was in Rheinau that he realized that schizophrenics could not be "demented" (Bleuler, 1991, pp. 2–3).

Prouty introduces his model by asking a question suggesting that teaching preparatory interpersonal skills will be important. He asks, "What are the necessary *pre-conditions* of a therapeutic relationship?" (1994, p. 36). His answer is a treatment plan designed to teach patients to meet his precondition criteria. As stated above, he assumes that patients who are viable psychotherapy candidates must be able to make reality, affective, and communicational contact with therapists. In turn, therapists must enact intensely personal, nondirective, verbal, and nonverbal "reflective behaviors" in order to awaken patients' awareness of these contact functions. Space limitations preclude further description of Prouty's concepts and methodology, but a presentation of one verbatim case vignette "illustrates contact reflections (on the part of the therapist) resulting in the restoration of the contact functions in a chronic schizophrenic woman" (Prouty, 1994, p. 42):

Case

Dorothy was an older regressed patient on the ward. The therapist could hear specific words within her confused pattern of speech. Reflecting (by repeating word-for-word) the words which could be understood and using bodily movements to mirror (reflect) the body movements of the patient resulted in Dorothy saying a complete sentence after about ten minutes. The example illustrates movement from a pre-expressive communicative state to an expressive style of communication—autism (loss of contact with the world, self, and the other) in this instance gives way to existential contact (contact with the world, self, and the other).

Client: Come with me.
Therapist: Come with me [The patient led me to the corner of the day room. We stood there silently for what seemed to be a very long time. Since I couldn't communicate with her, I watched her body movements and closely reflected these.]
Client: [The patient put her hand on the wall.] Cold.
Therapist: [I, using body reflections, put my hand on the wall and repeated the word.] Cold.

[She had been holding my hand all along, but when I reflected her, she would tighten her grip. Dorothy began to mumble word fragments. I was careful to reflect only the words I could understand. What she was saying began to make sense.]

Client: I don't know what this is anymore. [Touching the wall: *reality contact*.] The walls and chairs don't mean anything anymore. [Existential autism.]
Therapist: [Touching the wall.] You don't know what this is anymore. The chairs and walls don't mean anything to you any more.
Client: [The patient began to cry: *affective contact*. After a while she began to talk again. This time she spoke clearly: *communicative contact*.] I don't like it here. I'm so tired . . . so tired.
Therapist: [As I gently touched her arm, this time it was I who tightened my grip on her hand. I reflected.] You're tired, so tired.
Client: [The patient smiled and told me to sit in a chair directly in front of her and began to braid my hair.] (Prouty, 1994, pp. 42–43)

Teaching novel contact behaviors to regressed schizophrenic and psychotically retarded patients means that we depart from the mainstream of psychotherapy practice. New therapist roles sometimes emerge during these occasions when old methodologies do not work, and this model is a case in point. The pretherapy model requires practitioners to make themselves available to patients on interpersonal levels not usually encountered in daily practice. For example, physical contact and proximity are often necessary, sessions are sometimes carried out in the home, and the therapist must be able to experience as well as to disclose personal feelings, thoughts, and concerns that he or she has for the patient. These patients necessitate a therapist's willingness to share in the most horrible dimensions of human experience as well as the ability to tolerate slow and tedious progress.

That Prouty's pretherapy method transcends the personal involvement taboo is not surprising. The reasons why are important. The therapist role prescriptions are informed by the psychological and learning needs of patients. By beginning treatment on the patient's level rather than requiring the patient to fulfill preset psychological and professional criteria, Prouty achieved remarkable results with two populations Rogers and Gendlin had excluded from their purview.

Kent G. Bailey's Kinship Psychotherapy

Bailey is an evolutionary paleopsychologist and psychotherapist (1987, 1988, 1997, 2000, 2002; Ahern & Bailey, 1997; Bailey & Wood, 1998; Bailey, Wood, & Nava, 1992; Gilbert & Bailey, 2000) who introduced a general approach to human behavior called *paleopsychology* (Bailey, 1987) and published the initial article on *kinship psychotherapy* in the late 1980s (Bailey, 1988). He writes that both "empirically and theoretically, the relationship is central to virtually all forms of professional helping and psychological treatment" (Bailey et al., 1992, p. 125). Standing within the alliance tradition, his writings and research illuminate, from a paleopsychological point of view, *why* the personal involvement dimension is so crucial. Bailey assumes that all helping relationships are based on a natural human propensity to form psychological "kinship" or "kinship-like" relationships with significant others.

Two kinship categories are described in Bailey's work: biological and psychological. Biological kinship, although somewhat similar to psychological kinship, differs in significant ways. The former denotes the degree of genetic relationship one shares with another and entails a classification of the other "as family." Psychological kinship, on the other hand, describes "a universal, natural means of interpersonal valuing whereby persons classify others first in terms of in-group versus out-group status . . . and then further in terms of differential value with the respective status. Thus, one may 'love' (value biopsychologically) with differing intensities within the in-group, and 'hate' (disvalue biopsychologically) with differing intensities within the out-group" (Bailey, 1988, p. 133). Psychological kinship feelings and attachments clearly account for the widespread human tendency to include nongenetically related individuals (Bailey's list includes friends, lovers, marital partners, coworkers, adopted children, military buddies, athletic teammates, persons bound by mutual suffering, etc.) into the psychological in-group and classify them "as family" (Bailey, 1988) in a "kin-like" category (Ahern & Bailey, 1997).

According to Bailey, kinship displayed by a psychotherapist would include a long list of attributes or behaviors:

- Strong sensitivity to the patient's need to "be family" (e.g., patient's attempts to deepen the intimacy of dyadic contact)

- Careful monitoring of the sexual transference and countertransference domain so as not to cross the "incest barrier"
- Efforts exerted to increase "bonding" between practitioner and patient
- Avoidance of a "double standard" when ethical or moral issues arise (e.g., not holding one set of rules for his or her family and another for patients)
- Extending of a compassionate and caring style
- Integration of the patient's biological family into treatment whenever appropriate
- Sensitivity to a minority patient's racial issues (i.e., sensitive acknowledgment of cultural differences/nuances)
- Behaves authentically (i.e., does not play a "therapist role")
- Does not overemphasize techniques
- Gears treatment goals to engender "hope, faith and healing."

Bailey (1988) derives four assumptions from his premise that we universally tend to form psychological kinship relations with nonbiologically related others and, more specifically, with the "helper" in helper–helpee relationships. He assumes that (1) patients (helpees) desire a kinship relationship with psychotherapists (helpers) because they desire to move from an out-group position to in-group status; (2) the desire for kinship varies proportionately to the degree of mental or physical stress/suffering; (3) minority groups are likely to gravitate toward kinship forms of treatment because their life situation includes high levels of stress; and (4) many psychotherapists (helpers) do not recognize or desire psychological kinship relationships with patients. Bailey's approach represents a clarion call for therapists to recognize how important a role they play in the lives of their patients and then find ways to integrate this recognition into the therapy process.

A case description from Gilbert and Bailey (2000) is presented next to illustrate psychological kinship when it is actualized to a maximum degree. I paraphrase some of the case from Bailey's description and quote him in other areas.

Case

Jennie was a difficult challenge from the day she entered the office. She was belligerent, argumentative, appeared to be high on drugs, and thought the counseling process was a sham. Her history was sordid: substance abuse, minor brushes with the law, antisocial behavior, and suicide attempts. She was a native of backwoods Alabama and as an infant her "mother had cast her off" to an aunt and uncle. They had raised her in a rigid and unaffectionate manner. Jennie ran away from home as a teenager and was informally adopted by Wanda, a loving but mentally ill older lady. She still feels that Wanda is her "true mother" (i.e., closest psychological kin). During early sessions, Jennie was administered a battery of tests (MMPI [high F: Infrequency scale]) and significant clinical elevations on Scales 2 (Depression scale) and 4 (Psychopathic Deviate scale); Draw-a-Person; TAT [deep longings for love and acceptance]; Rorschach [impulsivity and psychological impoverishment]). The data suggested that she met criteria for borderline personality disorder, moderate, and was probably alcoholic.

When treatment began, the only significant others in Jennie's life were Wanda and the therapist—who came in a very distant second. However, Wanda lived in another city, so Jennie "grabbed on to me as a lifeline" (Gilbert & Bailey, 2000, p. 59). The patient–therapist relationship would prove to be pivotal in the early stages of her therapy. Jennie entered the sessions loud and boisterous, expressing extreme ambivalence about being in the room, and released her rage and anger at the only person in the room—the therapist. Bailey writes that "warm emotionality was low . . . as we struggled to find something to base a relationship on" (p. 59). In terms of kinship status, the relational dynamic was confusing. The patient seemed to perceive the therapist as a potential kinship object and enemy at the same time. Bailey confided that the only emotion he experienced at this point was a deep professional obligation to the patient. Her tirades seemed to be sort of "a test, to see if I really cared." In the early stages, his "goal was to hold firm and try to win her trust" (2000, p. 59).

During a session in the fourth month of treatment, Jennie became angry over probing questions and ran from the room screaming epithets at the therapist. She returned 20 minutes later looking sheepish, subdued, and trying to figure out how the therapist would react.

At that time, I felt that this was the moment where the relationship would stand or fall. I firmly stated that there was nothing she could do to get me to give up on her, so she might as well just knock it off. Surprisingly, she seemed very pleased with that and promised to be back next week. In retrospect, I can now see that this was the very deep "kinship" affirmation that she had sought all along from others and myself. (Gilbert & Bailey, 2000, p. 59)

The therapeutic bond was affected suddenly and deeply during that session. Subsequently, Jennie began to dress more attractively, made a few new friends, and found employment. At therapy outcome, her MMPI scores on Scales 2 and 4 had dropped significantly, indicating that she was no longer depressed and blaming others less frequently for her problems; however, she was unable to overcome alcoholism. Nevertheless, therapy had helped provide her with a sense of meaning and had terminated the downward spiral of self-destructive behavior. Jennie was accepted into the military shortly thereafter and became one of three female helicopter mechanics in the U.S. Army. Serving 8 years with distinction, she was promoted to sergeant. Following a failed marriage of 1 year, she lapsed back into alcoholism and accepted a medical discharge from the army.

She continues to keep in touch with me and my family, and she will occasionally call or come by my home for a visit. She continues to classify not only me but my wife and daughter as "family," and we see her as something more than a previous therapy client. This is probably the only true psychological kinship I have developed with a client, and I have been willing to accept the obligations and occasional inconveniences that go with it. (Gilbert & Bailey, 2000, p. 60)

In this instance, a "psychological kinship" or kinlike relationship appeared to bring a degree of relief and psychological improvement into the patient's life.

The psychological kinship role can be thought of as a continuum ranging from *very little* to a *great deal*. From Bailey's point of view, however, kinship issues pervade every nook and cranny of the practice of conventional psychotherapy. The role of both participants in regard to felt kinship or personal involvement will be determined largely by the needs of the patient and the interpersonal capabilities of the clinician.

Summary

In this abbreviated history we have reviewed 100 years of the personal involvement taboo: from the rigid proscription of classical psychoanalysis forbidding personal involvement, to the work of Rogers and the mainstream therapeutic alliance research tradition that have fostered the personal involvement taboo in psychology and psychiatry, to the innovative work of interpersonal psychologist Don Kiesler, who opened the door for therapeutic personal involvement, and concluding with the pioneering work of Prouty and Bailey, who describe methods in which personal involvement can be actively incorporated as an integral part of treatment. Prouty and Bailey have demonstrated that there are obvious degrees of personal involvement and psychological kinship in all varieties of helper–helpee relationships. Some patients need more of a *kinship-like* relationship with therapists than others. Similar variability in the degree of kinship present also occurs in relation to various therapeutic techniques with their respective outcome goals. Some techniques may require therapists to generate personal involvement with patients to achieve therapeutic outcome goals. Others need only a modicum of therapist personal involvement—one that extends no further than having a detached concern for the person's welfare.

In demonstrating that various techniques require differing amounts of therapist neutrality, Prouty and Bailey have also enabled us to transcend our ingrained all or-none thinking about personal involvement. There is no longer a "one-size fits all," to borrow a marketing phrase. Our century-old proscription must be revised in light of new data. It is clear that the decision to employ personal involvement with patients depends on complex parameters: (1) the diagnosed disorder; (2) the needs of the patient; (3) the technique being used and the goals of treatment; and (4) the interpersonal capabilities of the clinician. All four domains must be considered as informing sources whenever we speak of therapist personal involvement with patients.

Lastly, I discussed how learning concerns were largely absent during the 20th century in psychotherapy training, research, and practice. The one exception is the behavior therapy movement—which, ironically, never addressed the personal involvement issue. In the chapters that follow, learning issues are presented as salient and as informing therapist choice of personal tactics as well as how case outcomes are evaluated.

Chapter 3 begins by discussing the dangers of overestimating the chronically depressed patient's capabilities. I illustrate how, in overshooting the patient's reach, we sabotage our teaching efforts. A brief description of the psychopathology of the chronic disorder follows. Once the pathological needs of these patients are understood, it is easier to see why I recommend that CBASP therapists administer disciplined personal involvement with their chronically depressed patients. The final section discusses the interpersonal isolation of this patient population to illustrate why I think disciplined personal involvement is a necessary treatment component.

3
Treating the Chronically Depressed Patient

Psychological modifications can occur in later life through the influence of one or more "new" attachment figures combined with the development of formal operational thought.
—Katherine L. Schaefer (2004)

Therapists cannot adequately treat the chronically depressed adult without a thorough understanding of the patient: (1) what cognitive–emotional limitations he or she brings to treatment; (2) the nature of his or her psychopathology and the debilitating effects of the disorder; and (3) the extent of the interpersonal trauma and isolation experienced. Healing patients' trauma and overcoming their isolation often require disciplined personal involvement because, not infrequently, the clinician becomes the first authentic friend the patient has ever had. The goal of Chapter 3 is to paint a picture of the chronically depressed adult to help the reader understand why I advocate disciplined personal involvement in CBASP therapy.

Overestimating the Capability of the Chronically Depressed Patient

Every CBASP psychotherapist makes overestimation errors when it comes to evaluating the cognitive–emotional–behavioral capabilities of his or her chronically depressed patient. I have watched thousands of hours of videotaped CBASP sessions, and I frequently observe even veteran therapists overestimate their patients' ability in the way they conduct treatment. Several forms of the overestimation error are presented in the following material.

1. *Use of causal language.* One form of overestimation occurs when therapists talk to primitive-thinking patients using sophisticated "if this ... then that" causal language in an attempt to interpret *why* particular events happen or *what might happen* given certain circumstances. One of the most difficult lessons CBASP trainees must learn is to self-monitor the way they talk with patients. We are so used to speaking abstractly as well as thinking in probabilistic terms that it is not surprising we often fail to recognize that we leave patients at the perceptual starting gate. CBASP methodology is designed to help clinicians inhibit these tendencies.

2. *Preemptory provision of information.* Another overestimation error takes place when therapists impart information without previously assessing how much the patient knows about the subject matter. CBASP training stresses the importance of providing information only after evaluating what the patient knows. Telling patients something without prior knowledge of their understanding is always a "shot in the dark." More often than not, we overshoot patients with our information dissemination. For example, I observed a therapist describe to a patient an appropriate way for couples to settle arguments. The patient listened quietly. Later in the session, it became clear that the individual not only did not know how to identify when his wife was upset, he also didn't have the empathic skills to acknowledge her distress. The therapist's instruction was presented in an exemplary manner. Problems arose because of the patient's inability to process and understand the information. On such occasions, patients will often listen passively, then change the subject at the first opportune moment.

3. *Jumping the gun.* The most frequently observed overestimation error committed by CBASP therapists occurs when they "do the work of therapy" for their patients. In these instances, therapists either tacitly or explicitly assume that patients have mastered learning material when, in fact, they have not. CBASP is, in large measure, a didactic model in which the therapist's role is that of a teacher or guide. *Doing the work of therapy* means that clinicians, instead of teaching the coping method and allowing patients to practice until mastery is achieved, correct patient mistakes themselves—thereby precluding practice and mastery from taking place. This error occurs in another form when therapists actually provide coping answers for the problem at hand; both forms usurp the patient's role as learner.

These overestimation errors are subtle and hard to self-monitor. In fact, errors are usually detected only by supervisors who watch videotaped sessions and call attention to them. One reason overestimation happens so frequently in this area is because the acquisition learning process of chronically depressed patients is a slow one. All of us tire of the laborious process; we become impatient and, all too often, we move in and do the work. It must also be said that many patients pull strongly for us to assume a take-charge role; their interpersonal submissiveness and passivity constantly pull us into a complementary dominant role. Refusing to assume the dominant role is a never-ending challenge, and CBASP teachers must continually strive to master this overestimation behavior.

4. *Informational and perceptual overload.* A fourth example of the overestimation error is seen when the clinician tries to accomplish too much during the hour, assuming that patients can follow and assimilate multiple session goals. This error leads to sensory and informational overload and precludes effective learning from taking place. As a supervisor, I constantly encourage therapists to try to accomplish only one goal per session. If they conduct therapy in this manner, the patient more often than not learns the subject matter of the session. Not long ago I attempted to teach a patient to talk assertively with her mother, without screaming or losing her focus on what she wanted to say. She and I role-played a frequent scenario that took place between the mother and daughter (the patient). My session goals were too ambitious, and the therapy hour was not successful. The role-play goals I formed

included (1) to teach assertive behavior, (2) to teach the patient to monitor her emotional arousal during the role play, and (3) to remain problem-focused during the interactions. I tried to achieve too much too quickly. Mary Jane subsequently reported very little learning during the session. Constructing a reasonable goal for the therapy hour (e.g., just teaching assertive behavior), carefully thinking through what learning steps are needed, and then implementing the plan will often prevent the error of information overload.

In summary, overestimating the capabilities of patients at the outset of therapy can manifest itself in several ways. I have categorized overestimation as a therapist behavioral error. Such errors are usually the first problems CBASP supervisors tackle when training new therapists. CBASP, unlike many therapy models, has a specified learning agenda designed to resolve the psychopathology of the patient. Being able to teach the agenda effectively means that trainees must inhibit the tendency to assume that patients naturally function on their sophisticated levels. They do not. Instead, therapists must move to the patient's level and begin there. CBASP *therapist rules* and concomitant *patient goals* (McCullough, 2000; see also Chapters 6 and 7) assist practitioners to develop this ability. Furthermore, trainees must learn to achieve an optimal teaching pace with each patient in order to maximize learning.

Psychopathology of the Chronically Depressed Patient

During CBASP training seminars, I begin by having therapists list the challenges they face when treating chronically depressed patients. The audience usually produces a list that includes many of the following items:

- Not motivated to change
- Overwhelming feelings of helplessness and hopelessness
- A generalized pessimistic conclusion that nothing can be different
- Traumatic developmental history
- Feelings of inadequacy
- Expectation of rejection from everyone
- Pervasive self-rejection
- Feels like a failure
- Feels guilty about the state of his or her life
- Angry at one or more significant others
- Pervasive negativity
- Feels unlovable and believes that no one could/should care for him or her
- Suicidal ideation (runs on a continuum from mild to dangerous)

When we discuss the relationship challenges, many therapists highlight the following interpersonal difficulties:

- "The patient makes me feel helpless by saying that he or she knows that I will end up rejecting him or her (like everyone else)."

- "I feel incompetent and hopeless when patients keep telling me that nothing they do matters—that nothing will ever make a positive difference."
- "I often feel 'put in a box,' closed out and interpersonally pushed away by the detached style of the patient."
- "I feel frustrated and angry by his or her lack of motivation."
- "I feel tired, drained, and worn out—I often feel that I'm pulling a dead weight during the session."

Preoperational Functioning

A unique picture of psychopathology unfolds when we listen to, and observe, the way patients with chronic depression talk and behave. The picture is one of an isolated individual who is detached interpersonally, talks in a monologue fashion using a well-rehearsed script that has little or nothing to do with the actual interpersonal behavior of others, and exists in quiet despair within a self-contained, solitary world that is not informed by the external world. Nothing new enters or leaves the phenomenological orbit. The sensitive therapist will be impressed by each patient's terrible sense of "sameness." Existentially, these patients describe a lifestyle that makes time appear to be stopped—the present reflects the past and the future bodes only more of the same. I (McCullough, 2000) described this temporal outlook as a "snapshot" view of reality. These internal snapshots capture moments in time and freeze-frame them forever.

Piaget's (1926/1923, 1967/1964, 1981/1954) structural description of the maturational stage of *preoperational functioning* denotes a thinking and functioning style that is dominated by the individual's immediate perceptual experience—a style of functioning that provides an apropos description of the chronically depressed patient. Preoperational functioning accurately depicts the individual's phenomenological perspective. Patients think in a *prelogical* and *precausal manner,* drawing conclusions about their world without any hypothesis testing; the world is simply the way it is because patients believe it to be this way. Because their worldview has little, if anything, to do with any present interpersonal reality, logical or causal reasoning fails to modify the primitive structural set. Recently, for example, a chronically depressed patient viewed a CBASP videotape in which the narrator presented, "in a hopeful manner," the treatment the patient was about to undergo. Robust outcome data were presented from an earlier treatment study, suggesting that the therapy method would, more than likely, be helpful. After the tape ended, the patient commented, "I have no hope that anything will change." Reasoned viewpoints by others have no informing effect on the refractory perceptual outlook of these patients.

Chronically depressed patients' preoperational behavior can be seen in their *pervasively egocentric lifestyle.* All roads lead to the self. As noted above, the interpersonal environment exerts minimal-to-no influence on the person's outlook, because he or she is perceptually disconnected from the environment. When listening to beginning patients talk, I rarely hear comments that shift the attentional focus from a self-absorbed domain to the interpersonal realm. *I, me,* and *my* sentences abound. Only later will the individual begin to use *we, our,* and *their* pronouns in an informing way.

Another preoperational feature of the disorder is the inability to *generate empathy* for others. Emotional sensitivity must not be confused with empathy. Patients are emotionally sensitive to interpersonal rejection and seem magnetically drawn toward every word, expression, or look that might suggest such rejection.

In summary, the abilities to be informed by logical causal reasoning as well as by the reactions of others, to transcend egocentrism, and to generate empathy for others all require a perceptual structural capability that patients with chronic depression do not possess. Formal operational behavior—that is, the ability to disengage from the present moment, take a step back, and consider alternatives—is a skill that patients will acquire over the course of treatment. A maturational shift in psychological structure from preoperational thinking to formal operations thinking helps the individual overthrow his or her disorder and move toward remission.

Abstract thought must also be in place before emotional regulation is possible. *Dysfunctional emotional control* is a prominent feature of adult preoperational functioning. Before emotional regulation is possible, however, patients must first acquire the ability to disengage perceptually from their snapshot view of reality and consider alternative behavioral strategies in a planful, problem-focused manner (Folkman & Lazarus, 1988).

I (McCullough, 2000) describe how, during sessions, CBASP patients move from preoperational levels of functioning to formal operational behavior by repeated exposure to behavioral consequences. Maturational structural shifts are well documented in the Piagetian therapeutic literature (e.g., Cowan, 1978; Gordon, 1988). The CBASP construct of *perceived functionality* denotes the acquired ability to identify the environmental consequences of one's behavior. Perceived functionality is synonymous with formal operations functioning in the CBASP system. When patients recognize that their behavior has consequences, the recognition indicates that an informing environmental connection has now reached the level of perceptual awareness.

Etiology of Early- and Late-Onset Chronic Depression

What etiological events derail normal maturational development in the social–environmental sphere and entrap individuals at a preoperational level? Piaget (1981/1954), Spitz (1946), "failure to thrive" researchers (e.g., Drotar & Sturm, 1991; Money, 1992; Money, Annecillo, & Hutchinson, 1985), and Cicchetti (Cicchetti, Ackerman, & Izard, 1995; Cicchetti & Toth, 1998) all suggest that excessive emotionality, adverse familial circumstances of long duration, and severe neglect or trauma interfere with normal cognitive–emotional maturation as well as physical development and can derail or retard normal developmental processes. When a child's environment becomes an obstacle course with no resolution, normal growth and maturation are thwarted. Under such circumstances, surviving "the hell of the family," not normal growth-directed behavior, becomes the goal. The hallmark emotions of chronic depression—helplessness and hopelessness—are appropriate childhood and adolescent reactions to a developmental world that offers "no exit" (Sartre, 1961).

I (McCullough, 2000) hypothesized that most early-onset chronically depressed adults have undergone severe trauma and long-term adverse home environments. The individual exits childhood and adolescence as a structurally and functionally damaged adult. Cicchetti and Barnett (1991) identified four categories of childhood maltreatment frequently reported in the histories of early-onset patients: *emotional maltreatment, physical abuse, sexual abuse,* and *physical neglect.*

A recent research report (Nemeroff et al., 2003) ranked four modal forms of childhood trauma among 681 chronically depressed outpatients. The sample included both early- and late-onset outpatients. Trauma events occurred before age 15, and 64% of the sample reported some form of childhood trauma. Physical abuse (43.5%), parental loss (34.1%), sexual abuse (16.3%), and neglect (10%) were the most commonly reported traumata. Another study (Horwitz, 2001), comparing the two chronically depressed onset groups, investigated the extent of adversity in the childhood home environment. The most common "major" adverse events associated with *both* groups were impaired parent–child relationships, verbal abuse and constant criticism, domestic violence in the parental relationship, psychopathology in at least one parent, and divorce/separation from at least one parent. Several significant differences emerged when comparing the early- and late-onset groups. The early-onset group reported almost twice as many major adverse events when they were children, a greater incidence of verbal abuse, sexual abuse, and a greater dysfunctional relationship with the mother. These subjects also described a more "severe" childhood developmental milieu than late-onset individuals.

Consistent findings about the effects of trauma and the early-onset of the disorder have been reported in several other studies. For example, Lizardi et al. (1995) found significantly greater physical and sexual abuse, a poorer quality of relationship with both parents, lower levels of maternal and paternal care, and greater overprotection on the part of both mothers and fathers when early-onset outpatients were compared to normal controls. A more disturbed childhood and a poorer quality of parental relationship were also evident when the early-onset patients were compared to patients with nonchronic, episodic major depression. The authors concluded that the childhood home environment plays a highly significant role in the development of early-onset dysthymic disorder. Brown and Moran (1994) as well as Kendler, Walters, and Kessler (1997) wrote that the early home environment and, more specifically, *early childhood adversity* were associated with the development of chronic depression. In a similar vein, Durbin, Klein, and Schwartz (2000) showed that the presence of childhood adversity and familial psychopathology were more powerful predictors of the absence of remission among dysthymic outpatients than either clinical or demographic variables. Their patients were monitored during a $2\frac{1}{2}$-year naturalistic study.

An extensive review of depression in children and adolescents (Cicchetti & Toth, 1998) reiterated the above conclusions concerning the effects of childhood adversity and its association with early-onset depression. In summary, the authors noted that an adverse early home environment negatively impacts homeostatic and physiological regulation (Cicchetti & White, 1988; Davidson, 1991), affective differentiation and modulation of attention and arousal (Schore, 1996), the quality of the attachment between the child and the primary caregiver (Ainsworth, Blehar, Waters, & Wall, 1978; Bowlby, 1973, 1980; Hammen, 1992), and self–other differentiation (Hammen, 1988; Garber, Quiggle, Panak, & Dodge, 1991).

Early-onset chronically depressed patients frequently bring the "imprint" of a catastrophic environmental experience to treatment. Their developmental course precluded normal growth and maturation and, more than likely, dictated that they expend an inordinate portion of their growth energy just trying to survive.

The late-onset patient usually describes a *milder developmental history* (McCullough, 2000). This view has recently been supported in the research of Horwitz (2001), who reported that late-onset subjects recalled fewer major adverse childhood events, less parental verbal abuse, significantly fewer instances of sexual abuse, and less dysfunctional relationships with their mothers. Early home life was also described as "not as severe." In a literature of chronic depression determinants, Riso, Miyatake, and Thase (2002) identified several causal hypotheses that might account for some instances of the late-onset chronic disorder. The researchers suggest that *chronic environmental stress* (e.g., interpersonal problems, medical illness, longstanding medical issues in relatives, unabating unemployment, family conflict and discord) coupled with *heightened stress reactivity* (e.g., the temperamental dispositions of introversion and neuroticism; Kagan, Snidman, Marcel, & Peterson, 1999; McCullough et al., 1988; McCullough et al., 1994a; McCullough et al., 1994b) may, over time, erode the individual's self-worth as well as extinguish the available environmental resources. A "resource deterioration" model (Holahan, Moos, Holahan, & Cronkite, 2000) appears plausible from what we know of individuals who report no depression during childhood and who have their first major depressive episode around 25 years of age (McCullough, 2000; McCullough & Kaye, 1993). More often than not, this group, in contrast to the early-onset group (McCullough, Roberts, et al., 1994), can identify a stressful event as precipitating their depression. Of this late-onset group, approximately 23% who are treated for their first major depressive episode do not fully recover. The episodic disorder then takes on a chronic course (Keller & Hanks, 1994; Keller, Lavori, Rice, Coryell, & Hirschfeld, 1986).

Late-onset individuals are now faced with an unprecedented and refractory emotional condition that overwhelms their baseline cognitive–emotional regulatory functioning (Cicchetti et al., 1995). The resource deterioration model of Holahan et al. (2000), in which heightened emotional reactivity is coupled with chronic stress, may partially explain the vulnerability of this specific group. The pernicious dysphoric process leads to the conclusion that not only is one's world unworkable (hopelessness), its problems are irresolvable (helplessness). Unable to call upon coping reserves to solve the refractory, out-of-control emotional state, normal cognitive–emotional functioning deteriorates and the individual returns to a preoperational stage of functioning. He or she begins to emote, think, and behave like the early-onset chronically depressed adult. At the bottom of this slippery slope, the person's perspective shrinks to a snapshot view of reality: *The way things are now is the way they will always be*. The once-adequate representational worldview has imploded under affective bombardment, and the individual turns inward and disengages perceptually from the environment. The final result of this deteriorating cognitive–emotional process is the loss of the depressed person's environment. Said another way, the person's world and those who inhabit it lose the capacity to inform the person's behavior. The late-onset process leaves the adult feeling helpless, hopeless, and with no sense of the future.

Moderate to severe psychosocial impairment also characterizes the chronically depressed population. In a recent review (Keller et al., 2000) of 681 chronically depressed outpatients, the Global Assessment of Function scale (GAF: American Psychiatric Association, 1994), operationalized for this study, was administered to all patients at baseline. The mean score of the entire sample was 54 (SD = 5.6). The 51–60 range on the GAF indicated that patients either spontaneously or upon questioning stated during the interview that they were unable to function adequately because of their depressive symptoms. Interference of functioning was readily observable, such as missing some work, some school, or some social contacts.

Interpersonal Isolation of the Chronically Depressed Patient

When a therapist sees a chronically depressed adult for the first time, he or she meets a patient who thinks, talks, and emotes in a primitive, preoperational manner. The structural cognitive–emotional dilemma precludes normal interaction because the social–interpersonal world has no informing influence on behavior. Felt hopelessness will be articulated early in the session. Hopelessness arising from the out-of-control mood state also stems from entrapment in a preoperational snapshot view of reality. Salient feelings of helplessness will also be described. Feeling powerless to change anything, the beginning patient demonstrates little motivation to tackle the hard work of treatment. The universal mantra of the chronically depressed patient is the oft-heard comment: "It doesn't matter what I do, I stay depressed." Interpersonal empowerment as well as hope for a future come from being able to recognize the differential effects the person has on others—a perceptual view that beginning patients do not have.

As noted, the history of many depressed patients, particularly early-onset individuals, includes a sordid developmental background that left attachment bonds shredded in some instances and dangerous in others. The clinician begins therapy with someone who learned early that personal survival was contingent on maintaining interpersonal distance from others. Childhood emotional attachment with significant others led to maltreatment more often than not, resulting in prolonged and irresolvable suffering. The interpersonal consequences of these developmental histories frequently lead to an assumption of a hostile–submissive (H-S) interpersonal style (discussed in Chapter 2). Intimacy moments with therapists, or even the possibility of intimacy, may evoke reactions ranging from mild discomfort to outright terror. The same reactions often characterize moments when patients disclose their emotional needs or problems. Earlier attempts at disclosure with significant others usually brought ridicule and rejection. Many of these patients also recall childhoods in which making mistakes or breaking rules resulted in extreme punishment or serious rejection. Occasionally, a patient will say that, from time to time, he or she expressed anger over the mistreatment, and the consequences were either physical violence or rejection.

Further interpersonal deficits complicate treatment when we realize that our patients have never trusted anyone, have never known the experience of being loved or cared for. Still others I've treated were turned into sexual "servants" by significant others; not surprisingly, these patients often equate interpersonal relationship with sex. Some patients exhibit signs of emotional deprivation, of never having experienced human touch as a source of comfort, never recalling feeling safe and secure as a child, always fearing the next drunken rage, deliberately seeking isolation in order to survive. One patient stated that during the elementary school years, the only "safe spot" was at the top of the tallest tree in the neighborhood, where long hours were spent alone. If we listen to, and carefully observe, the way early-onset patients talk and behave, we will see evidence of growth stunting and maturational retardation. We find ourselves sitting in the room with an "adult child." As noted earlier, the late-onset patient usually presents with a milder developmental history, yet we will find the same primitive cognitive–emotive structural dilemma, which, as with the early-onset group, must become the focus of therapy.

These problems cannot be rectified by short-term therapy. Most chronically depressed patients in our national studies (Keller et al., 1998; Keller et al., 2000) have been depressed unrelentingly for 18 or more years. Several psychological goals must be reached before these patients learn to manage their lives and acquire the skills necessary to gain mastery over the ongoing emotional chaos they experience. First, the patient must be *perceptually connected* to the environment so that his or her preoperational worldview can be modified. Formal operational functioning is achieved by demonstrating, through repeated in-session exercises, that behavior has specific interpersonal consequences. As mentioned earlier, the acquisition of a *perceived functionality learning perspective* (McCullough, 2000) denotes that a patient can now recognize the effects of his or her behavior. Achievement of this first goal usually signals victory over the extreme hopelessness/helplessness outlook: the patient no longer feels hopeless/helpless when it becomes obvious that his or her problems are self-produced and self-maintained. The perceptual playing field is now transformed to one that requires a choice-point decision: *"If I don't like what I'm producing, then I must change my behavior!"*

The second goal entails the achievement of an attachment bond with the therapist, which is utilized to challenge and finally heal the interpersonal history with significant others. For the late-onset patient this may mean resolving current interpersonal difficulties resulting from divorce, being fired from a job because of inappropriate behavior, chronic physical illness, or conflicted relationships within the nuclear or extended family. Healing interpersonal trauma and helping to impart basic experiences such as *trust* and *being cared for* in both early- and late-onset patients do not happen by "talking about" such matters. Healing relational wounds interpersonally ineffectual, and somewhat emotionally distant woman who never disagreed with her husband. She described her mother as "tolerating her father" in a marriage that was not affectionate. Sara recalled feeling down during middle school. She said that she felt that something was wrong in her life because she was down most of the time, but she had no idea how to make herself feel better. Her high school years had been especially difficult. She made passing grades, but nothing she ever did pleased her father. He frequently accused her of being a "whore" or "slut" when she infrequently dated. She left home when she was 18 and moved to a nearby town, where she became a secretary in a construction firm.

Sara reported three episodes of major depression that always followed romantic breakups. During these episodes, which lasted 6–8 months, she would lose weight, be unable to sleep, feel generally worthless and guilty, and condemn herself for her mistakes and inability to succeed at anything. Making mistakes at work or in social relationships led to long periods of self-condemnation. She felt guilty most of the time now and had concluded long ago that she would always feel this way. She had never sought mental health treatment before, because of her conclusion that she would always feel depressed. The primary reason she had come for treatment now was because she was about to lose her job over missed work. Her boss, a kind individual, told her that he would not continue to keep her on the office staff unless she sought help for her depression. She saw Dr. Lee, a clinical psychologist, and spent the first two sessions discussing the course of her depression, describing her early developmental history, and telling the clinician what she had done since she left home. Her current relationships with her two siblings were not close. Sara had one close female friend, who had been a strong source of support.

At the end of the second session, during which she had described her relationships with her significant others (father, mother, one sibling, one aunt, and her maternal grandmother), Dr. Lee formulated a transference hypothesis (McCullough, 2000: Chapter 5). The core theme of the significant other history was the inordinate guilt and self-condemnation she felt for a life that she described as a "failure and mistake-ridden life." The transference hypothesis was as follows:

"If I make a mistake around Dr. Lee or do something wrong, then he will reject me or severely punish me in some way."

Using this transference hypothesis, Dr. Lee will look for *hot spots* (McCullough, 2000, Chapter 5) in subsequent CBASP sessions signaling that Sara has made some mistake, broken some agreed-upon rule, or done something wrong (e.g., been late for an appointment, forgotten an appointment, not completed her homework or done it incorrectly). Given her developmental history, Dr. Lee knows that whenever Sara does something that she perceives as wrong, she and he will find themselves transported to an old interpersonal arena that has been extremely problematical for Sara. Disciplined personal involvement can be used during such pivotal times to modify behavior, as shown in the following in-session verbatim exchange.

Dr. Lee: Did you complete your homework assignment?
Sara: No (*eyes on the floor; voice almost inaudible*). I feel so alone, so useless.
Dr. Lee: What happened to the plan to talk to your boss?

and imparting trust must be actualized by first-hand experience
type of relationship—more specifically, in a relationship in which
sonal involvement is present. The CBASP therapist must become
the patient and relinquish unilateral-type roles characterized by inte
behavior, warm empathic statements, the use of correct disputation:
or simply teaching appropriate coping skills. Comrades are authentic
are willing to interact on a reciprocal person-to-person basis in ways
explicit contrast to those of negative significant others.

As noted earlier, Prouty (1994) and Bailey's (2000) pioneering work
way to this new therapist behavior. Prouty's pretherapy model moves th
"toward" the psychotic patient so that treatment begins on a level that m:
patient's level of functioning. In Bailey's kinship model, the therapist n
the patient "like family" in order to impart a felt sense of kinship-like
ment. The chronically depressed adult cannot match the therapist's cognit
emotional pace, yet we frequently conduct treatment assuming that patiei
understand our interpretations, causal reasoning, or see problems the way
As noted earlier, these tactics overestimate the patient's ability. In a similar
many patients do not have essential *precedent* emotional experiences (e.g.
ability to trust another individual, knowing what it's like to be loved and cared
in their learning repertoires. The CBASP clinician must not assume that the pat
has any skill in his or her repertoire until assessment has determined whether or
the skill is present. Once the assessment has been conducted, the practitioner c
proceed on a level that matches the functional capability of the individual. CBA
trainees must learn the difficult lesson of checking out their assumptions when
comes to the cognitive–emotional–behavioral abilities of the patient. By teaching
patients how to interact reciprocally with us, we become viable alternatives to
maltreating significant others. We also set the stage for the healing of trauma by
creating new interpersonal realities between patients and therapists.

The following case of Sara illustrates how disciplined personal involvement was
administered to a 31-year-old chronically depressed, never-married female who
had been diagnosed with "double depression" (recurrent major depression without
full interepisode recovery and with antecedent dysthymia). Sara reported first
becoming depressed during early adolescence and described being continuously
depressed for almost 20 years.

Case History: Sara

Sara was the oldest child in a family of three children. Her father was a
construction engineer who had been an alcoholic throughout the years she lived at
home. He had "an explosive temper" when intoxicated and during these periods,
he physically beat all the children. Precipitant events resulting in the beatings
were any type of misbehavior or mistake a child made around the house. Sara
recalled being terrified of her father and avoiding interactions whenever possible.
She still felt fear whenever she spoke of her father. Sara's mother was a passive,

Sara: I don't know (*eyes on the floor*). I didn't know how to talk to my boss about how he had been treating me.

Dr. Lee: Last week you seem determined to talk to him.

Sara: I was, until I realized I didn't know how to do it (*eyes on the floor*).

Dr. Lee: Sara, will you please try to look at me?

Sara: I can't (*voice almost inaudible*).

Dr. Lee: Why not?

Sara: I'm ashamed about not doing the homework (*voice a little louder; eyes still on the floor*).

Dr. Lee: Please try to look at my face and tell me what you see.

Sara: (*Gradually Sara raises her head and looks at Dr. Lee's face.*) What do you mean, what do I see?

Dr. Lee: Tell me what you see in my face.

Sara: (*softly*) You look like you're feeling uncomfortable right now—like something is wrong.

Dr. Lee: I am feeling uncomfortable. What you said about not doing your homework because you didn't know how stopped me dead in my tracks.

Sara: What do you mean?

Dr. Lee: I feel like I've done something wrong here. Somehow, I agreed with you on this assignment, and I think I expected too much of you. I feel guilty about it.

Sara: I don't want you to feel guilty (*voice a little louder; more eye contact*).

Dr. Lee: You can't control how I feel—I feel guilty right now.

Sara: I feel terrible about what I've done to you.

Dr. Lee: Wait a minute! Are you saying you realize that you have an effect on me? That what you do can affect the way I feel!

Sara: You just said it did.

Dr. Lee: Do you believe that my guilt right now is tied up with what you and I agreed that you would do last week?

Sara: Yes, and I'm sorry about that.

Dr. Lee: If you can affect my feelings, what does this mean for us?

Sara: I'm not completely sure, but it seems that what I do is somehow important because it affects the way you feel.

Dr. Lee: You're right! You have very specific effects on my emotions here. Now, how have I affected the way you've felt over the last 15 minutes?

Sara: It's really weird, but I feel a little better than I did when I first started today—a little lighter, more hopeful.

Dr. Lee: Do you think it might be connected with realizing that you and I affect each other?

Sara: Maybe, I'm not sure. I just know I feel a little better. I don't feel so alone anymore.

Dr. Lee: I think we've stumbled onto something important here—that you're not operating alone in this relationship. You've got company, and maybe this is the first time you've realized this. It almost seems like you've been able to see you're not by yourself here. Now, let's talk together about a better way to approach your homework plan during our remaining time.

Commentary

At the beginning of the session, the patient was perceptually disconnected from Dr. Lee; unable to make eye contact. Her shame about not doing the homework potentiated her felt isolation. The content of the transference hypothesis, based on her Significant Other History, suggests that Sara and the therapist are in a *hot spot* area. Concentrating on his own emotional reactions, Dr. Lee moves the attentional focus away from Sara's shame to his own discomfort and experienced guilt. The attentional shift initiates a discussion implicating the *Person × Environment* (P × E) connection that exists between Sara and the therapist—an association of which Sara has been unaware. Recall that the basic assumption of CBASP is that until the patient (Sara) is perceptually connected to her environment (Dr. Lee), she will remain interpersonally isolated and uninformed by the consequences of her own behavior. In this session, Sara became inchoately aware that her behavior had affected Dr. Lee. This perception will have to be strengthened. Once she acquires the ability to recognize the consequences of her behavior with Dr. Lee, as well as with others in her life, Sara will begin to overthrow the chronic depressive predicament dominating her daily existence: That is, she will no longer feel helpless. Another positive outcome to this exchange occurred when Sara said that she felt somewhat better. Terminating felt discomfort by more adaptive interpersonal behavior strengthens the newly learned skills.

In summary, disciplined personal involvement was used to consequate in-session behavior by demonstrating that Sara's words and actions had a specific effect on the therapist. Said another way, personal involvement required that Dr. Lee be aware of his guilt feelings, be willing to disclose them to Sarah, and then help her recognize the association between *what she did* and *how he felt*. Finally, he focused Sara's attention on the implications of the new *P × E* perception. The outcome was Sara's first in-session experience of recognizing that what she does affects Dr. Lee.

Applying the Interpersonal Discrimination Exercise

Let's look at a second way Dr. Lee used disciplined personal involvement to differentiate himself from Sara's maltreating father, who punished his daughter for any mistake. Dr. Lee used the CBASP interpersonal discrimination exercise (IDE: McCullough, 2000, Chapter 5) to accomplish the task. In the IDE patients are guided through 4 steps:

- The situational context (the hot spot) is made explicit.
- Patients are asked to recall how specific significant others reacted to them in the hot spot situation.
- Next they are asked to describe how the therapist just reacted to them.
- The final step is to compare and contrast the therapist's behavior with that of significant others while considering the interpersonal implications—that is, discriminate the therapist's behavior from the significant other(s).

The setting for the following verbatim exchange occurred during the ninth session. Sara accidentally slept through her alarm the previous week and on her drive to the clinic, traffic was so congested that she was 45 minutes late for the appointment. She and Dr. Lee agreed to meet the following week. Once again, Dr. Lee's transference hypothesis suggested that the patient's missed appointment would thrust both of them into an interpersonal *hot spot*. At the beginning of the session, Sara's depression intensity was elevated. She looked sheepishly at Dr. Lee when she sat down.

Sara: I really messed up last week, didn't I?

Dr. Lee: I was really sorry that we couldn't get together.

Sara: I mean, aren't you mad?

Dr. Lee: About what?

Sara: Because I screwed up. I made a big mistake by sleeping through my alarm.

[Sara was becoming more upset with herself. Dr. Lee knew exactly where she had learned to expect punishment for her mistakes, but he allowed her discomfort to elevate so that it could be reduced by more appropriate behavior with him.]

Dr. Lee: You made a mistake. I've made plenty of them myself.

Sara: But aren't you going to punish me for messing up? I mean, I messed up your hour and probably threw your schedule off for the rest of the day (*begins to cry softly*).

Dr. Lee: Let me ask you something. How would your father have responded to you, had you slept through some prearranged event with him? [Dr. Lee begins the *discrimination exercise* by prompting cognitive–emotional memories colored by the hurtful recall of the earlier abuse.]

Sara: (*Draws a sharp breath and becomes silent for a moment.*) Oh, God, he would have beat me! He did it all the time. I would have ended up screaming and running into my room. I wouldn't come out for the rest of the day. I was terrified of what he would do to me next. I can still remember those times as if they happened yesterday. Why would he want to hurt me like this?! (*She stopped abruptly and slumped down in the chair. Her discomfort was obvious, and it made Dr. Lee uncomfortable.*)

Dr. Lee: I want to ask you another question, but I also want to ask you to look at me when you answer it. (*A brief time elapsed before she looked at Dr. Lee.*)

Dr. Lee: Did I acknowledge to you that we didn't meet last week? [Now Dr. Lee will begin to help Sara discriminate between his reactions to her mistake and the way her father reacted to her for making mistakes. He will concentrate on any emotional differences he detects in Sara's response to him versus her older emotional patterns that involved the father.]

Sara: Yes, you said you were sorry we couldn't meet last week.

Dr. Lee: Now, look at me carefully and describe how I reacted to you over the missed appointment last week. Think carefully about my reactions last week, this week, consider my facial expressions, tone of my voice, and anything else that comes to mind. (*Sara stopped crying and looked somewhat perplexed.*)

Sara: I'm not sure how to describe your reactions.

Dr. Lee: Try, it's very important.

Sara: Well, you didn't punish me.

Dr. Lee: What did I do?

Sara: You said you were sorry we couldn't meet. You sounded like you meant it. Today, you didn't act like it was that big a deal—in fact, you said that everyone makes mistakes, even you. You were very calm, you didn't yell or hit me, or make me feel like a stupid fool. I don't know how to understand your reaction. I mean, it's so new. I've never had anyone treat me this way before.

Dr. Lee: Did I do anything like your dad used to do?

Sara: Good God no! You're different. You're not like him. I'm not afraid of you.

Dr. Lee: Why aren't you afraid of me, especially when you make a mistake?

Sara: I never thought about it before I said it. I'm really not afraid of you. I don't really think you would intentionally do anything to hurt me. I've never trusted anyone before, but I think I trust you. It's a new experience for me. It feels weird.

Dr. Lee: I'm delighted you have experienced these feelings with me. Tell me, if you're right about all the things you just said about me and the way you feel about me, what are the implications for you in this relationship?

Sara: I could relax and be myself with you. I don't think I have ever had a relationship with a man when I haven't been afraid.

Dr. Lee: You've walked into a different room with me today. I'm amazed at all the discoveries you've made about us. We'll keep working on these issues and see how far you can take them. I want to sit here for a moment and enjoy what's just happened between us.

Sara: I began the session feeling terrible. You know, right now, I'm actually happy. I don't remember the last time I felt this way.

Dr. Lee: Have you ever been happy *while you were with* someone else before?

Sara: I don't think so.

Dr. Lee: Enjoy it, Sara, just enjoy it. I'm happy too.

Commentary

CBASP therapists use the IDE to attack the old emotional bonds that have entrapped patients intra- and interpersonally. Using disciplined personal involvement, clinicians challenge formidable odds of dissolving emotional patterns that have usually been maintained by multiple significant others. Certainly the lone therapist is outnumbered in this endeavor from the outset. However, when patients discover that the therapist is qualitatively different from those who inflicted the emotional injuries, the odds begin to shift. The one thing psychotherapists have in their favor—and it is made explicit through the IDE exercise—is the powerful exhilaration and relief that arises from discovery that an end to the chronic disorder is possible. In learning terms, these moments are negative reinforcement events: that is, aversive emotions are terminated when therapists guide patients to discriminate them from negative significant others. Strengthened motivation to bond with the therapist coupled with an increasing capacity for formal operational functioning finally undercut enmeshment in the old interpersonal realities that have enslaved the patient.

By establishing himself as an alternative interpersonal reality, Dr. Lee offers Sara another way to experience herself in the world. The new interpersonal reality also means that Sara must learn another set of interpersonal behaviors and skills, perhaps for the first time in her life—skills that are growth oriented, not survival oriented. Ultimately, Dr. Lee will have to help Sara transfer the new interpersonal learning to her relationships in the outside world.

Summary

Personal involvement can function as a robust change vehicle for chronically depressed patients as long as the therapist (1) does not overestimate their cognitive–emotional abilities, (2) addresses appropriately their core psychopathological issues, and (3) uses personal involvement strategies prudently and with discipline. Disciplined personal involvement can be effectively administered to demonstrate that behavior has consequences. Once this perceptual outlook has been achieved, patients are on the road toward interpersonal connection with others—a crucial goal in CBASP treatment. This usage was demonstrated in the first verbatim example with Sara and Dr. Lee. Personal involvement also offers a powerful tool with which to create a new interpersonal reality for these patients, who desperately need to see that there is one human being who is qualitatively different from their significant others. The second example showed how the IDE is used for this purpose. To strengthen this discrimination, patients must be assisted to differentiate the therapist from negative significant others. This work is not complete until the in-session learning is transferred to the patient's social network, wherein he or she can now establish new relationships based on sound interpersonal foundations.

Disciplined personal involvement also means learning to be oneself with chronically depressed patients. Becoming comfortable with this form of therapeutic role is not easy. It is novel and different for professionals who are introduced to it in CBASP training. Especially is this the case for those whose training labeled any kind of personal involvement *verboten, taboo*. I have supervised excellent psychotherapists who have been unable or unwilling to become personally involved with patients in this disciplined way. This is not a reflection of personal inadequacy. The CBASP model is simply not for everyone.

Training in personal involvement is discussed in the next chapter. Key issues our trainees experience when they are exposed to personal involvement techniques are explored. The essential content of the chapter comes from many colleagues whom I have trained and who, in addition, have provided written descriptions of their experiences.

Part II
Pedagogy of CBASP Training

4
Disciplined Personal Involvement Training

Personal involvement went against my understanding of the therapist–patient relationship. I was quite apprehensive about sharing any part of myself with a patient. I felt that there was a certain boundary a therapist must stay within in order for psychotherapy to be effective.
—DPG, clinical psychology practicum student (2004)

CBASP is known primarily for its Situational Analysis (SA) technique that teaches patients to recognize the consequences of their behavior. What is often overlooked in the model is the unique way in which the therapist role is conceptualized and administered. Therapists use the personal relationship they achieve with patients in a disciplined and contingent manner to modify behavior. In the CBASP therapist–patient relationship, the natural behavior of one interactant (the patient) elicits contingent personal reactions from the other (the therapist), which moves the patient in predictable, goal-oriented directions. Bandura, Lipsher, and Miller (1960) and Kiesler (1983, 1996) describe how these action–counteraction interpersonal response patterns predictably shape behavior. Because the patient's behavior and the therapist's personal reactions are perceptually and empirically *separable* (Bandura, 1977; Kiesler, 1983, 1996), the therapist's reactions are conceptualized in CBASP so that his or her behavior can have *intended* modification effects.

All psychotherapy techniques can be described as involving reciprocal response patterns between therapists and patients to one degree or another. CBASP is no exception. However, CBASP techniques differ from other psychotherapy techniques in that the therapist role involves disciplined personal involvement. Personal involvement is employed to (1) modify maladaptive interpersonal behavior, and (2) heal earlier trauma by producing a creative emotional experience for the patient (Toshiaki Furukawa, personal communication, June 29, 2004).

Chapter 4 describes the pedagogy employed to teach psychotherapists to enact the disciplined personal involvement role. The chapter is divided into three sections. The first section presents a rationale for a training pedagogy to help professionals engage patients on a personal level; the second addresses the issues and questions that therapists in training frequently raise; and the third section summarizes material furnished by 22 previously trained CBASP therapists, who describe their reactions to the pedagogy of personal involvement training and supervision.

Rationale and Pedagogy for CBASP Training

CBASP assumes that a *Person* × *Person* interaction or, expressed another way, a *Person (patient)* × *Environment (therapist)* interaction, characterizes all therapeutic activity. Under normal (i.e., nonpathological) interpersonal conditions, a *bidirectional view* of social control (Bandura, 1977; see Chapter 6) appropriately illustrates the major sources of control in the human social arena. This view also predicts the directions normal human interactions are likely to take. The following diagram illustrates the bidirectional nature of normal interactions.

$$\text{Person} \quad \overset{\rightarrow}{\underset{\leftarrow}{\times}} \quad \text{Person}$$

Because of the preoperational structural functioning of the chronically depressed patient, Bandura's bidirectional model of human interaction cannot be used when treating the chronically depressed patient. The therapist–patient interaction is reconceptualized in CBASP so that we can modify the patient's unique psychopathological style—a style that precludes "normal" social bidirectionality. At the outset, the therapist encounters individuals who are perceptually disconnected from their interpersonal environment; people whose behavior with others results in consequences that have no informing influence on what the person subsequently does or does not do. The egocentric circular functioning of these patients results in a refractory emotional disorder characterized by inflexible cognitive patterns and rigid interpersonal behavior. The upshot of the chronic predicament is that the patient orbits in an interminable circle of *sameness* because interpersonal consequences stemming from the reactions of others (e.g., the therapist, coworkers, spouse) never "get through" to the person or penetrate the barrier that bars informing feedback. The *blocked* environmental feedback pathway looks something like this:

Repetitive Patient Behavior] ← Environmental Consequences

The perceptual disengagement of the person with his or her environment is the major reason CBASP therapists conduct treatment from a unidirectional perspective. Practitioners use disciplined personal responses in contingent, unilateral ways to inform the interpersonal behavior of patients and to break through the preoperational barriers that inhibit bidirectional engagement. Moving patients into bidirectional engagement with the therapist, as well as others, requires the acquisition of formal operational functioning on the patient's part—a cognitive–emotive capacity that is developed over the course of therapy. At the outset, unidirectional control is used to achieve the following didactic goals:

1. Teach patients to recognize the consequences of their behavior—a perceptual skill they do not possess at the outset.

2. Teach patients alternative ways to behave with a therapist, who behaves toward them in personal ways—then transfer this relational skill learning to the daily living arena.
3. Help patients increasingly share in the responsibility for behavior change so that, by the end of therapy, they will have assumed full responsibility for their care (McCullough, 2000).

The pedagogy necessary for learning to enact the CBASP therapeutic role is qualitatively different from the training required to administer any other psychotherapy model. Not only do our trainees face the century-old professional taboo forbidding personal involvement with patients, they must also tackle personally held prohibitions derived from their clinical supervisors as well as from colleagues.

Our training pedagogy helps clinicians assume a role that enables clinicians to (1) *be themselves* with patients, which means being able to respond naturally and in a nonneutral manner; and (2) use personal responsivity *salubriously* and in a *self-disciplined* manner (this means knowing *when* and *when not* to respond, and when responding, to behave in a manner that facilitates healthy change or at least sets the stage for adaptable modification to occur). The personal involvement role requirements in CBASP are so demanding that I realized early that therapists in training must be exposed to pedagogical methods that would help them overthrow and neutralize years of prohibitory training and practice.

Training begins by addressing the issues and questions all trainees have about becoming personally involved with patients. The dangers of "a therapy without boundaries," "creating a sexually charged relationship," "making patients hopelessly dependent on the clinician," "receiving phone calls at all hours of the night," "losing control of the therapy session," "doing irreparable damage to patients," etc., are the issues that are always raised first. Discussions dealing with these matters must occur in an informal atmosphere in which participants feel that their questions can be raised, heard, and discussed openly. If the initial training phase is successful, *most* of the therapists' issues and questions about disciplined personal involvement will have been addressed and answered. The trainer's goal here is not to persuade; rather, it is to hear the question in a nonjudgmental atmosphere and to respond in an accepting manner. Not surprisingly, additional issues about personal involvement will emerge as training proceeds. Again, the trainer must stop whenever these questions are asked and engage in dialogue with the individual until the concerns are addressed to his or her satisfaction. I have learned in training over 100 CBASP therapists that personal commitment to administering personal involvement strategies never occurs during the training process. Personal commitment to employing these strategies only comes when clinicians see actual patients and experience firsthand the positive change effects their behavior can produce. Such moments often occur during the posttraining supervisory period and lead to productive discussions between supervisors and therapists.

I must also note that my usage of the word *pedagogy* in this chapter and in Chapters 5 and 6 is intentional and is borrowed from the pedagogical writings of Paulo Freire, particularly his book, Pedagogy of the Oppressed (2000). Freire faced the same training issues I do when he trained university (and highly literate) educational personnel to work with illiterate migrant workers in Brazil. CBASP trainees begin as highly functioning formal operational thinkers, whereas their patients function at primitive, preoperational adult levels. The learned habits of Freire's educators resulted in a proclivity to educate the workers by "telling" them things like how to live differently, "instructing them" to change their behavior with the landowners, or literally trying to find ways to "lift" or "pull" the workers out of their misery. Freire describes a teaching pedagogy to transform this "it's all up to me" teaching style to one in which the educators used a teaching method that enabled the workers to discover, over time, that it was up to *them* to change their lot with the landowners. What did they discover? Their status improved and their misery decreased when their behavior toward the landowners changed. Freire's pedagogical method was based on a somewhat similar assumption (i.e, workers are responsible for changing their conditions) that is highly familiar to CBASP therapists: Patients will increasingly assume responsibility for their depressive disorder and for the termination of their felt misery as they begin to recognize that the way they live and behave contributes directly to their chronic state of misrey (McCullough, 2000, pp. 15–16).

Freire showed his instructors *how* to create learning environments in which the workers "discovered for themselves" another way to live—a way that terminated their misery. CBASP training has similar training goals and teaches patients that they alone can terminate their felt discomfort. Freire's staff also learned that they must construct lesson plans that began on the workers' level. They could not do the reverse and require the students to match their thinking, emoting, and behaving levels. In a similar vein, CBASP therapists must learn to begin working on the patient's level—nothing else works. Finally, Freire taught his staff how to become *personally involved comrades* with the workers.

In summary, authentic pedagogy for Freire denoted the willingness to inter-act as an equal or comrade with his students, using instructional techniques geared to the students' level of functioning, and allowing students to dis-cover the truth about changing their predicament rather than merely telling them.

In a similar vein, CBASP pedagogy teaches professionals to relinquish their neutral role as a psychotherapist and to engage the chronically depressed pa-tient with disciplined personal involvement. CBASP therapists follow the pace of the individual without pulling, instructing, or feeling that they have to lift the person out of his or her misery, by learning to choreograph in-session dis-covery so that patients functioning at a preoperational level begin to perceive their world from a formal operational point of view. The ability to demonstrate to patients that *they* produce and maintain their misery and that nothing will change until *they* take specific steps to change their lot takes great patience and is not an easy skill to acquire. Our pedagogy of disciplined personal in-volvement training and supervision strives to help clinicians become this kind of psychotherapist.

Personal Issues and Questions of CBASP Trainees

I have never met a psychotherapist (psychologist, psychiatrist, social worker, psychiatric nurse, etc.) who has not been taught to avoid personal involvement. All of us have been schooled rigorously to maintain *interpersonal neutrality* in the therapy room. The power of this universal training stricture can be seen in the results of Borys and Pope's (1989) national, multiprofessional survey of 4,800 psychologists, psychiatrists, and social workers (return rate = 49% or 2,332 respondents: psychologists, 42%; psychiatrists, 27%; social workers, 31%). More than 65% of the sample said that disclosure of personal issues to patients was "never ethical" or "ethical under rare conditions." The prohibition or taboo against personal involvement has been ingrained in all of us, and the concerns and questions that arise during CBASP training are natural consequences of this past instruction. These same issues and questions are raised by professionals who attend my CBASP lectures, symposia, and workshops. The personal involvement topic is a "hot button" issue. I expect these reactions.

The issues/questions that psychotherapists raise when the personal involvement topic is discussed often fall into several categories:

1. Psychotherapy should focus solely on patient issues, not on the therapist's reactions.
2. There may be professional censure by colleagues for personal involvement practice.
3. Personal involvement might result in the patient's inordinate dependence upon the clinician.
4. "Personal boundaries" may become obscured and result in a destructive patient–therapist relationship.
5. Communicating anything to patients other than unconditional positive regard or positive reinforcement may be damaging.
6. Expressing personal reactions and emotions to the patient might overwhelm him or her.

This list is not exhaustive, but it does represent many of the issues that are expressed. A brief response to each issue is presented in the following material.

1. *Psychotherapy should focus solely on patient issues.* The general belief is that patients come to psychotherapy to resolve their problems and that therapists should not inject personal responses into the process. The neutrality view has several consequences: It leads to (1) the *blank slate role* espoused by psychoanalysts (one-way psychology), (2) the *limited approach* of Carl Rogers (unconditional acceptance role), (3) the two-way psychology of the therapeutic alliance tradition where the interaction and not the person of the therapist is highlighted, (4) Beck's cognitive therapy, and (5) Klerman's interpersonal psychotherapy where both Beck and Klerman's models maintain therapist neutrality. CBASP conceptualizes psychotherapy as a form of human interaction that uses unidirectional contingent

strategies to change behavior. Consequating interpersonal behavior requires that practitioners inject their personal responses into the change process.

2. *There may be professional censure by colleagues for personal involvement practice.* Not infrequently trainees report that they have had to justify personal involvement practice to colleagues who question their methods. Concerns about skepticism from colleagues are realistic and reflect prevailing views about therapist personal involvement. One of the major purposes of this book is to present a rationale for *disciplined* personal involvement to the field, which, hopefully, will result in greater understanding of why personal involvement with the chronically depressed adult is recommended. I encourage trainees to remind their fellow professionals that personal involvement is administered because of the patient's psychopathology, which is best modified through a contingent-based dyadic relationship.

3. *Personal involvement might result in inordinate dependence on the clinician.* Having never expressed their personal responses to patients, most therapists are, quite naturally, concerned about what will happen when they do. One fear is that personal responsivity may lead to excessive interpersonal demands for time, requests for personal meetings outside therapy, inordinate use of telephone mini-consultations, and an immoderate reliance on the therapist–patient relationship to meet social needs. This fear can be expressed in another, more down-to-earth manner: "*If I become personally involved with a patient by revealing my responses, I'm afraid I'll be faced with huge patient needs.*" My Answer: Choreographing contingencies for patients has nothing to do with fostering interpersonal dependence. It simply means that therapists begin to shape patient behavior by using themselves as interpersonal contingencies. It doesn't mean that I cease setting limits for inappropriate behavior, accede to all requests, stop providing feedback, or relinquish control of the therapy hour. If patients relate to therapists the way they have learned to relate to others (and I assume all do), then modifying their interpersonal behavior in the session is likely to correct their faulty interpersonal strategies. The reason inordinate dependence on the therapist is not the end result of CBASP disciplined personal involvement is because the final step in the contingent learning process is to transfer in-session learning to the patient's daily life.

4. "*Personal boundaries*" *may become obscured and result in a destructive patient–therapist relationship.* This concern is a crucial training and supervisory issue. Whenever clinicians use patients to meet their social–emotional needs, patient psychopathology is reinforced. Unfortunately, we have all heard patients recount unfortunate stories about previous therapists who *stepped over the line* and dated and slept with them, encouraged them to call at night to engage in long conversations, and, in short, required them to meet and fulfill the social–emotional needs of the practitioner. Such patterns are ones whereby therapists implicitly or explicitly communicate the following: "*If we work together, you must meet my needs.*" Many developmental histories of early-onset chronically depressed patients contain similar themes, wherein the child was thrust early into an abusive or caretaking role with his or her parent(s) or other caregivers. Developmental growth is precluded in these dysfunctional relationships. As discussed in Chapter 2, such behavior reflects the "subjective countertransference" problems discussed by Spotnitz

(1969), who defines subjective countertransference as the defensive and irrational reactions/feelings a therapist experiences with a patient. These behaviors result from the clinician's own intrapersonal conflicts and problems, and when acted out, denote a deviation from the "objective countertransference" (Winnicott, 1949) that derives from the patient's *actual* behavioral impact upon the clinician. Personal maturity is the sine qua non for disciplined personal involvement. CBASP trainers terminate training of individuals who fail to meet this essential intrapersonal requirement. These behavioral excesses on the part of trainees are usually observed during supervision, and they are either rectified or CBASP training is terminated.

5. *Communicating anything to patients other than unconditional positive regard or positive reinforcement may be damaging.* Affective constriction characterizes many psychotherapists. The allowable range of emotional expression most often includes either unconditional positive regard or some form of verbal or nonverbal positive reinforcement. Personal difficulties predictably arise when patients behave in ways that elicit frustration or anger. I've supervised many veteran psychotherapists who feel guilty when they become angry or, in candid moments, admit that they wish certain individuals would terminate treatment. These same clinicians frequently extend unconditional acceptance long after their *acceptance gas tanks* are empty.

Two problems underlie the use of a constricted therapist role with the chronically depressed adult: (1) Many practitioners have limited options, other than offering acceptance, in response to negative patient behavior (e.g., hostility); and (2) the fear that if the therapist responds honestly and expresses felt frustration and anger, he or she will psychologically damage the patient. Rogers' continuing legacy of inhibiting the considered expression of negative emotionality has limited the role alternatives available to practitioners who work with chronically depressed patients. In the face of this fear of hurting patients with emotional expressivity, CBASP trainees must be reminded of the *Person* × *Environment* model of behavior, which provides the essential rationale for the contingent use of disciplined personal involvement. Then they must be shown how to utilize contingent personal responsivity to modify the problematic behavior. Therapists overcome their fear of harming patients only through actual practice and supervision, through which they discover that judicious emotional responsivity does not injure; rather, it produces salubrious change.

Case Example

The following example of giving contingent feedback to a patient, "Bill," illustrates the training goal of supervisory feedback to change maladaptive behavior. Bill had been having difficulty with Situational Analysis because he wanted to discuss "all" of his problems in a global manner, not believing that addressing one problem at a time would help. He expressed frustration and anger every time Dr. Minor asked him to focus on one event. The clinician found himself caught between the proverbial rock and a hard place. He was also becoming increasingly frustrated and angered by Bill's repeated protestations at his requests for specificity and Bill's persistent global talk, both of which he knew would be counterproductive.

Bill: You keep asking me to focus on specific situations! It really frustrates me and makes me mad. I need to talk about *all* my problems! You assume that you can fix my life and all the problems I've got by focusing on one measly situation.

Dr. Minor: I can't help you fix anything by tracking all your problems at once.

Bill: What do you mean? You mean you can't?

Dr. Minor: No.

Bill: Then what am I going to do? I've got so many problems. I've got to get some help!

Dr. Minor: You're right when you say you've got many problems. I agree whole-heartedly.

Bill: Then why won't you let me talk about all my problems?

Dr. Minor: You've been talking about them. What have you solved?

Bill: Not much.

Dr. Minor: I can't deal with all your problems at once. I simply cannot.

Bill: Do you have some kind of learning disability?

Dr. Minor: Don't think so. I've never been able to solve more than one problem at a time. It's like trying to learn how to hit a baseball and having two pitchers throw two balls to me simultaneously. Can't learn to hit this way—I'd just duck out of the way. I also can't help you when you throw multiple problems at me at one time. You must think I'm some sort of magician. I ought to be able to do the impossible. Why do you treat me like I'm some sort of superman?

Bill: I didn't know I'd been treating you this way. I don't think of you as a super-man.

Dr. Minor: Then why do you treat me like one? Like I can do the impossible—solve everything at once.

Bill: I never thought that I was doing this.

Dr. Minor: This is the way you've made me feel with your protests every time I asked you to focus. I do it your way, which means I have to solve everything at once or else I'm a failure—which means I cannot help you. You've had me over a barrel, and I've been feeling very frustrated—I can't win with you. Let me ask you a question about us. Are any of the problems you've been talking about involving your wife and boss similar to what's happening between us right now? I mean, wanting to be understood and not feeling that you're getting what you want?

Bill: I usually think other people just don't understand me, they can't keep up with me—especially my wife and boss. Yeah, there's some similarity. I was thinking right before I came in here today that you can't keep up with me either, that you don't understand me.

Dr. Minor: I haven't been able to keep up with you. Do you think that your conclusions about me, your wife, and your boss might have anything to do with the way you present yourself when you want to be understood?

Bill: They might.

Dr. Minor: How are they similar?

Bill: Well, I end up feeling the same way—that no one can keep up with me or understand me.

Dr. Minor: Let's try to work back from the way you ended up feeling right now. Perhaps there is some similarity here in regard to what is happening between you and your wife, your boss, and me. You seem to be concluding the same thing with everyone—that is, we're not understanding you or can't keep up with you. Maybe if we took one person at a time and looked closely, you might be able to see if you're doing anything with the three of us that prevents you from feeling that you have been understood. Then you'd have a possible solution for all three people.

Commentary

It is possible to be personally honest with a noncompliant patient without counteraggressing or becoming interpersonally hostile, such that the individual is pushed away or made to feel that he or she has to make a choice between self-integrity (doing it his or her way) or self-surrender (doing it the therapist's way). In this instance, Dr. Minor told Bill that he simply couldn't do what he wanted or work with him on his terms. It was an honest personal statement of his limitations. Bill still had to make the choice about what he was willing to do. The practitioner's goal here was to make explicit *the interpersonal consequences for continued global talk*: "The consequences are that you cannot get what you want from me [i.e., to be understood] with global talk."

Disciplined honest responsivity that makes interpersonal consequences explicit puts patients in the "driver's seat" and allows them to make choices about what they want. Administering consequences in this fashion requires the CBASP therapist to give him- or herself permission to respond honestly, to be willing to take the time to learn to administer contingent interaction, and then to commit to the discipline of practicing the skills with patients.

6. *Expressing personal reactions and emotions to the patient might overwhelm him or her.* Several contemporary techniques do not require therapists to utilize their own emotional responses in expressive ways. Beck et al. (1979) and Klerman et al. (1984) encourage cognitive therapists and interpersonal psychotherapists, respectively, to avoid actively both transference and countertransference issues. Beck et al. wrote that patient *thinking errors* lead to both positive and negative transference issues, and that both should be subjected to "logic and the empirical method" (1979, p. 58). Therapists are instructed to resist all countertransference reactions that pull them out of the role of scientific observer of the patient's negative interpretations of the relationship. "In order to maintain an objective but empathic view, the therapist should remind himself that the patient's negative views are only cognitions and beliefs; i.e., they should be tested and either confirmed or disconfirmed" (Beck et al., 1979, p. 59).

Klerman et al. (1984) explicitly stated that the dyadic relationship is not in any way a transference or countertransference enactment: "the relationship is not seen as a fantasied reenactment of the patient's (or the therapist's) previous relationships with others" (Klerman et al., 1984, p. 214). In a manner similar to Beckian cognitive therapy, Klerman et al. (1984) defined the therapist's role as nonjudgmental and one that must extend warmth and unconditional positive regard. "In essence, the therapist is a benign and helpful ally" (Klerman et al., 1984, p. 214).

As noted in Chapter 2, in both models the emotional responses of the practitioner take a back seat to a heavy emphasis on technique administration. Not surprisingly, psychotherapists trained in these two traditions have never been schooled by supervisors who teach them to utilize emotional responsivity in contingent ways.

In contrast to these models, CBASP clinicians are reminded that in an interactional *Person* × *Environment* model, tracking (self-monitoring) one's emotional responses with the patient is essential. Practitioners must identify the specific emotional responses they experience while working with a particular patient. Kiesler's Impact Message Inventory (Kiesler & Schmidt, 1993) is an excellent supervisory tool with which to make explicit a therapist's emotional response to a patient's interpersonal stimulus value. More will be said about how CBASP utilizes the Impact Message Inventory in Chapter 5. For now, some readers may wonder what is meant by *tracking one's emotional responses*. The following verbatim example illustrates the responses one therapist had to her patient during a 10-minute videotaped segment. The *italicized text* set within brackets denotes the therapist's reported thoughts and feelings while interacting with the patient.

Dr. Bolton had seen Ted, a 38-year-old chronically depressed male, for seven sessions. He was diagnosed with an early-onset, double depression disorder. Ted reported two major depressive episodes over his lifetime. He was taking 150 mg of sertraline; he had never previously taken psychotropic medication or sought psychotherapy. During the eighth meeting, he began a Situational Analysis exercise in which he described an argument between himself and his wife. The argument had occurred the previous evening. He became angry while talking about the argument and then turned the anger on the therapist, whom he said reminded him of his wife. Dr. B watched the videotape of the session with her supervisor and described her thoughts and emotions during this segment of the tape.

Dr. Bolton: I see you completed a Coping Survey Questionnaire. Take me through the situation by telling me what happened.

Ted: My wife and I had another argument while we were eating supper. We were talking about her failure to log the checks she had written in our checkbook. She told me she was sorry, but that she just forgets to do it. I told her she messes up our balance every time she fails to write in her checks, and I end up overdrawing our account. God, she makes me mad. She's so stupid. Told her so. She started to cry and never said anything else. She got up from the table and went to the bedroom and closed the door. She didn't come out for at least an hour. She was all red-eyed, like she'd been crying the whole time. God, she's so incompetent! She can't even look me in the face and talk to me after she did something stupid like this. The situation ended when she got up from the table and went to the bedroom crying. I hate incompetent women! Why I married her I'll never know!

Dr. Bolton: *[I'm getting frustrated and a little angry with Ted's boorish behavior. He has no idea how strong he comes on or his stimulus value for his wife. He overpowers her with his anger and hurtful comments and then expects her to talk to him. No one can talk to him when he becomes this angry.]* Tell me the thoughts and feelings you had during the situation; that is, what did the situation mean to you?

Ted: Dammit! You don't understand a word I've said to you! I've just told you what a stupid bitch I have for a wife, and you want me to tell you what this situation means to me! You're just like my wife. You ask me to do things and don't even understand what's going on!

Dr. Bolton: *[Ted has just put me at the supper table with him! He's going to replay this situation with me! I'm angry with him now. He's also hurt my feelings with his comments, and I've got to figure out a way to consequate his anger without counteraggressing. Anger-for-anger would just play his game. I want to avoid this if I can. I've got to figure out what I want to do. Need some time here.]* You're angry with me, Ted. Why?

Ted: Because of your stupid question about what the situation means to me. You just don't get it, do you?! I'll bet you'll even side with my wife.

Dr. Bolton: *[There's almost a whine in the tone of his voice. Sounds like a plea of some kind. What's going on? He's confusing me. His anger has just decreased a little. Mine hasn't. What a jerk he is! Talk about someone who doesn't get it! What do I want to do with his anger? Stay focused on the effects he had on me.]* Why did you just punch my lights out with your angry comments?

Ted: What do you mean?

Dr. Bolton: I mean, you just turned on me in anger and let me have it right between the eyes. I want to know why?

Ted: You've been trained to handle these situations.

Dr. Bolton: I'm going to ask you again, because you haven't answered my question. Why did you just berate me in anger? I want to know.

Ted: Did I hurt your feelings?

Dr. Bolton: Yes, you did. You also made me angry. Why would you do this to me? I'm still waiting for your answer. *[Personal honesty here is the only way to go with this—got to see if I can get Ted to deal with me.]*

Ted: I don't know, I just lost it, I guess.

Dr. Bolton: *[His anger has lessened, and we're talking again. My anger has also decreased. I've got his attention now. Stay with the focus on the consequences he had on me.]* What effect do you think you just had on me when you attacked me this way?

Ted: I guess I hurt your feelings and made you mad.

Dr. Bolton: *[Can't let his indecision go. Stick with the consequence focus. I've calmed down now, and we can go to work on what's just happened between us.]* You're saying, "You guess." You're not sure what effect you just had on me. What are you not sure about?

Ted: I did hurt your feelings and anger you, didn't I?

Dr. Bolton: Yes, you did. You did it very well, too. Ever had anyone deal seriously with you, face-to-face, during one of your outbursts?

Ted: Frankly, no. Looking at what I've done here makes me feel sort of stupid.

Dr. Bolton: *[He's beginning to deal seriously with the consequences of his behavior. Stay with this focus and then look for any alternatives that might open up. I'm feeling okay now, no longer angry.]* Why do you feel stupid right now?

Ted: It's like I just crapped on the floor, and I'm looking at it. You're here too and also looking at it.

Dr. Bolton: *[He's got it! Staring right into the consequences of his behavior! Stay with it.]* Smells up the place pretty bad, doesn't it?

Ted: I've never been through something like this before. I'm not mad anymore. What's happened here?!

Dr. Bolton: Let's look at it and see what we can learn. I think you and I have stumbled upon some rich territory and the emotional control possibilities for you look good. After we make sense out of what's happened between us, let's get back to the situation you brought in with your wife.

Commentary

This is an example of how tracking one's emotions and then making the emotions explicit in the session can be used to consequate behavior. Modifying behavior this way requires that therapists continually monitor their emotional responses to the patient and then be willing to present those responses in a contingent manner. Once again, the goal is not to counteraggress but to *modify behavior*. What was made explicit to Ted was the association of his anger with the interpersonal effects he produced in Dr Bolton: *hurt and anger.* Ted had not made this association before and when faced with the connection in an unavoidable therapy situation, he was embarrassed. Reducing the discomfort of embarrassment (aversive state of affairs) by engaging in more adaptable behavior was now possible because Dr. Bolton refused to counteraggress or interpersonally withdraw; instead, she disclosed how Ted's behavior had affected her. In summary, Dr. Bolton created a negative reinforcement condition and set the stage for behavior change by contingently making explicit her personal reactions to Ted.

CBASP Therapist Responses to Personal Involvement Training

Twenty-two CBASP therapists answered several of my questions about their responses to disciplined personal involvement training and supervision. The questions were as follows:

1. What *initial personal issues/problems* arose when you were encouraged to administer personal involvement strategies with your chronically depressed patients?
2. What were the *phases/stages* (if any) you processed through before you could express your personal feelings/responses contingently to patients?

3. What were the *problems* you faced when you began to deal with patients on a personal basis? How did you *resolve* the problems?
4. *Where do you stand now* in regard to disciplined personal involvement?

1. *Initial personal issues problems*. Anxiety, fear, and insecurity were the modal emotional reactions expressed by the majority of training therapists. The anxiety reactions were expressed in a nonspecific way and were associated with feelings of dread for engaging in behavior that "just doesn't feel right" or that "seems to run counter to my previous training." Fears were tied to (1) making themselves feel emotionally vulnerable, (2) being unsure what to do with negative emotions such as feeling angry, (3) anticipating that patients would quit if faced with "reactant" therapists, and (4) worries over patients becoming "symbiotically" dependent. One veteran psychotherapist described the dilemma in this way: "I feel that letting a patient get to me and allowing myself to feel angry is unprofessional."

Other fears were expressed over concerns about psychologically hurting the patient and focusing on the therapist during the session. Another experienced therapist disclosed that she had actual sweat attacks during sessions. "I could literally feel myself sweat when I expressed personal feelings because I feared creating something I wouldn't be able to handle." Others admitted being afraid of "allowing myself to experience discomfort during the session" or of "disclosing negative affect with patients." One clinician said, "It's easy for me to express positive feelings such as pleasure or verbally reinforce patients for behavioral gains. Expressing negative responses such as 'I don't like . . . ' 'You've hurt me' or 'You scare me when . . . '—that's the problem." Fears of being honest in instances where the practitioner did not like the patient posed difficulties for several persons. Another bothersome task involved having to revise their approach to psychotherapy from focusing *soley* on the patient to considering an interactional perspective in which their own feelings and responses play a significant role.

A salient fear for some was *being different* and behaving in a way that took them out of what they felt was the professional mainstream. Several reported that their patients responded with astonishment when they expressed themselves personally. "No therapist has ever been honest with me before," one patient exclaimed, "what's going on here!" Another retorted, "I've never been treated this way by a therapist. Is this supposed to help?" The therapist admitted candidly that she was unable to answer satisfactorily—she wasn't sure either. A number of individuals said that they felt most patients don't expect practitioners to play a personal role in their therapy. One individual described it this way: "Patients come to treatment with a preconception that the clinician's thoughts and feelings will not be a part of therapy." Several expressed a fear that they might not be able to differentiate their personal issues from those of the patient if they responded honestly and directly. More specifically, the fear was that the treatment goals would be obscured or even lost.

Expressed insecurities were numerous. Most had to do with practicing something or doing something that was "unknown," "uncharted," "nonempirically based," "professionally out of the mainstream," and "being asked to behave in ways that made one rethink the nature and goals of the patient–therapist relationship." "It's all so new and goes against everything I've ever been taught."

One therapist summed up his initial reaction to personal involvement training this way:

The thought of being myself with patients makes me anxious. But I also thought, now I can finally be myself in the therapy session. All along I've felt I had to assume an *action-oriented stance* with patients that has meant just "sucking it up" when confronted with a lack of motivation, lack of progress, or with interpersonal insults, slights, and other inappropriate behavior. I had no alternative (I thought) but just to try harder. My work with difficult patients frequently led to my becoming angry and finally to interpersonal withdrawal and detachment. Now I have permission to be myself, and I can deal directly with negative interpersonal problems by shaping behavior and use the same negative responses that have been problems for me in the past.

2. *Phases/stages (if any) preceding expression of personal feelings/responses contingently to patients.* The responses of therapists came as a result of a training sequence that required several steps (Bandura, 1977): (1) a rationale was first presented for the personal involvement techniques; (2) the skills were modeled under simulated role-play conditions (a highly effective didactic exercise) that included two-person role plays and the use of videotapes on which trained clinicians demonstrated the techniques; (3) performance-based feedback was provided to trainees while they role-played with colleagues; and (4) intensive supervision was provided when the therapists worked with actual patients.

Many therapists said that they proceeded through several phases/stages during training. The phases were not uniform, and few clinicians moved easily from the classroom to the therapy room without one or more stops in between.

The first phase one trainee described was feeling compelled to *revise a strongly held view* that if the in-session focus highlighted the therapist's thoughts and feelings, the clinician would be inappropriately calling attention to him- or herself. After listening to me say that if specific steps were not taken to differentiate the therapy relationship from significant other relationships, then the patient would fail to perceive the differences, this trainee remarked, "I would feel like I'd be bragging if I called attention to the special quality of the relationship I had with a patient." His family had taught him that calling attention to oneself was a form of bragging and hence should be avoided. This aversive reaction had to be overcome through supervision before he was able to use his personal response contingently. "My comfort with personal involvement has increased as I've seen the way it strengthens the therapeutic alliance."

Another phase that was frequently described was a period during which individuals had to learn, many for the first time, *to take seriously their emotional responses to patients*—a difficult task if previous supervisors never made this practice area a priority. It was a novel experience for many persons when CBASP supervisors concentrated on personal responses and raised questions about how therapists felt when patients behaved in certain ways. One therapist described his experience this way:

First, I had to learn to attend to what emotions the patient was pulling from me moment-to-moment. Next, I had to decide what I wanted to do with those responses. I was looking for a *teachable moment* because I feel that timing is important in responding contingently. After I felt more comfortable being myself with patients, I realized that I would have to teach many of them how to deal with me interpersonally. This was a new experience—I had never done this before except when I conducted various sorts of role-play exercises. Even then, the focus was not really on me. I got to where I encouraged patients to practice most of their new skills on me before they transferred the new learning to others on the outside. Most patients told me I was a very different kind of therapist—they had never experienced anyone like me before.

Knowing one's stimulus value to patients also becomes an important goal in personal involvement training. It's risky to respond contingently in the session until the therapist knows the interpersonal impact he or she has on others. Some practitioners talk in a harsh manner; others speak in ways that sound pleading and overly submissive; still others make comments that sound somewhat detached. Interpersonal styles such as making poor eye contact (or the opposite, excessive eye contact), slouching in the chair and leaning away from the patient while responding, or always sitting behind a desk may communicate disinterest or excessive formality. These impacts mitigate the effectiveness of personal involvement responsivity. Many well-meaning therapists are unaware of these behaviors and how they affect others. This is why educating therapists about their stimulus effects is a crucial part of the training process. This learning task is the reverse of helping therapists identify the patient's stimulus effects. Contingent interaction methodology requires that clinicians be clear about their emotional responses to patients, what patients do to elicit these responses, and the likely stimulus effects their responses will have. Finally, contingent methodology requires that practitioners make the stimulus effects of patients explicit and then discuss and role-play alternative interpersonal strategies.

One practitioner listed the learning phases she experienced during training:

(1) I had to get to know myself first—what effects I had on others when I was being myself. (2) Next, I had to learn when to respond contingently and when to hold back—this was not easy. For example, if a session had been difficult and the patient was tired, I would not respond contingently; instead, I would wait until another session, knowing that the target behavior would present itself again. (3) I had to learn to teach patients to recognize their stimulus value for me and then for others on the outside—in addition, I realized I had to teach them to use their stimulus value in effective ways. (4) Doing this kind of therapy made me realize that I must learn to take care of myself psychologically. I discovered that conducting therapy in this manner was personally draining. (5) Finally, I found that I had to explain and even defend myself to colleagues who questioned my professional conduct.

Dealing with *hostile patients* is always difficult and stressful. Clinician stress becomes obvious when supervisors watch session replays on videotape. A veteran psychotherapist stated that the hostile-dominant patient gave her the most trouble. The challenge she faced here was to force herself to remain in personal contact and not withdraw. These patients make demeaning comments, challenge clinicians' feelings of competence, and frequently protest that therapy is a waste of time. The therapist who stands his or her ground usually feels exposed, with no place to hide. Personal involvement first requires that the clinician be able to tolerate *the hurt* stemming from the attack. It takes discipline to stand directly in the line of fire, and if the therapist is able to tolerate the discomfort, feeling *vulnerable* and *incompetent* is the interpersonal consequence. The reactions of others to the patient's hostility have usually been to counterattack or avoid any contact. Not only do others keep their distance, these patients successfully maintain interpersonal distance from others as well. It is this interpersonal distance that will be challenged by the therapist's personal response. At some point, the therapist will inquire of the individual: "Why do you want to hurt me this way?" Nothing else is done until the patient answers this question. Frequently, the question must be asked several times over protests such as: "You sure are thin-skinned"; "You've surely been trained to handle this stuff"; "Aren't I paying you to make me feel better?! You're not supposed to react to me like that!" "Don't take personally what I say"; and so on. Personal response tactics with hostile-dominant patients are always difficult to enact and supervision is required because of the degrading nature of these encounters. The essential requirement for the response strategy is that the therapist keeps the patient's expressed hostility focused on an interpersonal level and refuses to talk objectively about the behavior (i.e., as an observer). Both of these strategies are enacted in order to maximize the interpersonal consequences for the patient! More is said about this technique in Chapter 5.

Another therapist remarked that before she could engage patients on a personal basis, she had to admit to herself that *her dyadic relationship with the patient was qualitatively different and better* than most of the relationships the patient had reported. Her first reaction to this thought was "I'm being grandiose, self-serving, and excessively flattering of myself." As she, with supervisory assistance and support, realized the unique and differing interpersonal quality of what she and the patient shared, she felt less inclined to downplay the relational accomplishment. Many therapists have difficulty accepting—much less admitting to patients—the significant role they (the therapists) play in the healing process. Once practitioners are able to be honest about their significant contributions to treatment, they have an easier time teaching patients to discriminate between the old and the new interpersonal relationships.

Many trainees opined, and I fully agree with them, that *patients must be instructed early* about the personal involvement component of CBASP therapy; in addition, they felt that patients should be told explicitly that personal involvement is an essential component of the treatment procedure. Instruction should be provided and patients shown that the role enactment is based on a Person × Environment view of interpersonal reality. One trainee summed up her feelings about introductory instruction this way: "Patients must be told early what happens in CBASP therapy. We must try to help them understand why personal involvement is used and what the goals are. In this way, we help prepare them for the interpersonal experience."

Experienced therapists often feel more comfortable with personal involvement strategies as they come to realize that *the goal is to modify patient interpersonal behavior* and *to heal earlier trauma*. Describing his personal responses to training, a therapist delineated the stages he went through:

My first reaction was astonishment: "I can do that!", I said to myself. Then came the hesitation, self-doubt, and discomfort over being too self-centered during the session. I was afraid I would end up making therapy about myself and not about the patient. Once I began to see that the goal of contingent personal involvement was helping the patient, I started taking my training more seriously. Finally, I became excited and confident when I saw the interpersonal results with actual patients. I saw behavior change right before my eyes! I also needed continual reassurance from my supervisor that what I was doing was acceptable. Old prohibitions die hard.

Other individuals said that they continued to *feel uncomfortable* about personal involvement strategies throughout the training period. One behavior therapist reported: "The only way I overcame my anxiety was by just making myself do it with chronically depressed patients. It was an exposure-like procedure I repeated until I began to feel more comfortable. The more it worked, the better I felt." In extinction-like fashion, it took repeated trials with actual patients for the anxiety and discomfort to decrease, until the negative affect associated with the method was extinguished.

One final response must be mentioned. Several clinicians have argued that personal involvement responsivity must not be administered until the therapist feels that the *interpersonal bond* with the patient is solidly in place. "It's my acknowledgment of Rogers' contribution to the therapeutic alliance issue," a therapist said. "I must have a sense that the patient feels that I am his or her ally before I can react contingently to his or her behavior."

As is obvious from the above comments, most therapists did not complete training without a personal struggle that involved anxiety and self-doubt. Some questioned the professional ethicality of the procedures. Therapists' reactions to training and supervision often came in phases/stages:

a. Feeling discomfort with all or parts of the didactic training;
b. Questioning and revising their theoretical perspectives;
c. Learning to take their emotional responses to patients seriously;
d. Learning their stimulus value for patients and then learning to teach patients how their (patients') stimulus value affects the clinician;
e. Advocating that patients be instructed that personal involvement is an essential part of treatment;
f. Feeling that an interpersonal alliance should be in place before contingent responsivity was administered.

3. *Problems faced and resolutions found.* Patients are often surprised or astonished when practitioners respond to them personally. It takes time for many individuals to realize that their therapists are affected by how they behave toward them. The way psychotherapy has generally been practiced in the United States as well as portrayed in the popular media leaves most consumers assuming that therapists are unaffected, unfeeling observers of behavior—professionals who mostly sit in their

chairs, take notes, and listen. It is not surprising that, in general, patients expect to go to psychotherapy and just talk about their problems. Going to a practitioner who interacts with them on a personal level is totally unexpected. When the common assumption of just talking about problems is contradicted by personal responsivity, the consequences are sometimes overwhelming. Because one of the major goals of CBASP is to teach patients that behavior has consequences, practitioners must be ready to address and manage the surprise, astonishment, and emotional flooding that frequently accompany personal—though disciplined—responsivity from the therapist. When disciplined responsivity results in excessive reactions (shock, fear, etc.), the therapist must stop and address the patient's response. Historical origins for such reactions are often present and, whenever possible, these origins must be exposed and discussed. A therapist now has the opportunity to make explicit that he or she is not a maltreating significant other, therefore the earlier and hurtful interpersonal outcome will not be present. Ineffective management of these patient reactions poses problems that may lead to premature termination.

The biggest problem a number of therapists said they faced was experiencing discomfort with the personal involvement role. Typical comments such as these were heard: "At first, I was afraid of going too far and 'pushing patients over the edge' or hurting them psychologically. Once I began to respond contingently and subsequently helped patients understand why I had done so, I realized that I somehow knew when to back off and stop. I also discovered that sharing myself in honest ways was a definite *helping tool*." Another said, "I still feel awkward any time I disclose anything personal with my patients."

Fearing initially that one's personal responses might not be valid was also problematical. This issue usually receded in importance once practitioners began responding contingently. Problems sometimes arose when patients asked questions about the personal life of the clinician. This concern was short-lived once practitioners realized they had a choice about whether or not to answer the question.

One interesting problem that was described had to do with patients who didn't take the personal responses seriously; instead, they thought the therapist was playing some sort of joke on them. As it turned out, most of these individuals reported never having had the experience of being taken seriously. It took repeated trials for them to believe that they were having actual effects on the clinician. To this type of patient one therapist said, "This is a professional relationship, but I care about you and have constant responses to what you do when we are together. You can learn about yourself from my responses when I share them with you."

Another therapist described his initial problem with personal involvement this way:

Disciplined personal involvement was effective for me from the beginning. My biggest problem, however, was myself and my hesitation to respond personally. I was fearful I would hurt patients or that they wouldn't like me. To jump-start myself, I began saying, "I value you and our relationship. Because of this, I'm affected by what you do. I'm going to let you know from time to time how you affect me, and then we'll talk about it and discuss the implications. We'll also see if my reactions are similar to others with whom you interact outside of therapy." I also found that understanding the rationale underlying the personal involvement techniques made it easier for me to hurdle the initial hesitation.

An interesting strategy was employed by one of our therapists who reported few difficulties administering the personal involvement techniques.

When I disclosed my responses to the patient's behavior, I also taught the person to begin disclosing his or her responses to my behavior. It takes a while for patients to begin to open up, but most of them finally come around. These interactions brought us closer together. It also made our in-session consequation work more meaningful. Now I could show them how to use their knowledge of interpersonal impacts to make sense out of their social relationships. Patients would come back later and say they were beginning to read other people better.

Summarily, other than the initial patient surprise, most of the problems discussed above involved trainee difficulties with the process of actualizing a new therapeutic role. After the training sessions end, supervision must continue to address the personal problems until therapists feel comfortable being themselves with chronically depressed patients. Periodic supervision will also be needed by therapists who work with this patient population. I recommend monthly supervision because of the idiosyncratic stress chronically depressed patients impose on CBASP psychotherapists.

4. *Perspectives regarding disciplined personal involvement following training.* To avoid repetition of material that has already been presented, I include only those responses that contain new content. First and foremost was a strongly worded empirical concern related to the Interpersonal Discrimination Exercise which relies on the transference hypothesis that is formulated following Session 2. This exercise, which is used to heal early trauma experiences, asks patients to discriminate between the hurtful behavior of significant others and the salubrious behavior of the clinician. The goal is to ensure that clear distinctions can be made between the old interpersonal realities and the new therapeutic relationship. One therapist proposed that following training, a reliability test should be undertaken to assess the reliability of therapists to select *the salient domain* for subsequent transference hypothesis construction. Videotaped samples of self-reported significant other material could be used as a basic content for the ratings. Therapists would view the tape samples, then select one of the four domains (i.e., intimacy; disclosure of personal need, wants or concerns; making mistakes around the clinician; having negative feelings toward the therapist) that should be used to construct the transference hypothesis. Kappa coefficients would be run to assess domain agreement. Low kappas would indicate that additional training was needed in the transference construction area. These recommendations will be heeded and implemented in future training programs.

It was clear that most therapists believed that personal involvement was not necessary for all psychopathological conditions. Others felt that efficacy data for the techniques should be obtained in future dismantling studies (see appendix). An interesting response was proffered by one individual, who said that he has been comfortable using personal involvement strategies:

I found that contingent personal responsivity was an effective way to teach the patient how to establish effective interpersonal boundaries. For example, I was treating a homosexual male who had recently broken up with his partner. The patient complained that he'd had to do everything in the relationship. He had to wash the dishes, take out the trash, see that the bills were paid, and wash the clothes; emotionally, he described himself as the responsive and reactive one, whereas the partner was lazy and held back. According to him, he did everything and the partner did nothing. *I realized he was doing the same thing with me!* He was answering my questions before I even finished the sentence. He was watching the clock to make sure that we stopped on time. He was worried that I was working too hard, and [*without asking me*] he was automatically certain that he was too much of a burden for me—he didn't want to give me any more trouble than he knew I already had with my other patients. I began to react to his excessive caretaking by expressing displeasure and frustration that he was thinking for me and not asking; behaving for me and not asking; assuming he knew my feelings without asking; and generally taking care of me at every turn without asking whether or not I wanted to be taken care of. The upshot of my responding in that manner over several sessions was a growing realization on his part that I was going to handle 50% of the relationship, and all I expected him to do was manage the other half. He was surprised to learn that his invasive style was aversive to me as well as others. He thought all along that he was just being helpful. Over time, the patient began to ask first and inhibit his strong impulsive tendencies to overmanage. He also reported that he was transferring this learning to his social life, and that he felt more relaxed.

Several persons said that one difference they noticed as a function of training was a desire that patients know them better. Another therapist put it more succinctly: "You will not dismiss or discount me; rather, I will teach you to deal with me and then help you transfer these skills to the outside."

Conclusions

Training in disciplined personal involvement obviously entails more than simply learning how to administer a technique. The difference is that personal involvement requires individuals to put themselves directly in the line of fire in the patient–therapist interaction. One can administer many techniques without stepping out from behind a wall of professionalism. This is not possible with disciplined personal involvement. Personal involvement training not only requires therapists to disclose their personal responses, but it also necessitates that they continuously track their thoughts and feelings in order to identify the perceptual connections between the moment-to-moment stimulus pulls of the patient and their own responses. In addition, therapists discover that training raises basic questions about their role as a psychotherapist, their emotional life with its strengths as well as limitations, and the nature of the dyadic interaction. Finally, training requires that practitioners make basic decisions about how much of themselves they are willing to share.

An interesting article just appeared in Psychotherapy Bulletin (Manning, 2005) discussing therapist personal self-disclosure. The author details some of the problems new psychoanalytic trainees encounter when they begin self-disclosing countertransference reactions to patients. The paper is mentioned here because the training problems Manning describes parallel several of the therapist training issues discussed above; for example, new training analysts fear transgressing the neutrality barrier; trainees are leery of becoming vulnerable when they disclose personal feelings and experiences; and the threat of weakening the strict boundary between the analyst and the analysand by using self-disclosure often evokes initial avoidance reactions. Based on the overall content of her article, the references cited, and because her focus ultimately concerns the patient–therapist alliance to the exclusion of any diagnostic concerns, Manning clearly stands in the *therapeutic alliance research tradition* (see Chapter 2). To her credit, however, a strong training emphasis on personal disclosure is evident throughout the article, and this accomplishment is laudatory.

In closing, I must emphasize once again that these CBASP techniques were designed specifically to address the psychopathology of the chronically depressed patient. Personal involvement makes health-generating contact in ways that other strategies do not. For this reason, and this reason alone, do I recommend personal involvement in the treatment of the chronically depressed.

We now move to Part Three, where I describe several ways that disciplined personal involvement can be administered in a contingent-based, in-session environment.

Part III
Pedagogy of CBASP Treatment

5
Creating Contingent Environments Using Contingent Personal Responsivity

There was an interesting article in the September 3rd *Wall Street Journal* concerning the therapist sharing life experiences with patients.... For those of us in the old school of psychotherapy this behavior of the therapist was shocking. For we had been taught that one does not talk about one's personal life during the sessions.

—Meredith W. Green (2004)

In Rogerian psychotherapy, patients receive unconditional positive regard and acceptance from their psychotherapists. In CBASP patients confront the consequences of their behavior, which are made explicit through Situational Analysis, the contingent personal responsivity of therapists, and the Interpersonal Discrimination Exercise. Behavior is consequated in the session to teach patients that they are bound to their world in inextricable ways. When the therapist personally responds to the patient's behavior, information is imparted concerning the individual's interpersonal connection to the therapist (Bandura, 1977). Consequation is used to modify maladaptive interpersonal patterns with the therapist as well as others, and in-session contingencies are employed to heal the affective wounds of developmental trauma.

All CBASP techniques have one common goal: to connect the individual with early-onset depression (or "reconnect," in the case of the patient with late-onset depression) perceptually with his or her environment. Connection is defined as the ability to recognize and identify the interpersonal consequences of one's behavior—a learning perspective labeled *perceived functionality* (McCullough, 2000). I argue that perceptual disengagement— that is, the inability to recognize the consequences one produces in an interpersonal encounter—is one maintaining variable in chronic depression (McCullough, 2000). The intractability of the disorder is related to the fact that the interpersonal environment has no informing influence on the individual's behavior. To remedy this dilemma and to replace disconnection with perceived functionality, therapists must first demonstrate to patients that *all human interaction is contingently related*. The perceptual connection is discovered, over time, through repeated exercises of Situational Analysis and by learning how one's in-session behavior affects the therapist. When patients focus on behavioral consequences, they learn that everything they do impacts others in highly specific ways.

In-session contingency demonstrations also facilitate the learning of new interpersonal behavior as well as enhance the experiential encounter of patients with their clinicians. I have noted elsewhere that *behavioral rigidity* characterizes the interpersonal life of the chronically depressed patient (McCullough, 2000). I make the assumption that maladaptive behaviors that are manifested in the session and that become problematical for the dyad also pose difficulties for the patient on the outside. Thus, by modifying behavior in the session and then ensuring that the new learning is transferred to relationships on the outside, therapists enable patients to revise the way they interact with others.

We learned in Chapter 4 that patients are often surprised by the personal response tactics of CBASP therapists. The century-old role of the "interpersonally neutral" or detached therapist, described in the popular media and newspaper cartoons (e.g., Bob Thaves' *Frank and Ernest* and Wiley Miller's *Non Sequitur*) as well as experienced by millions of patients, is well known. Most patients do not expect clinicians to disclose their personal feelings or responses. When CBASP therapists respond personally to patients for the first time, they may hear comments such as "I didn't come here to have to learn to deal with my therapist!" As noted earlier, patients must be prepared didactically for this new role strategy well in advance and given sufficient explanation as to why the therapist will behave in a personally contingent manner. Helping patients discover that the interactive CBASP session is an effective teaching environment wherein new interpersonal skills can be learned will take time. Using contingent personal responses to choreograph this type of learning environment is one of the pedagogical tasks the CBASP clinician must learn.

Therapist Role Characteristics

In this chapter we explore several examples of problematical patient behavior. The personal response strategies that were used have proved beneficial. In addition to modifying negative interpersonal behavior, instances in which contingent personal responses occur also can provide opportunities to help patients understand their inextricable connection to the environment.

As previously discussed, two therapist role characteristics are essential when using contingent personal responsivity: (1) the ability *to be oneself* with patients, which means being able to respond naturally in the moment (see Chapter 4); and (2) the ability to make *judicious* and *self-disciplined* use of personal responses. Said another way, the second characteristic means knowing *when to* and *when not to* respond, and when responding, being able to do so in a manner that facilitates behavior change. Two hypothetical case examples are presented below that illustrate how being oneself with the patient and responding appropriately set the stage for perceptual change.

Case 1

Patient: No one could ever care for me.

Dr. Zetner: I don't understand what you mean.

Patient: You know, *me*, no one could care for me.

Dr. Zetner: What you say makes no sense to me.

Patient: What is it that you don't understand?

Dr. Zetner: How you can sit there and make that statement?

Patient: Well, it's true, isn't it?

Dr. Zetner: No.

Patient: How can you say that? I know my life better than you.

Dr. Zetner: You do, but what you say is simply not true.

Patient: Okay, name one person who cares.

Dr. Zetner: You're looking at him.

Patient: Oh, yeah, but I'm paying you.

Dr. Zetner: You've just written off what I've said. You've just blown me off!

Patient: Well, it's true, I'm paying you to like me.

Dr. Zetner: You don't understand what I said. There's no way you can buy my feelings! I don't think you've thought about that.

Patient: Do you ever treat anyone you don't like?

Dr. Zetner: Not if I don't think that liking and caring about someone is possible. There are certain types of individuals I don't see because I know I won't like them.

Patient: Okay, then tell me what you see in me that you like.

Dr. Zetner: Are you saying to me that you might be interested in how I feel toward you?

Patient: I'm curious.

Dr. Zetner: I'm glad you are; let's talk about it.

Dr. Zetner was completely himself in this exchange. He did care about the patient and was not hesitant to disclose it at the appropriate moment. However, the discipline in his contingent disclosure is seen when he disclosed his feelings indirectly ("You're looking at him") and allowed the patient to discover the ramifications of a caring relationship. Had the disclosure been more direct (e.g., "I care about you" or "Why is it hard for you to believe that I care about you?"), the optimal discovery moment might have been lost as the patient negated the therapist in the first instance or "talked about" the subject in the second. First, Dr. Zetner let the patient "play his cards" and pose the problem of the fee; it was apparent that the personal response would have to be differentiated from the monetary issue. Once both issues (money and caring) were on the table, the two could be disconnected, and the caring response could be highlighted. Let's look at a second example and see how another therapist dealt with the same issue.

Case 2

Patient: No one could ever care for me.

Dr. Ball: I don't understand what you mean.

Patient: You know, *me*, no one could care for me.

Dr. Ball: What you say makes no sense to me.

Patient: What is it you don't understand?

Dr. Ball: How you can sit there and make that statement.

Patient: Well, it's true, isn't it?

Dr. Ball: No.

Patient: How can you say that? I know my life better than you.

Dr. Ball: You do, but what you say is simply not true.

Patient: Okay, name one person who cares.

Dr. Ball: You're looking at her.

Patient: Oh, yeah, but you're a psychotherapist. You've been trained to like all your patients.

Dr. Ball: Let me be sure that I understand what you just said. You think I've been trained to like people. Do you really think that's possible?

Patient: I don't know, but I don't think you would tell one of your patients that you didn't like him.

Dr. Ball: How do you know?

Patient: I can't imagine you doing that.

Dr. Ball: You really don't know very much about me, do you?

Patient: Not really.

Dr. Ball: Are you interested in getting to know me and trying to understand what I mean when I say that you're looking at someone who cares about you?

Patient: It's *sorta scary* to think about someone caring for me.

Dr. Ball: It's different than just saying no one could, isn't it?

Patient: It feels very different.

Dr. Ball: We've got a lot of work to do.

Here the therapist again assumes the naïve follower role and allows the patient to make the first move, thus discovering and identifying the problematical issues surrounding the topic of others caring for him. The therapist will know how to respond personally once the patient's concerns are clear. The individual's problem lay in his perceived role of the psychotherapist and the quality of interpersonal honesty he thought would be forthcoming. Not surprisingly, in a developmental history devoid of caring, interpersonal therapeutic honesty takes on heightened significance; such was the case here. As noted in earlier chapters, *trying to make a "neutral" therapeutic response* (e.g., "Why is this issue so important to you?") to deflect the focus from the therapist back to the patient versus *responding personally in a disciplined manner* are two very different strategies. Dr. Ball was herself throughout this session, as she followed the individual's pace to see where it led.

She also avoided becoming entangled in the "hypothetical" question of whether or not she would tell patients if she didn't like them; instead, she remained focused on the issue of caring. Her effective response to this off-task query was that he didn't know her very well (this was true), nor did he understand how she could care for him (this was also true). Another disciplined aspect of Dr. Ball's work is seen in her reticence to "tell" or "explain logically" *how/why* she cared about this patient. Had she elaborated on why she cared, her remarks would have been verbally deflected by what followed ("You've been trained to like all your patients"). At the end of the scenario, an underlying issue emerged when the patient remarked that sitting with someone who cared for him was " *sorta scary*"—a response that was qualitatively different from his opening comment that "no one could ever care for me."

Years ago, Johnny Mercer and Rube Bloom wrote a wonderful song entitled *Fools Rush in Where Angels Fear to Tread.* This theme offers an applicable caveat for therapists to keep in mind when responding personally. If one wants to create a salubrious contingency environment, personal responding must be done gently and with a keen eye on the state of the patient at every given moment. Clinicians must inhibit the strong pull to rush in and say or do something. Setting the stage on which patients can discover the truth about their behavior (Freire, 2000) and the effects it has on therapists takes patience and discipline. Contingent personal responding (on the part of therapists) creates an awareness of one's interpersonal "stimulus value" (on the part of patients) that can only be acquired over time—*never* in one trial. Many practitioners often behave to the contrary. We frequently act as if knowledge can be "dumped" into someone's brain by telling or instructing; most psychotherapists, including myself, love to expound. Effective perceptual change, however, occurs when individuals are allowed to discover the truth about relationship in the presence of a person who facilitates the discovery process with discipline and sensitivity. Simply stated, brief sentences and probing questions, delivered at the right time, are the tools we need. When it comes to the *pace* therapists should maintain when personally responding to patients, the title of the song implies the correct way to proceed: *Wise therapists proceed slowly and identify the essential issues before rushing in and reacting rather than responding with discipline.*

Situational Examples of Contingent Personal Responsivity

Introduction

Ten verbatim case scenarios involving personal responses from therapists are presented below. At the beginning of each case, brief demographic and clinical case information is provided, followed by descriptions of the peak octant scores patients obtained when the therapist rated him or her on the Impact Message Inventory (IMI: Kiesler, 1996; Kiesler & Schmidt, 1993). Of particular interest to us as we explore personal responsiveness in the scenarios are the *complementarity pulls* (action tendencies) on the therapist that are inferred from the IMI peak octant scores (see

Figure 2.2, Chapter 2). As noted in earlier work, I reported that submission (S) and hostile–submission (H-S) are the peak octants that characterize most chronically depressed patients (McCullough et al., 1988, 1994a, 1994b). In Chapter 2 we learned that the complementarity pull for submission is dominance (D), whereas hostile–dominance (H-D) is pulled by hostile–submissive (H-S) behavior. Thus, when responding to patients who have peak IMI scores in either the S or H-S octants, psychotherapists must consciously avoid assuming the complementary D or H-D role. D and H-D reactions (as opposed to disciplined responses) to patients have very serious and destructive consequences. On such occasions when unwitting clinicians assume or imply either a D ("Do what I say and you'll be okay") or an H-D ("Your efforts are disappointing; I'll have to do it myself") stance, the patient's interpersonal psychopathology is reinforced. D and H-D personal reactions reinforce submissive behavior (S) and potentiate greater interpersonal detachment (H-S) and anxiety behavior (H-S).

The IMI is used in CBASP to help therapists define the *interpersonal boundary markers* for contingent personal responsiveness. The instrument is completed and scored by the CBASP therapist following the second therapy session. Avoiding excessively dominant and hostile-type reactions with chronically depressed patients is mandatory (McCullough, 2000). I label both styles "lethal." We train therapists to assume a *task-focused interpersonal stance* toward patients (remaining mildly dominant and, alternatively, mildly submissive), all the while remaining on the friendly side of the IMI circle. The optimal, task-focused IMI profile for personal responsivity is illustrated in Figure 5.1 (McCullough, 2000, p. 178).

At the end of each scenario, the therapist's contingent personal responsivity behavior is described.

The Empty Tank

Case Scenario 1

The patient, Fred, is a 34-year-old Caucasian male who has been married for 12 years. His wife was his adolescent sweetheart and "is the only girl [he's] ever loved." They married shortly after they both graduated from the same university. They have two children in elementary school. His wife is a CPA working in a large accounting firm. Fred graduated with an outstanding record in chemistry. He also ran the 10,000 meters on the track team and won a number of collegiate track meets in his specialty. His work history has never reflected his abilities, however. He is currently a route manager for a large metropolitan newspaper, where he has worked for the past 8 years.

Fred is very shy and quiet, saying little unless others take the conversational lead. He would be described as a "follower type" of individual; in interpersonal conflict situations, he usually withdraws into himself. His health is good, and he jogs several miles daily. He has one close male friend he sees on a regular basis. He was diagnosed with early-onset recurrent major depression with antecedent dysthymia (double depression). He became depressed as an adolescent but couldn't explain

Profile Summary Sheet
IMPACT MESSAGE INVENTORY: FORM IIA OCTANT VERSION
Donald J. Kiesler and James A. Schmidt

Therapists: Twelve B-MS Site Supervisors
Rater: B-MS Psychotherapy Coordinator (JPM)

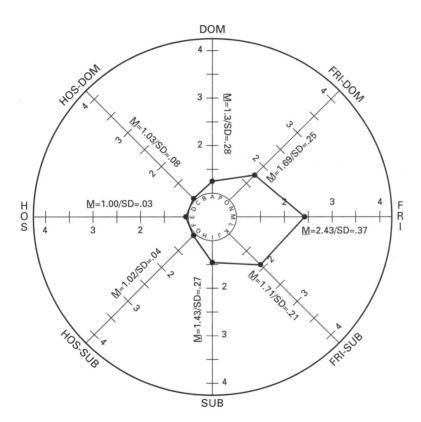

FIGURE 5.1. The "optimal" CBASP therapist IMI profile, based on mean data taken frem JPM's ratings of the 12 site supervisors during the sixth month of the Bristol-Myers Squibb Company national Chronic Depression study. Reproduced by special permission of the publisher, Mind Garden, Inc., 1690 Woodside Road, Suite #202, Redwood City, CA 94061: (650) 261-3500: from the *Impact Message Inventory: Form IIA Octant Scale Version* by Donald J. Kiesler, PhD. Copyright 1993 by Dr. Donald J. Kiesler. All rights reserved. Further reproduction is prohibited without the distributor's written consent.

why. During the history-taking interview, he described both parents as emotionally aloof. He talked more about his father, whom he described as very punitive and "never cutting [him] any slack." He also said he never understood why his parents married, because they never seemed to love each other; instead, they argued and fussed all the time.

He was dysthymic throughout high school and college and had his first major depressive episode when he was 25 years old. Since then, Fred has had three major episodes and received medication that brought the major depressions under control but never alleviated the dysthymia. All of the episodes followed job crises with his supervisor. He was unable to describe how the crises were resolved, saying only, "They just sorta went away." He had never received psychotherapy until now. Fred's motivation level for change appears to be moderate to low, and he often remarks that he feels that trying to stop the depression is a waste of time; however, he always comes on time for his appointments. Today is the sixth session.

His peak octant (highest scored octant) on the IMI was hostile–submissive (H-S), suggesting that he is experienced as interpersonally nervous, tending to withdraw from problematic issues, feeling generally inadequate, and making the practitioner want to do something to put him at ease. As noted above, the therapist faces two strong complementary action tendencies. One is to assume a dominant stance and tell Fred what he should do; the second stems from a felt frustration that makes it difficult not to point out Fred's obvious faults (e.g., his feeble efforts at completing homework assignments and his passive–nervous demeanor that leaves the therapist feeling that any change Fred makes is up to the doctor). Avoiding the assumption of a hostile–dominant (H-D) role with Fred is the major and ever-present interpersonal challenge.

At the end of the previous session, a conflict arose between Fred and Dr. Long. Fred asked if he could change his appointment the following week. After looking at the calendar, Dr. Long told him that he was sorry but he was booked solid. Fred became noticeably angry and made an off-handed comment (while looking away) that he had expected this kind of reaction. He brushed aside Dr. Long's efforts to explain. The two parted and agreed to meet at the same time next week. The following verbatim exchange started at the beginning of the next session.

Dr. Long: You sure threw a zinger at me last week—it stung.
Patient: What do you mean?
Dr. Long: The comment you made when I couldn't schedule you this week at an earlier time.
Patient: It was no big deal.
Dr. Long: Your words stung me.
Patient: You're making me feel guilty.
Dr. Long: About what?
Patient: About throwing a zinger at you.
Dr. Long: Why do you feel guilty?

Patient: I don't want to hurt you. I just didn't think before I said it. I'd like to talk about something else and move on.

Dr. Long: I'm still bothered by your comment. I don't think I can brush it under the rug and play like it didn't happen.

Patient: What can we do about it? There's nothing I can do to change what I said.

Dr. Long: True. But there's something we can do instead of just going on to something else.

Patient: What's that?

Dr. Long: Let's see what it says about the two of us. Did you have any idea that you could hurt me with your words?

Patient: I never thought about it.

Dr. Long: Think about it. What does the fact that you can hurt me say about us and about our relationship?

Patient: I'm not sure—that maybe you're a sensitive person or something like that.

Dr. Long: I didn't ask what it says about me but what it says about *us*. What does your comment and my response say about the two of us?

Patient: I'm not sure what you're getting at.

Dr. Long: You do something and it has an effect on me. What does that imply about us?

Patient: That I can hurt you by what I say.

Dr. Long: Yes, that's exactly what it says. But that's just one part of it. The other part is that your reaction when I told you that you had stung me—you mentioned a minute ago that it made you feel guilty.

Patient: I did, but it's funny, I don't feel guilty anymore. Wonder why?

Dr. Long: Where do you think the guilt has gone?

Patient: Somehow you don't seem all that hurt about what I said.

Dr. Long: As I said, it stung me but right now I'm more interested in us learning something about the exchange we had and are having now—something that involves both of us and the way we affect each other.

Patient: You mean the fact that you were affected by me? I never thought that was possible.

Dr. Long: Think about what we've been talking about. What effect did I say you had on me?

Patient: That I stung you with a zinger comment.

Dr. Long: That's a real effect and when I told you about it, what effect did I have on you?

Patient: I felt guilty.

Dr. Long: That's the effect I had on you when I told you about last week. We both affect each other moment-to-moment by what we do. We don't have a choice about this. It's just the way things are. And all this time you felt that what you did had no effect on me. Amazing!

Patient: Therapists are not supposed to be affected by their patients. I just assumed . . .

Dr. Long: I've been affected by you ever since you first walked in my door. Some time you might even be interested in some of the effects you've had on me.

Patient: I'm not sure I want to know.

Dr. Long: My point is that what you do to me as well as to others, has *effects*. I'm in the same boat because I have the same effects. That's the kind of world we live in. I'm glad we didn't brush this aside and go on to something else. What's your response to talking about this the way we have?

Patient: I'm not sure about all these things you say. Thinking about affecting you and others is new. I'm just not sure. I still wish we had talked about some other things. It's hard doing this.

Dr. Long: Maybe the hardest thing you'll ever do. We'll keep working on it. My goal is to help you see how you affect others and how they affect you. Okay, we'll go on to something else. Did you bring in a situational event we can work on?

Commentary

Dr. Long successfully avoided assuming an H-D stance with Fred; rather, he remained on the friendly side of the circle and at times assumed a mildly dominant role (e.g., he wouldn't talk about other matters before addressing this situation; he encouraged Fred to focus on the "guilty" effects he had had on him). At the end of the scenario, Dr. Long became mildly submissive as he followed Fred's wishes by changing the focus of their conversation to another subject. Fred's comments made it clear that he would need more exposure to the contingency-training techniques of CBASP before he would be able to recognize the interpersonal effects he had on others. Dr. Long wisely stopped, refusing to rush in and push for further understanding. He and Fred would have ample opportunities in the future to cover the same ground. He also matched Fred's pace (i.e., he "walked" with Fred through a recounting of the conflict, rather than striding out front to explain what had led to what; Fred's responses to his questions throughout the dialogue dictated his next move). This scenario illustrates contingent personal responsivity in its simplest form: "You did this, and this was the effect you had on me." Its simplicity can be misleading if one misses the fact that Dr. Long disclosed his own personal feelings to Fred ("You threw a zinger at me and it stung") and used the disclosure to open the discussion of the contingent dynamics of their relationship.

The Worm

Case Scenario 2

Susan is a 42-year-old African American female who was recently divorced. The marriage had lasted 15 years. Her husband had walked out because "he got tired of living with a depressed woman. I deserved his leaving me. I am nothing but a worm." The patient and her 11-year-old daughter are currently living with her mother, with whom she does not get along. They argue frequently about how to raise the daughter and over the problems the patient's depression causes in the home. The mother thinks she should just "get over it" and get on with her life. She is currently taking classes at a state university to get her degree in elementary education. She has held several nonprofessional jobs (secretary, clerk, office manager for a small construction firm, and, until recently, driving a delivery truck for a local pharmacy), has never been fired, and has worked at each job for several years. Susan never had difficulty obtaining positive recommendations from her supervisors when she stopped work.

Susan described her developmental years as "chaotic," with frequent fights occurring between her mother and alcoholic father. The father used to verbally berate Susan when he was drunk, calling her a "whore," "slut," and a "bitch daughter." Her mother repeatedly told her that she was a "disappointment" to her and that she would never make anything of herself. She described the relationship she had with her mother as "never close" and said that she "never felt [she] ever had a real mother." The father left the family when she was in her first year in high school. She rarely saw him after he left and didn't know if he was still alive. The mother didn't like her daughter's husband and never spoke to him after the wedding.

Susan's depressive onset began during her sophomore year in high school, and she reported feeling down "ever since." When asked if her depression had ever become more severe, she recalled that it had, usually on the heels of boyfriend breakups. As best as the clinical interviewer could determine, she had had three or four major depressive episodes that overlay an early-onset dythymia course. Her diagnosis was recurrent major depression with early-onset, antecedent dysthymia. Susan cried intermittently during the screening interview and was extremely abasive, making repeated self-derogatory comments about herself (e.g., "I'm a worm," "I don't deserve anything good," "I'm a loser," "I fail at everything I try to do").

Susan obtained extreme peaks on two octants of the IMI: hostile–submissive (H-S) and submissive (S). The H-D impacts were uneasiness in the presence of Dr. Hebert, going out of her way to remind the therapist that she was inadequate, and interpersonally holding back (remaining detached), which was evident in the way she talked. Susan never made declarative statements. Everything she said was qualified by "I think," "It might be," "I'm not sure," "You're probably right," "I might have," etc. Susan's S impacts made Dr. Hebert feel strongly that the therapist was in charge, that she could say anything and Susan would agree, that Susan felt that the therapist had all the answers, and that Susan obviously saw Dr. Hebert as a superior authority figure. Dr. Hebert faced two strong complementarity pulls that would make treating this patient difficult: (1) The first pull stems from the H-S octant and poses a temptation to express frustration and anger (H-D behavior) over the patient's detachment. Such behavior may arise from two sources: One might involve frustration over Susan's lack of initiative to complete homework or her failure to initiate any action to feel better; the second might come from her extreme self-derogation and abasiveness. Frequent self-effacement comments may cause Dr. Hebert to try to persuade Susan to think more highly about herself. Sitting with persons who repeatedly castigate themselves often prompts others to point out their positive characteristics.

(2) Dr. Hebert faces a second interpersonal obstacle. Susan's extreme submissiveness will make it easy to take the lead in the sessions, dominate and direct the flow of the conversation, provide information to Susan about taking better care

of herself, and pontificate about things she should do to feel better—in short, reinforce the submissive behavior of the patient with dominant behavior. Teaching Susan that she produces and maintains the dilemma she complains about will be difficult. Demonstrating to extremely helpless-behaving patients that their actions have negative consequences takes skill, patience, and considerable effort. In such instances one walks the razor's edge between pushing the person into greater despair versus opening doors of empowerment. The hopelessness-to-hope moment is created whenever patients begin to recognize the consequences of their behavior. On such occasions, the perceptual landscape is transformed from one where individuals conclude that it doesn't matter what they do to one where they recognize that what they do matters because of the obvious effects that they see produced. This scenario occurred during the tenth session.

Patient: I'm such a nothing. I hate myself.

Dr. Hebert: You confuse me.

Patient: What do you mean?

Dr. Hebert: Just what I said. You really confuse me.

Patient: I don't understand, you'll have to explain yourself.

Dr. Hebert: What I'm confused about is the way you feel about yourself and the way I feel about you.

Patient: You've got to think I'm a nothing, so what's confusing about that?

Dr. Hebert: I don't feel that way at all. What confuses me is that I don't feel toward you the way you feel toward yourself. I'm not sure why.

Patient: Now I really don't understand what you're saying.

Dr. Hebert: I really like you, care a lot about you. What's confusing to me, and I'll say it again, is how I can feel that way about you with you feeling that you're a nothing. How can someone really like someone who thinks of herself the way you do? How is that possible?

Patient: You just don't know me very well.

Dr. Hebert: Oh, I know you probably better than most. You've shared a lot about yourself with me, things you told me that you've told no one else. I know you pretty well. I just don't understand my feelings toward you, that's all.

Patient: You mean, how you could like me when I don't like myself?

Dr. Hebert: Yes. I'm not sure how that's possible. Why don't I hate you or think you're a nothing?

Patient: Now I'm confused.

Dr. Hebert: About what?

Patient: About what you just said.

Dr. Hebert: What did I say that's confusing?

Patient: That you can like me with my not liking myself. I don't know how you can like me.

Dr. Hebert: Why would you care? Why would it matter? You've already closed the door on yourself in this regard.

Patient: Are you asking me why I would care if you liked me?

Dr. Hebert: Yes.

Patient: I do care.

Dr. Hebert: Now you're really confusing me. Your jury is already in and you've decided you're a nothing. Now you want to open up the case again about how I feel about you?

Patient: Sounds crazy, doesn't it? But I do care how you feel about me.

Dr. Hebert: I don't see why. Whatever I say about that, you'll just dismiss it. You'd reject whatever I think and feel about you unless it fits your viewpoint—that makes me uneasy talking about how I feel toward you.

Patient: Somehow this conversation has gotten all twisted around.

Dr. Hebert: Yes, it has. You've just encountered someone who feels differently about you than you feel about yourself. And the strange thing is, that you care how I feel about you—how I feel really matters. Why is it important how I feel about you? I would think that how I feel wouldn't matter.

Patient: It does matter. I can't lie and tell you it doesn't.

Dr. Hebert: Susan, have you ever felt that anyone ever cared about you?

Patient: No.

Dr. Hebert: No wonder it's confusing to you to think about my caring for you—it doesn't fit, does it? You couldn't feel any other way about yourself. Your feelings are totally appropriate. I'm becoming a little less confused now.

Patient: I'm still not clear about what's going on here.

Dr. Hebert: It seems that I've responded differently to you than anyone you've known. And somehow it matters to you that I care about you, even though it's clearly a different sort of experience. You've met someone in me who hasn't treated you like you've always been treated—like a nothing. Is this what's going on here?

Patient: I think so. It's just very different to be talking to someone about all this.

Commentary

Dr. Hebert became "a problem for the patient" (McCullough, 2000, p. 264) in this exchange. Rather than try to counter the patient's self-perception with a different opinion or logically dispute the thought behind the comment, she framed the self-negation statement as an interpersonal problem for Susan to resolve. The problem was this: *"How is it possible that I can care about you when you don't care about yourself?"* Refusing to shift the focus away from the problem—a tactic similar to Dr. Long's refusal to change the subject in the scenario above—Susan was faced with two dissonant pieces of information: Her dysfunctional history dictated that no one could care about her, but Dr. Hebert obviously did care about her. Susan tried to discount Dr. Hebert's position with the deflective comment, "You just don't know me very well." Dr. Hebert held the focus, and in doing so, increased the intensity of the dissonance.

In most instances such as this one, something has to shift in the perceiving eye of the patient. Either the patient will make further deflective comments denigrating the veracity of the therapist, or he or she will complain that a therapist *has* to like his or her patients. If the therapist can tolerate the obvious discomfort of the moment while holding the focus, patients such as Susan will find it increasingly difficult to tolerate the dissonance, especially with the interpersonal alternative staring her in the face. Dr. Hebert held the line, and the essential issue finally emerged: Susan had never felt cared for and didn't know what to do when faced with a relationship in which caring was offered. If a patient has never experienced this type of relationship, the therapist must be willing to choreograph personally the interpersonal opportunity for caring to be incorporated into the perceptual system. Until the actual experience *of being cared for in a relationship* occurs for Susan, no amount of logical argument or instruction will fill the void.

The Failure

Case Scenario 3

Becoming a problem for the patient offers yet another alternative tactic with which to tackle Susan's self-deprecating and submissive style. Susan didn't complete homework during the early sessions. When Dr. Hebert would inquire if she had completed a Coping Survey Questionnaire (CSQ) so that they could conduct a Situational Analysis, the patient would often become teary-eyed and whine that she never did anything right, she was a hopeless failure and probably the worst patient that Dr. Hebert had ever had. Dr. Hebert found these whiny and self-punitive outbursts both annoying and frustrating. Susan's helpless behavior, coupled with her severe verbal attacks on herself, often left the therapist feeling helpless herself and feeling pulled to say or do something to make the situation less stressful. The extreme S and H-S octant behavior evident in Susan's outbursts requires (1) the recognition on the therapist's part that she is being pulled into interpersonal arenas she does not want to enter (viz. D and H-D responses), and (2) the need to formulate an immediate plan of action to remain on the friendly side of the interpersonal circle, yet task-focused. In the fifth session's verbatim scenario below, Dr. Hebert consequates Susan's helpless and destructive behavior with contingent personal responsivity.

Dr. Hebert: Did you complete a CSQ for us to work on today?
Patient: I've failed again. I can't do anything right. I tried to do the homework, but I just can't do it. I'm a worm. I'm the worst person in the world (*starts to cry softly*). I ought to quit therapy. I'll fail at this like I've failed at everything else. I'm a hopeless bitch.
Dr. Hebert: You don't have any idea what effect you've just had on me.
Patient: What do you mean?
Dr. Hebert: For someone who feels so helpless, you certainly pack a heavy punch.
Patient: I don't understand what you're driving at.
Dr. Hebert: Your comments about how bad you are. They make me feel totally helpless to do anything; they leave me without any energy.
Patient: I feel the same way, too.

Dr. Hebert: What I'm trying to say to you is that the way you just behaved made me feel helpless—it's the effect you had on me. I wasn't feeling that way until you started beating up on yourself.

Patient: See, I've gone and screwed up again with you. I messed us up. I mess up everyone. I can't do anything right!

Dr. Hebert: You still haven't understood what I said to you.

Patient: You told me that I messed you up, made you feel helpless.

Dr. Hebert: That's not what I was trying to help you see.

Patient: But it's what you said.

Dr. Hebert: Let me try again. I said I was not feeling helpless until you started beating yourself up. When you first came in, I had energy and was ready to go to work. That changed when you started verbally abusing yourself and telling me how awful you are. That's when I started feeling helpless—like nothing mattered. Why do you want to do this to me? [*At this point, Dr. Hebert personalizes the consequences and makes the patient's behavior a problem for the therapist. She deliberately increases the intensity of the issue.*]

Patient: I do this to everyone. I'm just a loser [*a deflective ploy that has the potential of removing Susan from the "hot seat"*].

Dr. Hebert: Let me ask you again. Why did you want to make me feel helpless? [*The focus on the behavioral consequences is maintained.*]

Patient: I never thought about doing that!

Dr. Hebert: You never thought that what you do affects others?

Patient: No. How can a helpless bitch affect others?

Dr. Hebert: Now think back. What did I say about how you affected me when you started beating up on yourself?

Patient: You said I made you feel helpless—like nothing mattered.

Dr. Hebert: And what did I say made me feel that way?

Patient: You said my beating up on myself made you feel that way.

Dr. Hebert: Do you see any connection between what you did and the effects you just had on me?

Patient: Yes, I think so. When I beat up on myself, it makes you feel helpless.

Dr. Hebert: Now, let's turn it around. What effect am I having on you right now?

Patient: Well, I'm not crying anymore. We're just talking.

Dr. Hebert: Have I done anything that caused you to stop crying?

Patient: You're not punishing me for not doing my homework. You're trying to get me to look at myself.

Dr. Hebert: So just talking to you and not punishing you has resulted in your not crying.

Patient: I think so.

Dr. Hebert: That's an effect I've just had on you. Let me ask you another question that has to do with your not crying anymore. Look at yourself right now. Whom do you see?

Patient: I don't feel I'm as awful as I did a minute ago.

Dr. Hebert: Why not?

Patient: Because you don't make me feel bad about myself.

Dr. Hebert: You've just changed the way I feel, too.

Patient: How do you feel?

Dr. Hebert: I don't feel hopeless anymore, I've gotten my energy back because I feel like we're doing some good work.

Patient: I've made you feel that way?

Dr. Hebert: Yes. We really have effects on each other, don't we? Maybe you're not as helpless as you think.

Patient: I never thought that what I did mattered to anyone before.

Commentary

By personalizing the consequences and disclosing how Susan made her feel, Dr. Hebert made explicit the contingent, interactional nature of their relationship. The ultimate goal was to undercut the felt helplessness and hopelessness by demonstrating to Susan the interpersonal consequences of her own behavior—consequences that resulted from interpersonal power, albeit not an adaptive use of it. Dr. Hebert also refused to be pulled into a D role by trying to make the patient feel better. Ignoring the fact that Susan had made her feel helpless and drained of energy would have thrust Dr. Hebert into an inauthentic interpersonal role.

She had still another difficult obstacle to overcome. Had Dr. Hebert expressed her felt annoyance and frustration (H-D response) nonverbally, with a sigh of resignation or a look of frustration, she would have missed the opportunity to address directly Susan's feelings of helplessness. She made a wise decision and chose to consequate personally the patient's maladaptive behavior. To achieve the consequation goal, she helped Susan concentrate solely on her (the therapist's) responses and the reasons for them. At one point, Susan tried to deflect the focus by shifting the center of attention in a global direction ("See, I've gone and screwed up again with you. I messed us up. I mess up everyone. I can't do anything right!"), but the therapist maintained the focus ("You still haven't understood what I said to you") and stayed on task.

Dr. Hebert was willing to disclose personal feelings that nudged Susan into a highly charged participant role. The therapist's enactment of personal responses avoids "talking about" how he or she feels, which would leave the patient in an observer role. Instead, the therapist brings the consequences of the patient's behavior to the fore *now* in a disciplined manner and places them squarely on the table: "You made me feel *this* when you did *that*." Susan could not maintain her detached observer role or flee into whiny self-punishment (both characteristics of the H-S octant) when the clinician helped her see the effects of her behavior.

Shove It!

Case Scenario 4

John was an angry, 43-year-old engineer who reported being depressed since high school. His father was a marine drill instructor, and the family had lived in Paris Island, CA and Quantico, VA during John's childhood. The patient had one brother

2 years older who was "my dad's favorite son." The brother was an outstanding athlete, had done well in school academically, and gone to college on a football scholarship. John also played sports and obtained good grades throughout college. He attended a Southern university on a boxing scholarship and took a degree in mechanical engineering. He married right after graduation and divorced 10 years later. The couple had no children.

John had tried dating several women after the divorce but no lasting relationship had evolved; he would become angry at something the woman did and never call her again. He worked at a large construction firm where he had been promoted to a supervisory position 5 years ago. His promotion was presently in jeopardy because the people who worked under him complained that he did nothing but criticize their work. Morale in the department was poor, and several of his employees had quit the company and sought employment elsewhere. Their letters of resignation blamed John as their reason for quitting. He had few friends and lived alone. He told the clinical interviewer that he was known around his apartment as an "old curmudgeon."

He said that his father had demanded that everything in his room be kept spotless and orderly at all times. He described his home as a "marine barracks" and said his mother complied with everything his father said. He described his home in the following way: "There was a time to get up, a time to retire, meals had to be served on time, the dishes were washed promptly, homework was done by 10 P.M. and lights out by 10:45 P.M. Being on time and following the rules were God." John was never sure if his parents loved him. The "rules in the family" overshadowed everything—his feelings, his concerns, and the problems he had in school. He never asked for anything. He began to box in high school and continued to box on the varsity team at the university. John described his boxing experiences as a way to get rid of anger. Since graduation, however, he complained that he'd never found any outlet for his anger. When asked why he was so angry, he replied, "I've always followed the rules to the letter, and it's gotten me nowhere—I've lost my marriage, am about to lose my job, and I've ended up lonely and by myself." Both parents had died several years before, and John and his brother rarely communicated.

John entered treatment in a major depressive episode. He reported having had several major depressive episodes that "would just go away after a while." His depression began as early-onset dysthymia with three or four recurrent episodes of major depression (double depression). He reported never having sought formal treatment until now. "I've come to the end of my rope," he said. John never smiled, looked down most of the time, and made only infrequent eye contact with his therapist, Dr. Boudreaux. He looked angry, and most of his comments were terse, cold, and hostile. Rarely did he initiate conversation with Dr. Boudreaux.

When Dr. Boudreaux rated John on the IMI, he obtained a peak score on the hostile octant (H) because he made the therapist feel like a "stranger." Other hostile impacts left Dr. Boudreaux feeling that John wanted to be left alone and that he clearly desired no interpersonal involvement. Asking John questions also left the therapist with the sense that he was intruding. Summarily, the essential message John communicated to Dr. Boudreaux was "stay away from me" or "leave me alone." He also peaked on the hostile–submissive octant (H-S) because of his frequent comments about feeling inadequate, feeling like a failure, his verbal avoidance when asked about work problems, and his obvious unease and nervousness sitting with Dr. Boudreaux. Little progress had been made over 10 sessions. The 11th session began with an angry outburst because Dr. Boudreaux was 10 minutes late—detained by an emergency telephone call from another patient.

Patient: Dammit, you're late!

Dr. Boudreaux: Yes, I am.

Patient: I pay you to be here the entire time. I get short-changed if you run late.

Dr. Boudreaux: You mean it matters to you that you have the full hour with me?

Patient: Hell, yes, it does!

Dr. Boudreaux: You told me last week that you were wasting your time here. Now you're saying you want the full hour. What's going on? I'm having trouble following why you're so mad.

Patient: If I'm going to get my money's worth, I want to see you the full time.

Dr. Boudreaux: What does getting your money's worth with me mean?

Patient: I can't believe we're discussing this. You were late, and now you're asking why I want my money's worth.

Dr. Boudreaux: We're discussing this because this is the first time I've seen you act like you care about being here. You sound like you care about what goes on here. I'm amazed and impressed that I've done something that matters to you—even if it is negative.

Patient: That's bullshit! You're making no sense. I don't understand what you're getting at.

Dr. Boudreaux: What is it you don't understand?

Patient: Why it matters that I care about what you do here.

Dr. Boudreaux: Obviously it matters very much to you—when I was late, you got mad.

Patient: Hell, yes, it matters what you do here.

Dr. Boudreaux: There's something going on in you that I haven't seen before. You've let me see that something matters to you—namely, what I do here. You've really put your cards on the table. Now, why does what I do here matter? Why does my late behavior matter to you?

Patient: I don't want to talk about it anymore.

Dr. Boudreaux: Don't fink out on me like this. You're the one who brought this up. Finish it!

Patient: I . . . uh . . . I don't know what to say.

Dr. Boudreaux: I think you do. Just say it.

Patient: You're . . . you're the only hope I've got.

Dr. Boudreaux: What hope could you possibly find in me? You'll have to explain.

Patient: Most of me didn't want to go along with what you were trying to do. A little piece of me did. I've fought myself and you the entire time we've been together.

Dr. Boudreaux: If you had gone along, what would that have meant? Why the big fight?

Patient: I would have lost face, I would've had to admit that I needed help. I couldn't let myself admit this.

Dr. Boudreaux: Losing face and needing help—are they the same thing?

Patient: I've never asked for anything. Never did as a kid. It would mean that I was weak, not strong. My father would have laughed at me. I could never admit to anyone that I needed anything. I just had to produce and keep going. You know, "Damn the torpedoes, full steam ahead"—that sort of thing.

Dr. Boudreaux: Damn, you've really beat up on me for about 10 hours. I'm surprised I wasn't 30 minutes late! Today, I wasn't looking forward to getting beat up again.

Patient: I'm sorry I've been an asshole.

Dr. Boudreaux: I accept your apology. You have acted like an asshole, but I'm beginning to understand why. If you didn't fight and acted like you wanted help, you would have had to admit to yourself and to me that you're weak. That was unacceptable for you. You and I have had a tough time together.

Patient: Yes, we have.

Commentary

Anger is one of the most difficult emotions for most therapists to handle (McCullough, 2000, p. 177). I've seen some therapists withdraw (a passive–hostile maneuver), others try harder to be more accepting of the patient (you know the adage—"I accept you but not your behavior"—as if the two could be so facilely be separated), and a few counteraggress in an actively hostile way (always a destructive maneuver). None of these three reactions is productive. Dr. Boudreaux shows us a better way. He had received an emergency call just as the session with John was to begin. Unable to be empathic with Dr. Boudreaux (a behavioral deficit among chronically depressed patients at the outset of treatment), John became angry about the clinician's lateness. Dr. Boudreaux could have explained his lateness to justify his behavior, but look what would have been obscured and perhaps lost. John revealed over the next few minutes a lifetime dilemma of not being able to admit that he needed anything because to do so would have been an admittance of weakness.

Tolerating the discomfort of the moment and waiting until patients "play their cards" pays big dividends more often than not. Justifying our behavior usually shuts down this process of discovery. Dr. Boudreaux evinced discipline and restraint and waited. In addition, his resposes to John were determined solely by John's responses; nothing was added or deleted. At the risk of overstating this point, Dr. Boudreaux took John literally, every sentence, and responded only to what John said. This is usually the most productive road to take in such heated encounters. By taking John literally, Dr. Boudreaux observed and personally responded to John's major points:

1. Lateness mattered to John.
2. Dr. Boudreaux's lateness mattered.
3. Lateness mattered because Dr. Boudreaux was perceived as John's last hope.
4. Finally, John saw the consequences of his angry behavior and how it hurt. Dr. Boudreaux didn't minimize the hurt; John had to confront directly how he had mistreated his therapist.

The discipline of proceeding slowly and following the patient, however excruciating, takes practice and the ability to tolerate the "heat" of a hostile attack. The strong complementarity pull of such attacks is always to counterattack or withdraw. Dr. Boudreaux also remembered the H-S complementarity pull from John's IMI, which was his felt inadequacy and nervousness in being in relationship (an H-D response, either spoken or thought, would take this form: "Couldn't you see I was late because I had a patient emergency and couldn't get off the phone?") To deliberately avoid an H-D reaction (though he was clearly feeling like acting it out), Dr. Boudreaux tried to remain on the friendly side of the Kieslerian circle, and in a task-focused mode, but he didn't hesitate to disclose the effects John's anger had on him. In doing so, Dr. Boudreaux boldly expressed his own mild hostility in a comment he made: "Damn, you've really beat up on me for about 10 hours. I'm surprised I wasn't 30 minutes late! Today, I wasn't looking forward to getting beat up again." By being willing to respond personally and demonstrate behavioral consequences, Dr. Boudreaux was able to articulate the truth about the relationship with John—being with John had been aversive and difficult. Contingent personal responsivity was administered judiciously and effectively. This is always the ultimate test of the personal responsivity: *Do one's responses facilitate the possibility of positive behavior change in the patient?* If they don't, the therapist has likely failed to track correctly the patient's core issues and respond accordingly.

The Entertainer

Case Scenario 5

Phil was a 35-year-old actor who became depressed 10 years ago following his failure to obtain a part in a Broadway play. He had studied drama at an Eastern university and been highly successful while in academia. Following graduation, he spent 2 years at a Playhouse School in New York, "learning the acting ropes" from all angles: directing, lighting, prop choreography, music, dance, martial arts fighting, and the nuances of acting itself. He excelled at the playhouse and graduated with a certificate in acting. He stayed in New York and took bit parts in off-off Broadway productions and even in several off-Broadway shows. For 1 year he had prepared for an audition for the Broadway part he wanted "more than anything in the world." His failure to be selected left him discouraged about his career ever "getting off the ground." His disappointment resulted in a major depressive episode that lasted about 10 months; during that time he lost considerable weight, quit socializing with friends, and stayed in his apartment most of the time. He never saw anyone for his depression or took any medication. Phil reported that he has never felt right since the onset of the major depression—he has always remained "a little bit down." At the screening interview, Phil was diagnosed as having single episode major depression without full recovery. In short, he was a chronically depressed patient who came to the clinic because he was tired of feeling down.

Phil grew up with a mother whom he described as "very angry," alternating between "loving [him] with hugs and beating [him] with a switch." He learned to keep one step ahead of the anger outbursts "by trying to maintain peace at all costs." This meant extreme compliance with his mother's wishes. Resolving conflicts in the family was a skill Phil never learned. He said that his father taught by platitudes—"he had a saying for everything." He opined that they "had an okay relationship—at least he didn't beat me." Phil has held multiple jobs and tries to stay on the good side of his wife, to whom he has been married for 12 years. He has two younger brothers and one sister, none of whom contacts him with any regularity. Phil married a woman who was several years older than he. She is the bread winner in the family and actively discourages him from working. He does everything he can to please her and stay on her good side, usually by complying with whatever she wants. During the screening interview, Phil was chatty, outgoing, yet obviously sad over his life and the fact that he couldn't get rid of his depression. He was put on medication and referred to a psychotherapist for treatment.

The CBASP clinician, Dr. Robicheaux, rated Phil on the IMI after the second session. Phil peaked on the friendly–dominant (F-D) octant because he left the clinician feeling entertained. During the session, he acted like he was on stage cracking "one-liners" about his problems. Several times the therapist laughed out loud at his remarks. He obviously enjoyed the interview and remarked that others liked being around him because of his humor. Phil obtained equivalent scores on the submissive (S) and hostile–submissive (H-S) octants. The S octant was rated high due to his noticeable attempts to please the therapist and say what he felt she wanted to hear; he admitted candidly that this was a longstanding problem (i.e, trying to please others by saying the right thing). He behaved like he had all the time in the world, yet when the topic turned to serious matters involving his wife, he seemed unable to stand up for himself and what he wanted. He was rated high on the H-S octant due to his detachment and avoidance of any behavior that would have led to serious reflection about his problems. He seemed more comfortable chatting, entertaining, and making light of his obvious difficulties. Dr. Robicheaux concluded that helping Phil learn to take himself seriously would thrust him into unfamiliar territory and make him uncomfortable. He would no longer be able to please the other person; instead, he would have to look seriously at what he wanted and didn't want and behave accordingly. Avoiding Phil's entertainment pull for "an audience" (that would be a friendly–submissive complementary [F-S] reaction) and taking him seriously without laughter and jocularity must define Dr. Robicheaux's therapeutic role. The ultimate therapeutic goal would be to demonstrate to Phil that his behavior had predictable consequences with others. Based on what Phil said and intimated about his interpersonal relationships, others did not take him seriously; hence, none of his interpersonal problems was ever resolved. He remained "the clown" across all situations.

The following scenario occurred during the seventh session. Phil progressively escalated his entertainment behavior with Dr. Robicheaux, frustrating all her attempts to keep him task-focused on Situational Analysis. She was reaching the limits of her tolerance as she increasingly pushed back thoughts and impulses to move into the H-D octant and say "Your entertainment behavior is full of crap!" Dr. Robicheaux knew she couldn't avoid his behavior any longer. Here's how she handled her felt complementary H-D action tendency.

Patient: I can't quit laughing at my stupidity. It's ridiculous how I can't tell my wife that she upsets me. I mean, a grown man who can't even talk seriously with his wife. It's comic, that's what it is.

Dr. Robicheaux: (*Remains silent.*)

Patient: You are very quiet. Did I say something wrong?

Dr. Robicheaux: Yes.

Patient: What?! What did I say wrong?

Dr. Robicheaux: The way you talk about yourself.

Patient: What's wrong with the way I talk about myself?

Dr. Robicheaux: Do you have any idea why I've responded to you this way?

Patient: You mean, in telling me that I said something wrong?

Dr. Robicheaux: Yes.

Patient: I have no idea. Tell me.

Dr. Robicheaux: What did I say the last time you laughed off your difficulties and made jokes about them?

Patient: You said you found it difficult to listen to me when I talked like this.

Dr. Robicheaux: Do you know why I find it difficult to listen?

Patient: I'm not sure, except that you said you didn't find my comments funny.

Dr. Robicheaux: I still don't find them funny. I don't see anything funny about you or your problems. You keep acting like I do by the way you continue to joke about your problems. In fact, I get the feeling that it doesn't matter what I say to you.

Patient: It does matter.

Dr. Robicheaux: Then why do you keep laughing and making jokes about yourself when talking about your problems? You look right at me the whole time. What am I supposed to think about your reaction to what I say?

Patient: I don't know why I do this. It's stupid, isn't it? (*chuckles*)

Dr. Robicheaux: You just chuckled—why?

Patient: I'm nervous talking about this.

Dr. Robicheaux: Are you nervous whenever you talk to me about your problems?

Patient: Yes.

Dr. Robircheaux: Why?

Patient: I've never known how to talk seriously about my problems. I've always had to crack jokes.

Dr. Robicheaux: Have we put our finger on why you keep trying to be funny with me? Why you keep trying to entertain me with your jokes and put-downs?

Patient: Maybe.

Dr. Robicheaux: You're not making a joke of this. Why not?

Patient: I've never thought of this before.

Dr. Robicheaux: Think about it. Why haven't you made a joke of this right now?

Patient: It's sad to think about why I try to be funny. I don't feel like making a joke right now.

Dr. Robicheaux: I haven't felt like laughing since you first walked into my office. In fact, it makes me a bit sad to think how you've had to tell jokes to hide from yourself and others.

Patient: You're not mad at me?

Dr. Robicheaux: You've frustrated me with your humor because you've used it to run away. I'm tired of your running away every time we try to talk seriously.

Commentary

Have Dr. Robicheaux's comments simply replaced one type of "pleasing" behavior (telling jokes) with another (suppressing the jokes to please her)? Perhaps, in the short term. But extinguishing the joke-telling behavior offers Dr. Robicheaux and Phil another alternative. By interrupting his lifelong pattern, the therapist has given Phil the opportunity to look seriously at his interpersonal problems and learn how to solve them. Phil's use of humor as an avoidance tactic has had destructive consequences not only for him but for others. Phil has never learned to take himself and his problems seriously. His friends, instead of addressing his needs, concerns, and desires seriously, have laughed at him and played an audience role—they've missed the real Phil. Behind the mask of humor is a man who has never learned to obtain for himself what he wants and needs from others. By consequating Phil's behavior with honest personal response, Dr. Robicheaux initiates the process of modifying his behavior. She will help Phil learn that comic interpersonal behavior has one set of predictable consequences, whereas serious behavior has a qualitatively different effect on people. Then it will be up to Phil to choose how he wants to engage others.

Once again, the therapist focuses the patient on her responses to his problematic behavior. In doing so, she *becomes a problem for Phil* as she refuses to allow him to avoid her responses by countering with humor. The discipline involved in using personal response requires avoiding the complementary pulls for anger and dominance while still reacting honestly to the negative behavior. Dr. Robicheaux avoided the H-D complementary pull of an angry put-down (even though she wanted to express it) by presenting her protest to Phil in a task-focused manner (neither hostile nor excessively dominant).

Her reply was a simple "Yes" to his desperate question asking if he had said something wrong. She allowed the explanation of why she had responded in this way to unfold in the dialogue that followed. The query about what he had said wrong was followed by "The way you talk about yourself." Then, following his lead, she kept Phil in *a participant role* by guiding the conversation into a discussion of *why* she had responded this way. Making the interpersonal consequences explicit ("I get the feeling that it doesn't matter what I say to you") led to the core issue: Phil uses humor to reduce anxiety and avoid talking seriously about problems. In summary, Dr. Robicheaux's contingent personal response required that she be honest about the obnoxious humor, that she express her responses in a task-focused manner, and that she allow Phil's questions to clarify the problematic issue she had with his behavior.

The Seductress

Case Scenario 6

Tina was a 28-year-old female who presented for treatment with a longstanding history of depression that began as far back as she could remember. "I've always felt sad," she said, "and feeling sad is the normal mood for me." When asked if her depression had ever deepened and become more severe, she said "Yes, several years ago." A married man had broken off their relationship, and she had "felt really down ever since." Tina was diagnosed with double depression. She was currently in a major depressive episode that had lasted 5 years. The current episode was preceded by an early-onset dysthymia disorder. She had never sought treatment before. The reason Tina gave for coming to the clinic was "wanting to do something to stop the depression."

The male staff member who conducted the screening interview described her behavior as "seductive." She maintained eye contact with him for long periods of time; she wore a very short dress with no underwear and a tight-fitting T-shirt; her body posture throughout conveyed a highly suggestive interpersonal message of "look at my body." Tina behaved as if she enjoyed being the center of attention in the interview and answered questions with excessive emotion and sweeping gestures. The interviewer also noted that her emotions appeared "shallow" and labile. She described the affair with her last lover and remarked that she had been in love. Her tone of voice as well as her description of the relationship suggested otherwise, however. She seemed more interested in the lavish gifts he had bought her and the expensive restaurants and nightclubs they had visited. Tina described a history of many previous love affairs with married men. She talked about this area of her life, exhibiting both feelings of sadness and amusement. She was currently working as a masseuse at a message parlor in a part of town known for its pornography shops and parlors. She had worked in this capacity for 3 years. When asked why she worked at a massage parlor, she remarked: "It pays well, and I'm treated okay." She also met criteria for the Axis II personality disorder: histrionic personality disorder.

Tina's developmental history had been destructive. She had two older brothers whom she had never liked, adding that they had run away from home during adolescence. She could not tell the interviewer where either brother currently lived. She reported having been sexually abused by an alcoholic father, beginning at puberty. "He was never mean, he just wanted to see me bathe and do other bathroom things. Then he wanted to touch me, and we had sex for a while." Tina had been fond of her mother, a prostitute; however, the mother was in and out of the family so much that their relationship had never been consistent. It still wasn't. The father died 8 years ago. She told the interviewer that she had matured physically at an early age and noticed that all the boys in the school liked to look at her. "I've always been able to use my body to get anything I wanted from men," she said. She also reported that she'd never taken drugs or drunk alcohol excessively, and that she'd never been arrested or incarcerated. "Other than sex," she said, "I've been a pretty good girl." One final comment the intake staff made to Dr. Renaud concerned Tina's intelligence level. The interviewer felt she was very intelligent, based on the way she verbally expressed herself.

The clinic psychiatrist prescribed 50 mg of sertraline, which would be titrated to a therapeutic dose over the next few weeks, and her clinic psychotherapist, Dr. Renaud, began seeing her once a week. He completed an IMI on Tina following their second therapy session. Similar to Case Scenario 5, the patient peaked on the friendly–dominant (F-D) octant, followed by similar peaks on the friendly–submissive (F-S) and hostile–submissive (H-S) octants. The F-D score was obtained because of Tina's exhibitionistic sexual behavior toward Dr. Renaud. It was a take-charge type of role suggesting that she obviously anticipated he would be entertained by her physical charms. Tina seemed to enjoy talking about herself in the sessions and worked hard to be a charming and engaging patient. The only noticeable inconsistency in her exhibitionistic behavior was the mild to moderate dysphoria that was obvious in her nonverbal behavior (lowering of the eyes, drop in the inflection of her voice at various times, and sometimes staring off into space in a longing way). When Dr. Renaud spoke, Tina often moved into the F-S domain and would look longingly into his eyes. She took his every word very seriously (almost too seriously, with her constant eye contact), and she gave the appearance of trusting him totally. He scored Tina on the H-S octant because of the inauthentic way in which she presented herself. He felt that much of her presentation was "a show" and that the real Tina was somehow hidden beneath the layers of sexual suggestiveness, the way she dressed, and her attempts to manipulate him physically. The one authentic component in this otherwise consistent display was her obvious sadness, which she had experienced for many years.

Trying to remedy her behavioral shallowness and lability would be difficult for one major reason. Tina had no precedent experiences in her learning repertoire for authentic human encounter. Interpersonal intimacy for her had consisted of using others and being used. One positive variable Dr. Renaud could use was the patient's depression intensity. The depression would not decrease until Tina changed some things in the way she lived. If decreases in depression intensity could be perceptually linked to more adaptive behavior, he would have a chance to modify her behavior. This, however, would not be an easy task. Secondly, Dr. Renaud wanted to help Tina begin making discriminations between interpersonal authenticity and interpersonal manipulation. This goal placed a significant burden on the dyadic relationship because he would have to become perhaps the first authentic male relationship the patient had ever experienced. The verbatim exchange below occurred during the third session.

Patient: (*looking somewhat worried at the beginning of the session*) You're different, really different. I've never met anyone like you before.

Dr. Renaud: What do you mean?

Patient: You don't act like other men.

Dr. Renaud: I still don't understand what you're trying to say to me.

Patient: Are you gay?

Dr. Renaud: What are you saying to me with all this? Obviously, there's something going on that you're concerned about. Tell me what's bothering you.

Patient: I've never had a man react to me the way you have.

Dr. Renaud: How have I reacted? Can you explain it and help me understand? Then we may be able to clarify your concerns.

Patient: You haven't come on to me. You've been strictly business with me during the last two sessions. I've never been around a man for any length of time who hasn't come on to me. I still wonder if you're gay.

Dr. Renaud: Now I'm beginning to understand. First off, I'm not gay. I've been happily married for 19 years. Secondly, you're right. I haven't reacted to you in a sexual way. I'm really not surprised it's caught your attention. You want to know something?

Patient: What?

Dr. Renaud: You've worked hard at coming on to me sexually.

Patient: What do you mean?

Dr. Renaud: Well, the way you sit and dress. I can't miss your sexuality. I noticed, all right, I just haven't reacted the way others do.

Patient: Why not?

Dr. Renaud: I don't want to.

Patient: I don't understand why not.

Dr. Renaud: I bet you don't. That's got to make me different compared to other men you've been with.

Patient: You are different. You seem a little weird to me.

Dr. Renaud: Just a little weird?

Patient: A "whole lot" weird. I'm not sure who you are and what you're about.

Dr. Renaud: What if it turns out that I don't want to get to know you sexually? What would that mean?

Patient: I don't know. Never experienced a man like that. Every man I've known has wanted to get in my panties.

Dr. Renaud: By the way, you haven't worn any since you've been coming here.

Patient: You've noticed!

Dr. Renaud: Couldn't miss it. I'm just not interested in you this way. So, why don't you start wearing underclothes? Truthfully, I'd like that better.

Patient: Men want me to take my clothes off. You want me to put more on. I can't figure you out.

Dr. Renaud: You're right. Taking off your clothes is not what we're here for. I want to help you get rid of your depression.

Patient: You really think that's possible?

Dr. Renaud: I think so, but we're going to have to move beyond your sex stuff to do it.

Patient: I've never gotten very far away from sex—it's been my ticket for everything. I wouldn't know what to do in here without it.

Dr. Renaud: Damn, I believe you! Let's play your way for a moment. What would you want from me if I responded to you sexually?

Patient: Just to know you couldn't resist my body.

Dr. Renaud: That's all?! Good grief!

Patient: Isn't that what every woman wants? What more is there?

Dr. Renaud: But that's like smoke—it's vapor—it has nothing to do with who I am and who you are.

Patient: I don't know about all that, but that's all I've ever known. Men like my body—what else is there?

Dr. Renaud: Tina, I believe every word you say: Men have never known anything about you except your body. The real question is, is there anything else to Tina Smith except Tina's body? I'm talking about other things like dreams you might have for your life and thoughts about what you might have been like had you grown up in a different family and with different parents. Things like wondering if a man could really like you, love you, because of who you are?

Patient: I don't allow myself to think about things like that.

Dr. Renaud: Why not?

Patient: Because I am who I am.

Dr. Renaud: What does that mean?

Patient: It means that I cannot be any different.

Dr. Renaud: How do you know?

Patient: I don't think I can.

Dr. Renaud: Let's find out if you can change and see if your depression improves—I'm convinced it will.

Patient: I'm not sure I want to come back here again.

Dr. Renaud: Why not?

Patient: I'm not sure, I just feel real uneasy right now talking about all this.

Commentary

Tina's interpersonal style, like the interpersonal style of many chronically depressed patients, required that Dr. Renaud respond candidly and directly to the problematic behavior. In doing so, he refocused Tina's attention away from herself to him. She had never learned to deal with a man except in a physical way, so it was clear that Dr. Renaud quickly put Tina in unfamiliar waters by talking about his not wanting to respond to her sexual overtures. Dr. Renaud may have moved too quickly, but patients such as Tina frequently terminate early. Sooner or later such patients arrive at a *choice-point barrier* that they must hurdle if treatment is to continue. That barrier turns into a choice point when it becomes obvious to the patient that the therapist will not respond in the way the individual wants. My strategy has always been to exacerbate this choice point sooner rather than later. If

Tina refuses to see Dr. Renaud because he will not treat her as a sexual object, then the relationship ends. In this particular case, Tina made the decision to continue, and the outcome was positive. What might have been some of the variables that contributed to her decision to continue?

Dr. Renaud did not respond to her sexual exhibitionism by remaining in the F-S octant (i.e., by remaining in an "accepting" audience position). Neither did he move into the F-D octant when she behaved coyly with him and evinced F-S behaviors with her excessive eye contact and dramatic attention to what he said. He stayed task-focused, and when she inquired why he didn't respond to her sexually the way other men did, he said simply, "I don't want to." The other task-focused response occurred when she gushed "You've noticed!" (that she was not wearing underpants). Dr. Renaud's reply was a direct one: "Couldn't miss it. I'm just not interested in you this way. So, why don't you start wearing underclothes? Truthfully, I'd like that better." Responses such as these task-focused statements frequently carry significant impact. They follow immediately on the heels of what a patient has said and relate directly to the subject matter at hand. What is contingently communicated to the patient is this: "I'm not going to play your silly game here. I'm going to deal seriously with you, regardless of what you say or do." Perhaps Tina, at least on some level, interpersonally understood that here was a human being who was different, and this difference might spell *hope* for her. There is no way we can know this, but the verbatim dialogue certainly demonstrated that Tina had met someone who was not going to do things her way.

As stated above, the therapeutic risk in candidly saying "no" too quickly to a patient's modal behavior (e.g., sexual overtures) while simultaneously making the alternative explicit (i.e., relating without sex) is that the behavioral requirement may be perceived as too great a step and result in the person giving up and withdrawing from treatment.

Beyond Help

Case Scenario 7

Sam frequently reiterated his doubts that anything or anyone could help him overcome his depression. He expressed these doubts to the screening staff member, the pharmacotherapist, and to his psychotherapist, Dr. Marshall. The 63-year-old patient was diagnosed with late-onset chronic major depression, which had begun 10 years previously when his "beloved" wife Annie had died of cancer. He had taken several medications since that time, but nothing seemed to help. He decided to seek psychotherapy as a last resort. Sam was currently taking 20 mg of paroxetine. In the last 8 months, after a urology appointment that was precipitated by an elevated prostate specific antigen (PSA) score (score clearly above his usual PSA baseline), the urologist did a biopsy and found several sites in the prostate that were malignant. His Gleason Scale (cancer severity) score was in the "intermediate range," so the doctor recommended surgery rather than radiation "for a man his age." Radical prostatectomy surgery was scheduled 2 months hence.

Sam was a self-made-man-type of individual who had worked his way through college, obtained a degree in marine biology, and had had a steady and successful career with a salt-water diving firm over the past 22 years. He earned a substantial salary and, until his wife had died, he seemed to have felt that he had "life by the tail." The staff member conducting the screening reported that Sam had never allowed himself to grieve his wife's death. He went back to work the day after the funeral and had worked 12–14 hours a day since then. He never discussed his wife's death with anyone and felt that the best thing for him to do was "to put Annie's death behind me and get on with my life." He rarely went out, though he attended a Sunday class meeting and went to church regularly. When the clinical interviewer asked him to describe his marriage to Annie, Sam began to cry, which led to an outpouring of how much he missed her and how empty and lonely his life had been over the last 10 years. He talked about her as if she had just died, saying, "I don't know what to do or how I will continue living." The company president had been very supportive and encouraged him to seek psychotherapy.

Dr. Marshall completed an IMI on Sam after the second session. Sam obtained his highest IMI octant score on the hostile–submissive octant (H-S). Dr. Marshall rated him high on H-S because of his withdrawn and detached style. He also appeared nervous with Dr. Marshall, particularly when discussing personal matters. Sam often commented on his inability to deal adequately with the stresses of living since his wife's death. His second highest octant score was submission (S). During the first two sessions, Sam made it clear that Dr. Marshall was in charge. The therapist also had to inhibit strong pulls to point out to Sam that he had significant strengths and assets that were being overlooked—for example, he had the ability to focus and problem-solve at work, he had interpersonal social skills that made him likable, his general health was good, and he was an excellent golfer (5 handicap) but rarely played anymore. His passivity and compliance were expressed in his felt hopelessness over his current life situation and his stated feelings of helplessness to change anything. The cancer diagnosis had seemed like "the final straw." He confided that he didn't think he had sufficient strength to go through with the surgery. In addition, he said he was scared to death over "having the big 'C'— that's what took Annie." This verbatim scenario took place during the sixth session.

Patient: I don't think anything can help me. I'm a lost cause.

Dr. Marshall: What do you mean, "a lost cause"?

Patient: I'm beyond help. I lost my best friend when Annie died 10 years ago—now I've got prostate cancer. I feel hopeless. You've just met your worst nightmare with me.

Dr. Marshall: Lost your wife and now you have cancer. You ought to be feeling hopeless.

Patient: What'd you say?!

Dr. Marshall: I think you heard me correctly. I'd be surprised if you felt any other way. Your feelings are appropriate.

Patient: Whose side are you on?

Dr. Marshall: What do you mean?

Patient: You're not supposed to tell me that feeling miserable is okay.

Dr. Marshall: Why not?

Patient: You're a shrink. You're supposed to be against bad feelings. You're supposed to make them go away.

Dr. Marshall: How can you not hurt when you've just taken two severe hits to the gut? I'm interested to hear how you think you shouldn't be feeling bad.

Patient: I never thought about it that way. But you're just saying that to make me feel better. That's a therapy technique, right?

Dr. Marshall: Nope, it's called a dose of reality when you're getting beat up in multiple ways.

Patient: How would you know about this getting beat up stuff. What do you know about suffering and feeling hopeless?

Dr. Marshall: I've been where you are.

Patient: What do you mean?

Dr. Marshall: Well, I lost my wife, who died several years ago, and I've had prostate cancer. About the cancer, I was one of the lucky ones, and so are you. Your prognosis is good.

Patient: (*quiet for a very long time*) I didn't know. I'm sorry.

Dr. Marshall: You couldn't have known.

Patient: No, I couldn't. I just didn't think it could happen to you.

Dr. Marshall: Why not?

Patient: You look like you've got it all together—I just didn't think that . . .

Dr. Marshall: That I could have stood where you stand.

Patient: Yes, that you could be like me—and know the pain. It doesn't look like all that killed you. I mean, you don't act like you've given up.

Dr. Marshall: I haven't. But I felt like giving up for a long time.

Patient: Could we spend some time talking about how you managed to keep from killing yourself? Would you tell me how you made it?

Dr. Marshall: Sure. We can talk about what I did. In fact, what I wanted to do was help you learn how to manage this crap so you wouldn't go and do something stupid like killing yourself.

Patient: How'd you learn to live with your wife's death? It wasn't easy, was it?

Dr. Marshall: I'll tell you all about it. I'm also going to encourage you to talk about Annie, your life with her, her dying and what you did, and finally her death. You've never talked much about it before, have you?

Patient: Never, it was too painful. I'm not sure I can now.

Dr. Marshall: The only reason I can talk about my wife now is because I started talking about her several years ago. Now, it's easier. It doesn't mean I miss her less, it's just easier now. It doesn't bring my life to a grinding halt the way it used to.

Commentary

Facing the severe despair and retreat of the H-S patient elicits strong dominant action tendencies that often lead to the enactment of dominant strategies.

Anxiety is often aroused when our patients behave in ways suggesting that they are beyond our help. More often than not, we reduce our anxiety by trying to dissuade the individual from this perception. Remember how Paulo Freire describes traditional teaching and learning? It's up to the teacher to "pour" the right knowledge, thoughts, or facts into the brain of the student. CBASP pedagogy requires a different tactic; hence, Dr. Marshall illustrates an alternative route. He circumvented the H-S retreat of the patient and accomplished the task without assuming a dominant role. He did it using disciplined personal involvement.

First, he confirmed that the patient's feelings and despair were justified ("You lost your wife and now you have cancer. You ought to be feeling hopeless"). This tactic is based on an assumption expressed by Skinner many years ago: that patients are always where they ought to be, feeling the way they ought to feel, behaving the way they ought to behave. If changes occur, something must be *added to* the person or the situational context that evokes a different response. Skinner was not speaking of psychotherapy, but he might as well have been: "Eventually I realized that the subjects were always right. They always behaved as they should have behaved" (Skinner, 1948, p. 289). Dr. Marshall's personal response placed him within the orbit of the patient's dilemma. It was the disclosure that he had experienced the same slings and arrows of fate ("Well, I lost my wife, who died several years ago, and I've had prostate cancer. About the cancer, I was one of the lucky ones, and so are you. Your prognosis is good."). The personal disclosure stopped Sam's H-S retreat and moved the attentional focus from Sam to Dr. Marshall. It resulted in Sam questioning Dr. Marshall about how he had survived ("It doesn't look like all that killed you. I mean, you don't act like you've given up"). Sam followed with another question: "Could we spend some time talking about how you managed to keep from killing yourself? Would you tell me how you made it?" The patient's submission was also transformed into more dominant behavior.

The pedagogical method implemented here was to respond in a way that *normalized* the patient's dilemma by the therapist's injecting his own personal information that communicated the following: "You are not alone with these problems—I've stood where you stand and made it through." The strategy resulted in changing the attentional focus in the session from Sam (hopelessness) to the therapist (hope). It should also be noted that the shift occurred without removing the responsibility for change from the patient's court. Sitting with someone who has faced a similar problem and come through it successfully often imparts hope. Disciplined personal involvement allowed Dr. Marshall to choreograph just such a moment.

A caveat must be added to the success of this scenario. One reason Dr. Marshall was able to accomplish what he did was due, in part, to the characteristics of the patient: (1) Sam had a late-onset condition, which frequently suggests a milder and more nurturing developmental history; (2) late-onset patients often present with higher premorbid functioning levels, and Sam's work, social, and marital history certainly evinced these features.

The Abused

Case Scenario 8

Phyllis entered treatment when she was 26 years old. She presented with an early-onset history of antecedent dysthymia (began during middle school) and a 14-year history of recurrent major depressive episodes. She was diagnosed with double depression and currently met criteria for a major depression that had persisted for 6 months. She scored a 39 on the Beck Depression Inventory–II (Beck, 1996). Combination treatment was recommended, and her pharmacotherapist administered sertraline, an SSRI medication Phyllis had not taken before. She reported being in and out of psychotherapy since early high school and taking a number of psychotropic medications, "none of which did me much good." Her developmental history was dysfunctional, and her sexual abuse history was remarkable. She was the youngest child of four; she had one sister and two older brothers. She had been sexually abused by her father since elementary school. It wasn't until she entered middle school that she discovered that sex with one's father was not normal. She never told her peers about the abuse, but she heard them laugh about similar events that happened to other girls. They labeled it "weird," "crazy," and "dirty." As best as Phyllis could recall, her depression began after she heard her peers talk about fathers and sex. The abuse continued until she was 16 and left home to live with an aunt.

In addition, her oldest brother periodically abused her by beating her physically. She described him as having an uncontrollable temper, saying that he "took his anger out on me." Once he'd broken her arm by twisting it behind her back. Her mother was alcoholic throughout the patient's childhood and "stayed drunk most of the time." Phyllis described the mother as having very little influence in the family. "Everyone pretty much ignored her," she said. She also reported that she tried to avoid her father and older brother as much as possible, but "that was not realistic in our house because it was fairly small. We only had a three-bedroom house with one bathroom." She and her sister had been close throughout childhood and still were. Her sister knew about the abuse, and they talked on the phone several times a week and lived in the same town. Surprisingly, the father had never approached the sister in any sexual way. Her sister had married several years ago and worked as a secretary. Her two brothers had gone to college and "become big businessmen." They lived in another city and rarely contacted her or the sister. Her mother and father had died several years ago—the mother from alcohol-related complications and the father from a heart attack.

The current problem bringing Phyllis to the clinic was her relationship with a physically abusing boyfriend. Bob would get mad on a date when she wouldn't do what he wanted and physically beat her. She came to the clinic with a black eye and noticeable bruises on her arms. She repeatedly told the staff interviewer that he was "really a nice guy, he just had a bad temper." Phyllis also said earnestly that she believed Bob would change and stop hurting her. In the meantime, however, she was bothered by the physical abuse and wanted to learn how to make him quit.

She was assigned to see Dr. Baxter, a CBASP therapist with experience treating sexual abuse victims.

Dr. Baxter rated Phyllis on the IMI and gave her an extreme score on the submissive (S) octant. Her remaining octant scores were rated in the "mild range" and fell predominantly on the friendly side of the circle. Phyllis was socially affable, cooperative, but extremely passive and compliant. Dr. Baxter rated her high on S because she clearly waited for the therapist to take the lead, was extremely compliant, afraid to stand up for herself, and clearly thought that Dr. Baxter had all the answers. Avoiding the assumption of a dominant (D) role with Phyllis and telling her what to do would be difficult. Dr. Baxter's first covert reaction to the stories of Bob's abuse was "get rid of that son-of-bitch!" However, she knew that dominant behavior, such as telling Phyllis what to do, wouldn't solve Phyllis's abuse problem. The actual pain resulting from dating Bob (i.e., getting beat up and hurt) had, as yet, no informing influence on Phyllis's decision to go out with him. The therapist decided to address the abuse situation first before tackling other problems. Her strategy involved helping Phyllis become aware of the consequences of her dating behavior. She was fearful that Phyllis would be severely hurt if she continued to date the man. Dr. Baxter also knew that perceptually connecting behavior with its consequences (i.e., going out with Bob and getting hurt) would take time.

In Dr. Baxter's mind, perceptually chaining the dating behavior with the abusive consequences would look like this:

Going out on a date with Bob. *Pain: Getting beat up and hurt, leading ultimately to the avoidance of pain by avoiding Bob.*

The following verbatim scenario was one of many such dialogues that occurred between Dr. Baxter and her patient. After many weeks, Phyllis finally said "no" when Bob asked her to go out, and over time, Bob exited her life. The perceptual connection between behavior and the painful consequences was slowly acquired, and the result was avoiding Bob. Here's the way Dr. Baxter used graphic contingency demonstrations and disciplined personal involvement to teach Phyllis to make the P x E connection that ultimately modified her behavior.

Patient: Bob called me late and wanted to go to the movies tonight.
Dr. Baxter: And you said?
Patient: I said I'd go. He'll pick me up at 7:00 P.M.
Dr. Baxter: Let's go through our routine—you're learning it well.
Patient: I'm not learning it well enough—I keep going out and getting hurt. I keep wishing that Bob would change, that he'd be decent with me.
Dr. Baxter: You're still not sure about Bob. You want him to be different and not hurt you.
Patient: Yes, I keep wishing that he would change.

Dr. Baxter: Now, go up to the flip chart and write out what you just agreed to do with Bob.

Patient: (*Getting up, going to the flip chart, and writing, "Go out with Bob"*) That's what I agreed to do: go out with Bob.

Dr. Baxter: Now, based on everything you know—not what you think, but what you know about Bob's behavior—what's likely to happen to you tonight?

Patient: I'm going to get beat up and hurt.

Dr. Baxter: And how will that make you feel when you get beat up and hurt?

Patient: I will be in pain when he takes me back to the apartment. My arms and face will hurt.

Dr. Baxter: Write that on the flip chart after you draw an arrow between what you wrote first and what's likely to happen tonight.

Patient: (*Draws an arrow and writes "I'll be in pain when I come home"*) I'll be in pain after the date.

Dr. Baxter: Now, read what you've just written and explain to me what the arrow means. Let's go through it.

Patient: I wrote that I'm going out with Bob. The arrow points to what will happen when I go out. I'll be in pain after the date. He'll beat me up again.

Dr. Baxter: Are you sure this describes what you've actually experienced with Bob, let's see, how many times so far?

Patient: Too many times to count.

Dr. Baxter: So, you're going to get hurt tonight. Any idea what my response is to what you've just written?

Patient: Tell me again, I need to hear it.

Dr. Baxter: I'm scared and dreading tonight. I'm afraid of what's going to happen to you.

Patient: Before you, no one has ever cared what happened to me. It's hard for me to believe that you can really care what happens to me.

Dr. Baxter: I can believe that! Before we get into how I can feel this way, I want to ask you another question—then, we'll talk about why I care what happens to you. Let's say we're playing an unusual game and I ask you what's a sure way to get yourself hurt tonight—what could you do that's 100% guaranteed to get you beat up and hurt?

Patient: Go out on a date with Bob!

Dr. Baxter: Are you sure, really sure?

Patient: I think so, I'm pretty sure.

Dr. Baxter: Not totally sure, but pretty sure. What keeps you from being totally sure?

Patient: You know, it's that wish thing. I keep wishing Bob would be different.

Dr. Baxter: Given your wish that he would be different, on a 1–10 scale where 10 is totally certain and 1 is totally uncertain, how certain are you about getting hurt tonight when you go out with Bob?

Patient: About an $8\frac{1}{2}$.

Dr. Baxter: Whew, that's pretty certain. Now, let's talk about why you frighten me and why I care about what happens to you.

Commentary

Dr. Baxter avoided the strong pull toward dominance to tell Phyllis what to do with Bob; she knew from experience that it would do no good. She took an alternate task-focused route that didn't reinforce continued submissive behavior from Phyllis. Her tactic demonstrated repeatedly that Phyllis's behavior had specific consequences, a perceptual view of the world that Phyllis had not previously acquired. The patient's developmental world had taught her that she was no match for the environment. Her lessons in submission began early and were presently being acted out in the destructive relationship with Bob. Once *perceptual functionality* (McCullough, 2000) is acquired and patients learn to recognize the consequences of their behavior, empowerment follows because they can no longer hide behind the fiction *"It doesn't matter what I do."* Dr. Baxter's demonstrations showed Phyllis that how she behaved produced the hurt she felt and kept her in pain. Over time, the message of the exercises was acquired: *"If you get tired of the hurt and pain, you know what you have to do to stop it."* For the first time in her life, Phyllis came to realize that she had a choice, and with the help of some assertiveness training, she learned to say "no."

Celebration Time!

Case Scenario 9

Al, a 35-year-old minor league pitcher, has been pitching baseball for "more years than I'd like to remember." He was recruited by a major league team right out of high school and told that "I was an outstanding pitcher who had a guaranteed future in the major leagues." His dreams of becoming a big leaguer never materialized, however. Al amassed an outstanding pitching record in Triple AAA ball but, for some reason, it never resulted in a "ticket" to the big leagues. Al reported that he had been called up to pitch in "the show" several times during September, when the rules allowed major league teams to expand their rosters. These experiences always raised hopes that "my time has finally come." However, the next season it was always back to Triple AAA ball. These call-ups became fewer over the years, and his face showed the disappointment he felt as he talked about the experiences. He reported a history of depression that began during his early 20s following one of the call-ups and then the subsequent demotion back to the minors. The first major depressive episode never fully remitted and assumed a chronic course. Al had had two other episodes, which, like the first, had followed his demotion back to the minors. He was diagnosed with late-onset, recurrent major depression with incomplete interepisode recovery.

The patient appeared to have a stable marriage of 13 years. He talked fondly about his wife and two daughters, who were 7 and 10. He'd never liked the travel involved in baseball and being away from home had been a continual source of marital conflict. Al entered treatment in August at the end of the season. He'd never been to psychotherapy before but had been prescribed several SSRI medications for major depression. When asked if the medications had helped, he was unable to answer the question. The pharmacotherapist prescribed buproprion and then referred him to see Dr. Wilson, a clinical psychologist and CBASP therapist.

Dr. Wilson began seeing Al once a week and administered the IMI following the second session. The patient peaked on the hostile–submissive (H-S) and hostile (H) octants. Feeling that he wanted very much to put Al at ease, noting Al's discouragement and stated hopelessness over never doing well in baseball, and listening to his hostile self-rejection, Dr. Wilson rated Al high in the H-S octant. As we've noted before, interpersonal evasiveness and withdrawal often pull impatient hostile–dominant (H-D) reactions from practitioners. Some of the anger Al expressed in the sessions also left Dr. Wilson feeling that he didn't want to come to psychotherapy, that he clearly was not in the mood for interpersonal involvement, and that he was embarrassed talking about his problems. Thus, he was rated high on the H octant because of these hostile impacts.

This was not going to be an easy case because the patient was distant and withdrawn and his anger was associated, at least in part, with a perceived career failure. Dr. Wilson also realized that, given Al's age, he was facing the end of his career without ever having realized his goal of being promoted to the big leagues. The verbatim scenario occurred during the fourteenth session, following a meeting Al had had earlier in the week with his team manager, who had talked about his playing next season.

Patient: (*obviously excited/energized*) I'm getting tired of being depressed over this career thing. Dammit, I made a good move yesterday! I thought about my desired outcome before I met with Matt (team manager). When the situation ended, I got what I wanted. The AO = the DO! (McCullough, 2000, p. 147)

Dr. Wilson: Tell me about it!

Patient: Well, our season just ended. I won 15 games—about my winning average over the years and with teams that haven't been strong. We finished fifth in the overall league standings this year and didn't even win the division title, though we were in the playoffs. I also won two playoff games with very little hitting behind me.

Dr. Wilson: If it had been up to me, I'd have called you up to the big leagues years ago.

Patient: Man, I'm getting sick of even thinking about that stuff. So, I took a different route. As I said, I went to see my manager on Monday. He and I went out to lunch. I told him I was ready to retire—that I didn't want to pitch next year. He looked surprised and remarked, "Never thought I'd live to see you ever hang it up." I told him I had a request. I asked him if I could be his pitching coach next season—that maybe I could work my way up another route. Hell, I know more about pitching than anyone I know. With my experience, I could help the young guys coming up. That was my *desired outcome*: To ask Matt if I could be his pitching coach next year.

Dr. Wilson: What you have just done is absolutely fantastic!

Patient: Well, Matt said, "I'll sign you up now. I need to make a few phone calls to the front office, but I don't think this will be a problem. I'd surely like to have you running the pitching—we might win some more ball games next year."

Dr. Wilson: Al, you've just made my day. You got your desired outcome! That's the most fantastic plan I've heard in a long time. I think you've just worked yourself out of one royal mess.

Patient: Sorta gives me an opening, doesn't it? I keep doing something I really love, just plug in from a different angle. I'm tired of beating my head against the wall and trying to figure out the system. If this works out, it's like a fresh start, a new season.

Dr. Wilson: I'm dumfounded, I don't know what to say. How in the world did you come up with this? What prompted you to change directions?

Patient: You kept showing me that what I did had consequences. I started seeing I was not as helpless as I thought. I've been trying to work things out with a frigging system that wouldn't give me what I wanted. Did everything I was asked to do—it got me nowhere. I let that damn system define my life—make me feel less than a man. Once I started concentrating on people, I realized I've got a lot of know-how when it comes to pitching. I also realized that someone can use what I know to win ball games. So, I decided to begin with my own club and see what I could work out. Somehow, Matt seemed relieved with my decision. He really jumped at taking me on his coaching staff. He knows what kind of person I am. I've never had a beef with him. If it had been up to him, I'd have been in the major leagues a long time ago.

Dr. Wilson: Do you have any idea what effect you've just had on me?

Patient: You look surprised.

Dr. Wilson: Yes and what other effect do you think you had?

Patient: You're pleased.

Dr. Wilson: Yes! I'm not sure I would have had the guts to do what you did.

Patient: What do you mean?

Dr. Wilson: Had I been in your shoes—had I won the way you have and not been called up—I would have become one angry, cynical old fart. I'm not sure I could have gotten passed it.

Patient: You really think I've accomplished something, don't you?

Dr. Wilson: Honestly? I've been feeling that you wouldn't be able to pitch your way out of this one. I thought you and I had gone as far as we were going. I was at the end of my rope—didn't know anything else to do. I've been mad as hell about the way you were passed over. Someone in the organization should have told you to take a hike; instead, they just let you twist slowly in the wind. With the hand of cards you'd been dealt, I swear I thought we'd both hit a dead-end. Now, you come in here with this!

Patient: Never thought I'd get past this resentment. For the first time I feel bigger than *it* is. I have some options now. When we first started working together, I didn't see any.

Dr. Wilson: If I had some champagne, I'd break it out and we'd celebrate. How about a diet coke instead? That's all I have.

Patient: Let's pop one.

Commentary

At the beginning of treatment, Al's anger was normal. He'd been shabbily treated, and the confusing parent club never gave him honest feedback about his prospects of playing in the big leagues. When treatment began, his dream lay shattered, and, given his age, he knew he was close to the end of his career. Dr. Wilson began treatment deliberately avoiding the overwhelming career issue. The problem was too big to tackle at the outset; in addition, the problem was irresolvable because Al's environment (the baseball club) wouldn't give him what he wanted. The therapist began by teaching Al to focus on small interpersonal problems and used the Situational Analysis (SA) method to demonstrate that his behavior had specific consequences.

Undercutting the generalized sense of felt helplessness is a slow and tedious process with chronically depressed patients. At the outset, patients are indeed existentially helpless because they orbit in a self-destructive cognitive and behavioral spiral of negative functioning. The pernicious nature of the chronic disorder precludes any environmental feedback from informing behavior (McCullough, 2000); thus, nothing changes in their perceptual world. Breaking into this closed perceptual system requires an acquisition learning attack to demonstrate explicitly and repeatedly that patients are, in fact, producing and maintaining the disorder. By perceptually concentrating on one situational event at a time, individuals are taught how to achieve interpersonal mastery. These small mastery experiences, highlighted in therapy, slowly begin to generalize across areas of functioning. In the wake of these mastery experiences, patients realize that they are no longer helpless. CBASP therapists have to work assiduously to prevent patients from overlooking their successes, until finally the dam of despair breaks and a personal success track record modifies the perceived history of failure.

In Al's case, he acquired the ability to utilize the SA methodology quickly and palpably achieved greater interpersonal success; however, resentment over the career failure cast a continuous pall over any and all interpersonal accomplishments. His dilemma was a *"yes, but"* sort of entrapment. In resignation, Al would often say, "What I've done here is okay, but the real problem remains—I've failed in baseball."

Dr. Wilson was becoming increasingly frustrated, discouraged, and angry with Al's baseball organization. He understood Al's resentment, but he also knew that unless Al was able to transcend the career failure issue, it would mire his life in depression. Dr. Wilson felt he was running out of options, but he and the patient continued to work on situational problems using SA. He worked hard not to lose patience and plunge himself into the H-D octant by telling Al how to "fix" his life. Thoughts such as "You'll never get past this resentment," "Dammit, you've let them beat you!" and "I'm tired of listening to your whining and self-pity" were becoming more frequent. Impulses to tell Al that he (Dr. Wilson) had done all he could were also becoming stronger. Dr. Wilson was beginning to feel increasingly helpless in the face of the refractory resentment. As stated above, what he did in a disciplined, task-focused way was continue to consequate Al's behavior, using

SA to show him that the way he behaved with others made a difference in the way he felt as well as in the way others responded to him.

When the shift in behavior occurred, it was a genuine surprise to the therapist. Dr. Wilson was able to personally disclose his surprise and pleasure, as well as his concomitant feelings of helplessness and anger over the way the patient had been treated. Discipline personal involvement means that the good as well as the bad responses can be honestly communicated. In this case, Dr. Wilson's enthusiastic responses were made explicit as well as his admittance that he had been feeling increasingly helpless and angry. It was also clear that the cumulative effects of the previous consequation work had contributed to Al's shift off the "*yes, but*" baseline. There appeared to be no other historical changes in Al's life at the time (other than his behavioral innovation) that would have accounted for his felt increase in empowerment and corresponding decrease in resentment.

Dammit, Deal With Me!

Case Scenario 10

Bill was 39 years old and reported that he had been depressed since elementary school. He didn't remember exactly when the onset occurred, he just remembered feeling that "something was wrong and I was never happy." He described a home life that was hostile and punitive. He was an only child of parents who argued constantly. He was afraid of his mother when she became angry over "my messiness." She demanded perfection in his schoolwork and table manners, cleanliness, punctuality, and orderliness. His father was a lawyer and worked incessantly. He came home late at night and left for work early. Bill saw him on the weekends, when he wasn't playing golf with his friends—which was most of Saturday and Sunday. The family rarely took vacations. It was mostly Bill and his mother. Socially, he was correct in every way. He said the right things and behaved appropriately with the clinic staff. It was obvious to the staff that he was very sad, though he tried to keep a "stiff upper lip" and respond politely to the interview questions.

Bill was diagnosed with a current major depressive episode and a long history of antecedent dysthymia. He had recently broken up with a woman he had dated for several years, and this loss appeared to be the precipitant of the major depression episode. He was also given an Axis II diagnosis of obsessive–compulsive personality disorder. He was prescribed sertraline by the pharmacotherapist and referred to Dr. Brooks for psychotherapy.

Dr. Brooks noted early that Bill "lived in his head" and had never learned how to make genuine interpersonal contact with others; rather, he stayed a step ahead of others by *mind reading* what he thought others might say, think, and want. This made conversation with him difficult as well as superficial—in conversation, Bill seemed to react only to himself. It left Dr. Brooks feeling interpersonally isolated and alone. His self-descriptions were highly intellectualized monologues, and his socially polite demeanor was not particularly aimed at Dr. Brooks; rather, it reflected more of Bill's reactions to his own internal standards of behavior.

Dr. Brooks realized that Bill had sealed himself off from others years ago and lived alone in his private world of rituals and routines. The only favorable prognostic variable was Bill's present misery, which, hopefully, would keep him coming to therapy and which could be used to help Bill see that behavior change might result in less misery. Dr. Brooks scored Bill high on the hostile–submissive octant (H-S) because of his interpersonal nervousness, his avoidance of personal problems via a smokescreen of intellectual explanations, frequent comments of inadequacy, and the strong pull he (Dr. Brooks) felt to do something to put the patient at ease. The scenario took place during the eighth session, following Bill's avoidance of a comment Dr. Brooks had made to him.

Dr. Brooks: I tried to say to you that when I commented that you had not taken me into account when you said that no one takes what you say seriously, you just blew me off, made light of my comment.

Patient: Oh, I was trying to say I didn't mean you, everyone else.

Dr. Brooks: Then why did you say it the way you did?

Patient: I was just making talk.

Dr. Brooks: You mean, you were not serious about no one taking you seriously?

Patient: What does it matter?

Dr. Brooks: It matters to me what you say and what you mean, especially when it implicates me. Where do I fit in with not taking you seriously?

Patient: Oh, I know you take what I say seriously.

Dr. Brooks: How do you know?

Patient: Because that's your job. You wouldn't be a psychologist unless you took people seriously.

Dr. Brooks: Bill, I'm not talking about anyone but you and me. How do you know I take what you say seriously?

Patient: I just know.

Dr. Brooks: How?

Patient: Can we get off this subject? You know I know you take me seriously.

Dr. Brooks: You never answered my question. How do you know?

Patient: I wouldn't be coming here if you didn't.

Dr. Brooks: I want to know how you know that you are being taken seriously by me. Why are you so sure?

Patient: You mean, there's a chance you don't?

Dr. Brooks: Has that thought ever entered your mind before—I mean, that thought about me?

Patient: No, I've never thought about it before now. But you wouldn't be a psychologist if you didn't take what your patients say seriously.

Dr. Brooks: You're slipping out again and talking about people in general. What about just you and me—just stay focused on us. How do you know that I'm taking what you say seriously, really listening to you?

Patient: I never think about you in that way.

Dr. Brooks: I know. I really don't exist to you, do I?

Patient: Of course, you exist.

Dr. Brooks: I mean, as far as your considering me in anything you say and do here.

Patient: I don't think about you while I'm here.

Dr. Brooks: I know. That's why I feel I'm really by myself when you're here. You're by yourself, and I'm by myself while we're sitting in the same room together. Quite odd, isn't it?

Patient: I don't have any idea what you're talking about.

Dr. Brooks: You've finally heard what I've just said and you don't understand what I'm trying to say. That's the first time I've ever felt you heard and listened to a word I've said in this room. Bill, you've taken me seriously for the first time.

Patient: I don't understand.

Dr. Brooks: I'm sure you don't, but you just made contact with me again by what you said.

Patient: Please explain.

Dr. Brooks: *Contact* and *taking each other seriously* mean that you are affected by what I say, and I'm affected by what you say. These mutual effects then determine what we say next.

Patient: Are you saying that we've been out of contact all this time?

Dr. Brooks: I'm saying that I don't think you have any idea of what making contact with someone else is. In fact, and I'm not totally certain about what I'm about to say, you may have never made contact with anyone before this moment with me.

Patient: I'm not sure, and I don't understand all this.

Dr. Brooks: I'm not sure either, but let's stop for a moment and talk about what's just happened between us and see if we can make more sense of it.

Commentary

We have an example of primitive "parallel talk" in the conversation between Dr. Brooks and Bill. You say something and then someone else says something—that's all that happens. There is no verbal mutuality and no interaction. Bill cannot use language to make himself understood or to understand Dr. Brooks. He is perceptually disconnected from the interpersonal environment, and his verbal style is symptomatic of his general disengagement. Carefully listening to Bill's sentence structure reveals several primitive characteristics of preoperational functioning. Because Bill's speech is not influenced by others, he can easily inject two opposing statements in the same sentence ("everyone, but I don't mean you"). When he replied, "I'm not sure [if I've ever made contact with anyone else], I don't understand all this," he also exhibited an experiential developmental deficit in learning how to use language to communicate. If Dr. Brooks is to enter Bill's perceptual world, he will have to teach the patient to focus on his responses, communicated through language. At present, talk for Bill serves no interactive function. Dr. Brooks begins the process of teaching Bill to focus on his therapist by responding personally to Bill's disengaged style. It's not surprising that the patient doesn't understand what Dr. Brooks is doing. Dr. Brooks will have to teach Bill how to engage in interactive speech with him before the patient will be able to engage others in interactive conversation. Until the environment (the therapist) acquires entrée into the perceptual world of the patient, the therapy has no power to modify behavior.

Conclusions

The refractory nature of the chronic disorder is the first effect psychotherapists encounter when they begin working with the chronically depressed patient. Most patients describe feelings, thoughts, and memories they have carried around for a long time. Learning to administer CBASP requires one to adopt a pedagogical mind-set that is different from most other therapy models. The didactic mind-set is determined by the nature of the patient and disorder. Most patients begin psychotherapy with little or no motivation to actually make changes in themselves. In all likelihood, their motivation levels will remain the same until they encounter unmistakable evidence that what they learn to do in treatment alleviates felt discomfort. This learning requires that clinicians conjoin technique with demonstrated reductions in suffering. Until the individual makes the specific perceptual connection that *"if I do this, I will feel better,"* nothing is likely to change. In order to conjoin treatment with reduction in distress, practitioners choreograph behavioral contingencies in the session to demonstrate that felt distress is self-produced and maintained.

What I have tried to show in these scenarios is that the consequation of interpersonal behavior through contingent personal response is best accomplished when therapists bide their time and wait for optimal moments when specific behaviors occur that are interpersonally problematical. Personal response is not the final goal, however. Patients must then be assisted to make the connection between their behavior and the contingent personal response. Sometimes this connection requires repeated trials across sessions. I've also attempted to demonstrate how one "walks with" a patient, taking into account his or her circumscribed worldview and limited behavioral repertoire. Walking with patients also includes avoiding the strong tendency we all have to "paraphrase" and make the structure of the person's language fit our own. Learning the discipline of using the language of the patient is difficult. Patients cannot keep up with our language usage and all that implies—for example, our causal logic and our highly sophisticated reasoning skills. We function best with these patients when we try to enter their primitive worlds, walk at their pace, and continually make explicit (by consequation demonstration) the fact that their behavior has enormous interpersonal consequences even while they are feeling helpless.

My desired outcomes for this chapter are twofold: (1) to help readers understand the rationale underlying the CBASP pedagogy of contingent personal response; and (2) to communicate *a feel* or *sense* of what the methodology of contingent personal responsivity is like when administered.

6
Healing Interpersonal Trauma Using the Interpersonal Discrimination Exercise

If we are to use the methods of science in human affairs, we must assume that behavior is lawful and determined. We must expect to discover that what a man does is the result of specifiable conditions and that once these conditions have been discovered, we can anticipate and to some extent determine his actions.
—B.F. Skinner (1953, p. 6)

What really happens is not that the neurotic patient "transfers" feelings he had toward mother or father to wife or therapist. Rather, the neurotic is one who in certain areas never developed beyond the limited and restricted forms of experience characteristic of the infant.
—Rollo May (1958, p. 79)

The Interpersonal Discrimination Exercise (IDE) is the second disciplined personal involvement technique used in CBASP to connect patients with the interpersonal environment and to break the cycle of preoperational functioning. Discrimination learning is a process by which "stimuli come to acquire selective control over behavior" (Hilgard & Bower, 1966, p. 512). CBASP discrimination performance goals are realized when different emotional responses and behavior are consistently evoked in the presence of two different classes of interpersonal stimuli: *maltreating significant others* and the *psychotherapist*. The best treatment outcome occurs when the patient is able to respond to the therapist in positive ways that eclipse the older destructive reactions.

The purpose of the exercise is to teach patients to discriminate cognitive-emotionally and behaviorally between the person of the therapist and significant others who have maltreated them. During IDE work, patients focus on a partic-ular type of situation that evoked abusive reactions from significant others. One common pattern is related to receiving punishment from significant others for making mistakes. Patients also make mistakes while in treatment (e.g., forget an appointment date, arrive late, fail to complete homework assignments). If making mistakes has been one cause of maltreatment, therapists can target these situations when they arise and compare and contrast their personal responses to the hurtful behavior of significant others.

Teaching patients to recognize the differences between the way maltreating significant others made them feel and behave and the way they feel and behave now with the clinician opens new avenues of emotional responsivity. We have found that if we do not use the IDE to teach patients to make clear discriminations between previous hurtful encounters and facilitative therapeutic encounters, they tend to overlook or minimize the differences. Successful IDEs involve more than *subjective responses* or *intellectual insight* (Ferenczi, 1932). These terms are associated with psychoanalytic thought and signal interpersonal occasions where conflict elucidation occurs in the transference aspects of the dyadic relationship (Hoffer, 2000). Other analytic definitions of insight (1) describe instances when older memories associated with family members shed light on current behavioral practices and experiences (Freud, 1963), (2) suggest the "experience of grasping oneself" (May, 1958, p. 68), or (3) implicate times when sudden awareness breaks through consciousness to help the person understand his or her current style of living. IDE work, while it may involve these insight components, includes a greater focus on the person of the therapist vis-a-vis maltreating significant others than does the psychoanalytic tradition.

Being able to discriminate the therapeutic relationship from that of significant others also signifies more than does the frequently used term *cognitive restructuring*, a cognitive therapy construct (Beck et al., 1979; Guidano & Liotti, 1983; Mahoney & Mahoney, 1976) referring to the matching of one's intrapersonal cognitive and emotive behavior with reality. In CBASP, we want patients to learn how to make crisp interpersonal discriminations between *"This is the way it was when I behaved this way around my significant others"* and *"This is how I feel now when I behave this way around my therapist."* The final goal in IDE training is the transferring of the new learning to daily life so that patients are enabled to identify and experience new interpersonal realities with others. We turn now to a brief review of two models of emotional responsivity/reactivity: one involving the adult equipped with normal psychosocial functioning and the other, the chronically depressed patient.

Normal and Preoperational Models of Cognitive–Emotional Functioning

Two diagrams of cognitive–emotional functioning models are illustrated in Figures 6.1 and 6.2. Both models are based on Piagetian (1981) theoretical formulations describing the inextricable and omnipresent connection between cognitive and emotive behavior. In assuming that the chronically depressed adult begins treatment functioning on a preoperational cognitive–emotional level (McCullough, 2000), I rely on the work of Piaget (1981), May (1958), Cicchetti et al. (1995), Cicchetti and Barnett (1991), Cicchetti and Toth (1998), Spitz (1946), as well as the *failure to thrive* research tradition (e.g., Drotar & Sturm, 1991; Money, 1992; Money et al., 1985). I do not assume that preoperational cognitive–emotional functioning is a *transfer of learning problem,* meaning that the perceptual–structural problems of patients stem solely from the transferring of anomalous emotions or behaviors learned from significant others to persons in their current world. The

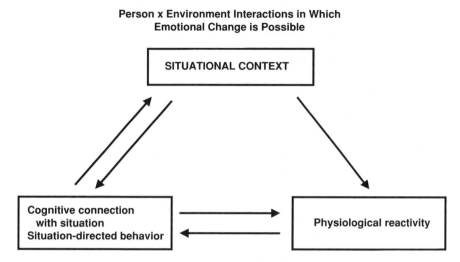

FIGURE 6.1. Model of normal cognitive–emotional functioning.

patient is functioning structurally at an infantile level in the interpersonal sphere because of earlier maltreatment that has led to maturational retardation; hence, the individual cannot cope with the demands of adult living and responds toward others in childish ways (McCullough, 2000). This structural developmental anomaly has been discussed at length in another text (McCullough, 2000, Chapter 3).

The first diagram shown in Figure 6.1 illustrates normal cognitive–emotional functioning and depicts foundational dynamics that give rise to a wide variety of

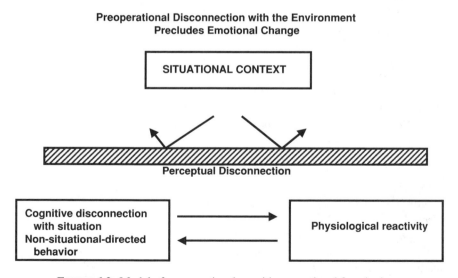

FIGURE 6.2. Model of preoperational cognitive–emotional functioning.

emotional responses. The second diagram, in Figure 6.2, illustrates the constricted and isolated cognitive–emotional world of the preoperational patient. The individual lives without an informing environment; thus emotional change is precluded and a pall of "sameness" characterizes the person's cognitive–emotional history. Each model is described briefly in order to compare and contrast normal and patient functioning. Keeping an eye on the standard for normal emotional functioning helps CBASP therapists gauge their progress as they move patients from preoperational reactivity to formal operation levels of cognitive–emotional responsivity (Piaget, 1981). The achievement of formal operational capability dramatically alters the patient's emotional landscape because it affords new mechanisms of emotional regulation while simultaneously opening the door for novel emotional experiences.

Close inspection of Figure 6.1 reveals multiple sources for emotional responsivity and regulation in adults who have the capacity to interact with others from a level of formal operational functionality. The *situational context* (viz. interpersonal interaction) provides the perceptual foundation from which variegated emotional responsivity and emotional regulation emerge. Said another way, without cognitive and situational-directed behavior anchored in and informed by one's interpersonal environment, emotional change, affective variability, and emotive regulation are precluded.

The environment provides continual feedback (information) about our emotional responses that reaches us through cognitive mediational processes (Bandura, 1977). Because our emotional and behavioral responses modify the environment in a reciprocal, interactive way (Bandura, 1977), ongoing information makes possible a continual stream of emotional experiences that is constantly changing in content, scope, and intensity. Let's look at some of the etiological sources for the emotional response.

The physiological work of Richard S. Lazarus (1966, 1984, 1990; Lazarus & Alfert, 1964; Lazarus, Opton, Markellos, Nomikos, & Rankin, 1965) demonstrates the informing power of cognitive interpretations arising from the *situational context* to steer autonomic reactivity in predictable directions. For example, we frequently observe athletes using self-talk and instruction to "psyche" their autonomic nervous system "up" or "down" in preparation for an athletic contest. The *left downward arrow* from the *situational context* to the *cognitive–behavioral* domain, then proceeding over to the *physiological reactivity* arena, illustrates the Lazarus type of emotional response. A second type of emotional reaction occurs when the *situational context* simultaneously impacts the *physiological reactivity* and *cognitive–behavioral* arenas. Emotional reactions arise here that are not immediately recognizable. Individuals then begin to scan the *situational context* to identify the cause of the arousal state (e.g., the *why am I so angry? why am I so afraid?* or *why am I so happy?* types of experiences). The *left upward arrow* from the *cognitive–behavioral* arena to the *situational context,* combined with the *right downward arrow* from the *situational context* to the *physiological reactivity* domain, continuing through to the *cognitive–behavioral* sphere, illustrate this circular emotional process. Stanley Schachter's (Schachter & Singer, 1962; Schachter,

1978) social psychological research describes such instances by illustrating how the cognitive and physiological domains interact to clarify emotional arousal.

A further source of emotional arousal stems from recalled memories involving oneself and another person. In such moments, we recall persons (or events) in the past or even anticipate future interactions with persons (or events) that generate highly specific emotions. Thinking of meeting a loved one who has been away and feeling the emotions associated with the anticipated reunion is a common experience. Such intrapersonal emotional responsivity is shown in the diagram by the *two horizontal arrows* moving in opposite directions between the *cognitive–behavioral* and the *physiological reactivity* domains. In our etiological delineation of reactivity sources, we have not described instances where individuals, within one situational event, experience several discrete emotions (e.g., the failure-to-success situation with the accompanying emotions of sadness and happiness; the confusion-to-clarification event involving frustration, then satisfaction; the anger-to-diffusion-of-anger encounter with the accompanying reactions of hostility and its felt diminishment; and the conflict-to-settlement situation that might result in the experience of hostility and then felt relief. Each of these simplified situational examples could be reversed and turned into a success-to-failure situation, a clarification-to-confusion event, diffusion-of-anger to the intensification-of-anger encounter, and a settlement-to-conflict situation).

The above illustrations of the etiological sources of the affective response reveal that the external and internal sources for emotional reactions and responses are multiple, involve many central nervous system processes (Izard, 1993), and implicate a whole array of nonverbal and verbal reactions (Kiesler, 1996; e.g., motor gestures, facial expressions, voice rate and variability, and speech) that have not been discussed. The diagram is simplified to show, in a limited way, the ever-changing emotional life most of us experience daily. The diagram is also based on my assumption that emotional variability, change possibilities, and mature emotional regulation are not achievable without a base of formal operational functioning.

The refractory nature of the chronic depressive disorder and the concomitant preoperational dilemma that maintains the disorder commingle into an altogether different picture of cognitive–emotional functioning. I illustrate my conception of the emotional landscape of the patient with chronic depression in Figure 6.2. Perceptual and behavioral disconnection from the *situational context* consigns the chronically depressed adult to a life of constricted emotionality; patients end up reacting to themselves and not to the world in which they live. I describe these refractory and stereotypic patterns of emotional behavior in the next section.

A refractory and dysregulated state of emotionality and a snapshot perspective of "time having stopped" characterize the emotional life of the chronically depressed adult (McCullough, 2000). At the beginning of therapy many patients describe an emotional history that I would paraphrase in this way: "What I experience emotionally in the *present* characterizes my experiences *yesterday* and predicts what my emotional life will be like *in the future*. It doesn't matter what I do because controlling my emotions is impossible." In their words, "No one could ever love me"; "Nothing will ever work out for me"; "I'll always fail"; "Life has passed me by"; "I've wasted my life."

The sad truth is that this description of the emotional predicament is an accurate one—these patients are stuck in a snapshot view of reality (McCullough, 2000). For psychotherapy to be effective, the therapist must overthrow patients' perceptual disengagement with the world and reconnect them to their environment. This achievement enables patients to break the chains of preoperational entrapment and helps them experience emotions other than depression.

The first aspect of the diagram that catches most people's attention is the horizontal "barrier" extending the width of the figure. The barrier represents the patient's perceptual disconnection from the interpersonal world and is intended to convey the preoperational dilemma. The interpersonal efforts of others cannot penetrate the barrier. The movement of the *situational context* toward and then away from the patient (denoting the environment's reactions/responses to the patient) is shown by the deflected arrows bouncing off the barrier.

Because the environment has no informing influence on the person and no interpersonal feedback penetrates the barrier, emotional reactivity remains unchanged. Not only is there an absence of *cognitive connection* with the *situational context*, there is no *situational-directed behavior* aimed toward interpersonal goals. The catastrophic implications of perceptual disengagement are realized when we imagine an individual who is incapable of responding to others in an appropriate manner due to an inability to modify the quality of the relationship with others.

As noted, the only cognitive–emotional–behavioral outlet patients have is to react to themselves. This self-referential component is illustrated in the diagram by parallel arrows moving in opposite directions between the *cognitive disconnection* and *non-situational-directed behavior* sphere and the *physiological reactivity* domain. The pathological quagmire is characterized by egocentricity, one of the hallmark features of preoperational functioning.

In this stagnant pool of emotionality (which is particularly common among early-onset patients) we find memories of abuse and the resulting feelings of hurt and fear that originated during the early developmental years. Because new interpersonal information has not been able to penetrate the egocentric system and the individual has not been able to modify any *situational context*, early traumata and hurtful memories reverberate back and forth in a never-ending orbit. Old *physiological reactivity* patterns continually impact the *cognitive and behavioral* domain, and vice versa. Thus it is not be surprising that when early-onset patients describe their dysfunctional childhoods and families, the stories of abuse sound like they happened yesterday.

The IDE is used when the patient enacts some situational behavior that historically resulted in negative consequences from significant others. The IDE shows how the response of the clinician to the patient in the targeted situation is unlike the reactions of significant others. In instances of making mistakes (e.g., forgetting an appointment date, arriving late, failing to complete a homework assignment, completing an agreed-upon assignment in an inept manner), the patient receives a nonjudgmental and facilitative response from the therapist. The therapist then inquires how one or more significant others would have reacted to a similar mistake.

For example, "How would your mother [father, brother, etc.] have reacted to you, had you forgotten some arranged activity the way you forgot your appointment with me?" After patients describe the punitive consequences they would have received (often accompanied by observed felt distress), the therapist then asks: "How did I respond to your forgetting our appointment?" Patients are thereby directed to focus on the therapist's positive responses and are asked to compare and contrast these with those of significant others. Sufficient time is spent in the discrimination task so that the patient cannot overlook the behavioral discrepancies or miss the point of the exercise.

The IDE is based on a well-known Piagetian technique (Cowan, 1978; Gordon, 1988; Nannis, 1988) that is used with adolescents who have conduct disorder to teach problem-solving skills. The technique is called a "mismatching" exercise: "If didactic exercises are 'optimally mismatched'—that is, are offered on levels exceeding the patient's current level of functioning—cognitive [emotional] operations will be sufficiently challenged and maturational-cognitive [emotional] shifts will follow" (McCullough, 2000, p. 77). Once patients learn to attend accurately to the clinician's positive responses as well as to the emotions evoked by these responses, the disengagement barrier becomes permeable. When the interpersonal barrier finally comes down during treatment and patients are able to connect perceptually with the *situational context* (viz. the clinician), cognitive–emotional behavior moves toward levels of functioning that approximate the first diagram (see Figure 6.1).

Sessions 1 and 2 of CBASP Therapy

Session 1. Diagnosing the patient (McCullough, 2001, Chap. 3; McCullough et al., 1996), explaining the general procedures of CBASP treatment, and asking patients to bring in a list of *significant others* are covered during the first session. Significant others (McCullough, 2000, Chap. 5) are defined as the "major players" in one's life—individuals whose roles have exerted significantly more impact than (other) friends or acquaintances. Clinicians further explain that significant others have influenced the patient to be who he or she is; they are individuals who have left their "stamp" or "legacy" on the patient, determining the interpersonal direction his or her life has taken. Therapists also stress that these role influences may be either positive or negative. Patients are requested to restrict their list to no more than six individuals.

The Significant Other History in Session 2. At the beginning of the second session, a Significant Other History (McCullough, 2000, Chap. 5) is conducted based on the patient's list. The major players are reviewed in the order they are listed. Taking the first name on the list, the clinician asks, "What was it like growing up or living around ____?" The question is framed to "warm up" and prompt whatever memories (thoughts, feelings, experiences) a patient may have about the target individual. Patients usually recount several memories or stories of previous experiences with each person on the list. As discussed in Chapter 3, most patients with early-onset depression recall negative memories that are personally destructive or injurious. This is not necessarily the case with late-onset patients, who, as noted, are likely to recall a less injurious developmental history (Horwitz, 2001; Holahan et al., 2000; McCullough, 2000; Riso et al., 2002) that includes one or more positive memories with significant others.

Clinicians then ask patients, "How did this person [parent, sibling, spouse, etc.] influence the course of your life? How did the person influence you to be the kind of person you are now?" (with an emphasis on RIGHT NOW) The goal here is to allow patients to formulate causal judgments about the specific effect(s) significant others have had on their current behavior. This "developmental analysis" procedure (Guidano & Liotti, 1983) provides rich sources of autobiographical information. Most patients are able to target at least one quality in themselves that originated from interactions with a significant other (e.g., "I learned not to expect anything good from a woman"; "I don't trust any man"; "I learned that if you ask for what you need, you open yourself to ridicule. I don't ask anymore"; "I learned that I must be perfect in all that I do"; "I can never get angry"; "I'm afraid to let anyone know who I am").

As noted, the Significant Other History procedure is a "mismatching" exercise (Cowan, 1978; Gordon, 1988), meaning that the preoperational patient is asked to think about his or her interpersonal history in an antecedent–consequent format; for example, "Growing up around my father resulted *in my feeling this way about myself* or is related *to what I expect from others.*" I call these self-constructed deductions or judgments *causal theory conclusions* (Giodano & Liotti, 1983; McCullough, 2000). The patient's causal theory conclusions that are made explicit here have usually determined his or her coping patterns in specific interpersonal contexts.

After patients leave the second session, the practitioner reviews all the causal theory conclusion material and, using his or her clinical judgment, decides what *interpersonal theme* best summarizes the patient's major or most salient causal theory conclusion. The theme should suggest (1) a *problem area* in which the patient interacted with one or more significant others (e.g., occasions of intimacy; instances when the patient disclosed personal information to a major player; times when the patient made a mistake or misbehaved; occasions when the person expressed negative affect, such as anger toward a significant other), and (2) the *negative consequences* that followed the interactive behavior (e.g., interpersonal intimacy led to physical or emotional abuse; disclosed personal matters resulted in ridicule or censure; severe physical or emotional punishment followed the making of mistakes; expression of anger or dissatisfaction led to punishment).

Therapists hypothesize that the salient interpersonal theme will play a negative role in the way patients go about constructing their relationship with them (i.e., their clinicians). This means that the early learning with significant others (identified in the causal theory conclusions) will become an interpersonal problem for patient and therapist. Targeting the primary interpersonal problem is the jumping off point that leads to the construction of one transference hypothesis.

CBASP therapists then construct one formal *transference hypothesis* that will inform therapist behavior with the patient and that will be used in the IDE exercise.

The hypothesis postulates the types of reactions the patient will probably expect from the therapist (based on previous learning with the major players) if this particular hot spot occasion arises. Interestingly, most patients are not consciously aware of the association between the problem situation and any expected negative consequences from the practitioner (e.g., expecting that getting close to a therapist or making mistakes will result in any negative reactions). Whether or not patients have consciously made these associations, the Significant Other History provides clinicians with autobiographical information with which to construct relevant transference hypotheses. Whenever these interpersonal hot spots actually occur in the session, the transference hypothesis is made explicit to the patient through IDE work. The utility of the Session 2 procedure will become clearer in a moment, when I illustrate the IDE exercise with several verbatim case scenarios.

CBASP Transference Hypothesis Construct

My view of transference is derived from Guidano and Liotti (1983), who suggest that patients' verbalized interpersonal worldviews as well as their current in-session behavior are valid reflections of their early developmental experiences. This assumption is particularly compelling in cases where individuals have been maltreated and evince manifestations of cognitive–emotional retardation as a result of injurious encounters with significant others (Conway, 1987; Kiesler, 1996; Mischel, 1973; Wachtel, 1993).

Patients with chronic depression become interpersonally attached to therapists, and the expectations or emotional reactions that originated in earlier attachment interactions will play a significant and informing role in the therapist–patient relationship. Said another way, patients transfer learned interpersonal expectancies to any significant dyadic encounter. Some patients will anticipate rejection at every turn, others will approach the clinician in fear and trembling, and a few are going to strive to be perfect. I've known patients who work hard to maintain a safe interpersonal distance by disclosing little about themselves. Still others assiduously avoid making demands on therapists and try to nurture *them* by focusing on their supposed needs—even going so far as downplaying their own issues so as not to burden the clinician. All of these transfer-of-learning patterns are clear interpersonal signals denoting the person patients learned to be during their formative developmental years. The purpose of the Significant Other History is to sensitize clinicians to these interpersonal patterns and to help them formulate transference predictions that can be used salubriously.

Bowlby (1969/1982) notes that many individuals correct and heal chaotic developmental beginnings by participating in constructive relationships, as adults, involving personal attachment—attachments that offer intrapersonal and interpersonal alternatives that were not previously available. The IDE is based on the premise that the therapist–patient relationship offers just such an opportunity; using it, the therapist proactively seeks to modify destructive interpersonal attachment patterns in positive ways. As choreographer of this process, the CBASP psychotherapist judiciously uses disciplined personal involvement to correct patients' limited interpersonal worldviews and behavior.

Four categories of trauma situations are used in CBASP. I briefly mentioned these four categories above. They are detailed here to show how CBASP therapists use the Significant Other History material to formulate and construct the wording for a transference hypothesis. Of course, there are many sources of patients' trauma (Cicchetti & Barnett, 1991); these are the four salient areas CBASP therapists look for during the Significant Other History:

1. Moments in which *interpersonal intimacy* has been experienced/verbalized between the patient and a significant other(s)
2. Moments in which the patient has expressed felt emotional needs or wants, disclosed problems or shared personal information, either directly or indirectly, to a significant other(s)
3. Moments in which the patient has *failed at some task*, *made an obvious mistake*, or *done something wrong* while with a significant other(s)
4. Moments in which the patient has *expressed negative affect* (e.g., fear, frustration, anger), either directly or indirectly, toward a significant other(s)

Intimacy issues typically accompany long histories of rejection or abuse. *Disclosure of emotional needs* or *personal problems* with significant others may be associated with earlier patterns of withdrawal by one or both parents or may have resulted in ridicule or punishment. Issues surrounding *failure* or *making mistakes* often result from chronic patterns of criticism or ostracism by significant others. Finally, the reluctance to express *negative affect* or the fear associated with such expressions is usually due to the infliction of punishment following negative behavior.

These interpersonal areas also come to the forefront during psychotherapy. Whenever a patient and therapist encounter a situation that has been targeted by the transference hypothesis, they have landed in a hot spot that signals the need for an IDE (McCullough, 2000, Chap. 5). Administering the IDE can transform a hot spot moment into a profound healing experience.

One aspect of the disciplined personal involvement component is revealed in the way CBASP transference hypothesis statements are worded; they are personalized in relation to the therapist and framed in an *if this ... then that* format. The following examples illustrate sample transference hypotheses for the four trauma situations:

- *Intimacy*: "If I get close to Dr. Smith, then he will reject me." (The consequences must mirror the previous consequences experienced with significant others.)
- *Disclosure of needs/wants/problems*: "If I let Dr. Riley know what I really need and want, then she will ridicule what I say."
- *Failure/making mistakes*: "If I make a mistake around Dr. White, then she will punish me with silence or disgust."
- *Express negative affect*: "If I let Dr. Matthews know that I'm mad at him, then he will refuse to see me again in therapy."

The IDE: Discriminating Malevolent Affective Experiences from Healing Ones

The negative phase of the IDE is seen when patients (1) recall some memory involving a specific behavior (e.g., "I asked for help with my homework"), (2) describe an injurious consequence administered by a significant other ("My father told me I was stupid and wasn't worth his time"), and (3) evince noticeable negative nonverbal or verbal affect produced by the hurtful memory (i.e., a painful expression, look of resignation, fear; or a statement such as "I never asked him for help again because I knew he would hurt me in some way"). The discrimination healing phase in the IDE is realized when the patient compares and contrasts the negative consequences with the positive interpersonal consequences delivered by the clinician in a similar situational context (i.e., disclosure of a need).

CBASP clinicians report that patients become intensely involved in these discrimination exercises and that a high state of negative arousal is desirable. By having patients recall the negative reactions they received from significant others under specific stimulus conditions, CBASP clinicians try to recreate the older emotional experience in the session. Then they focus attention on the positive interpersonal reactions they provided in the similar situational context. Why? As stated above, patients who have never experienced kind responses for simple requests such as asking for help with homework frequently overlook the positive responses of therapists when similar situations arise in the session. Chronically depressed patients begin receiving facilitative responses from therapists in the first session. In many cases these responses are "firsts." Patients must be guided to stop and attend to these positive events in the IDE or they will overlook salubrious therapist behavior. Repeated IDE training provides an acquisition learning process through which patients ultimately acquire the ability to discriminate between injurious reactions of significant others and the healing responses of therapists.

As I discussed elsewhere (McCullough, 2000, Chap. 5), these IDE healing moments involve a *negative reinforcement condition* wherein the aversive stimulus situation is alleviated by a redirection of attention to the facilitative personal responses of the therapist. The positive interpersonal consequences that are highlighted result in two intrapersonal shifts: (1) mitigation of the aversive internal state, and (2) the beginning acquisition of a connection between the old behavior and the new *situational context* (i.e., encounter with the therapist).

There is another reason we highlight differences between the therapist's responses and the negative reactions patients have received from major players. We want to make explicit that the new interpersonal reality present in the dyad offers unique growth possibilities. Several brief examples will illustrate some of these growth opportunities: (1) a recognition that there will be no undesirable consequences (e.g., anger) from the therapist for mistakes or errors enables some patients to attempt new behaviors without fear of rejection or ridicule; (2) mistrust and the intrapersonal isolation it fosters are often replaced with trust when patients come to realize that therapists are reliable in their positive responses; and, (3) felt anger toward significant others who have hurt the individual is mitigated and managed more effectively within an environment of safety, as the patient learns that the clinician remains positively predisposed toward him or her. All of these positive outcomes are acquired through IDE work.

Verbatim case scenarios are presented in the following material to illustrate how CBASP therapists administer the IDE. Consistent with the verbatim scenarios in Chapter 5, each scenario is introduced with a brief case history. Next, the patient's list of significant others is presented with some abbreviated information of each person on the list. The causal theory conclusion (CTC) the patient constructed for each significant other follows. Then, one transference hypothesis (TH), derived from the major interpersonal theme of the CTCs, completes the introduction to the scenarios. The TH is highlighted during each scenario. At the end of the IDE scenario, a brief commentary identifies the disciplined personal involvement maneuvers of the psychotherapist.

IDE Verbatim Scenarios: Demonstration of the Method

Case Scenario 1

Sue was 55 years old with early-onset depression; she reported becoming depressed at age 13. She was the youngest child of three, having fraternal twin siblings, a brother and sister 3 years older. The family lived in the Appalachian area of West Virginia, and her father was a coal miner and an alcoholic who verbally abused all the children when he was intoxicated. He physically beat his wife; the patient said that "[she] never heard [her] mother protest anything [her] father ever did." The family lived in a neighborhood that included the extended family. Both sets of grandparents lived down the street, and the families of both her father's brothers and her mother's sister lived in the neighborhood. All the men in the family had worked in the coal mines for several generations. On Sundays, the extended family gathered for a large meal, with the wives preparing the food and the men boisterously recounting the experiences of the previous week. The patient added an interesting comment here: "The men took great delight at making derogatory comments about the women in the family, young and old, in a no-holds- barred atmosphere." The patient attended the community school, which was understaffed and included several grades in the same room. Students who were not self-motivated to learn usually did nothing but mark time until the school bell sounded to end the day. The female teacher was strict, used a paddle for discipline, and screamed frequently at students for mistakes made on assignments.

The patient, of above-average intelligence, had done well in school and had applied for admission to a junior college in a nearby town. She was accepted and attended the 2-year college, graduating with honors. While there, she met a man, fell in love, and, in spite of the family's protests, moved to the West Coast. She had two children, worked as a secretary in a small corporation, and described her marriage as somewhat satisfying. She described her husband as a "perfectionistic individual" who frequently pointed out things she'd done wrong. She stayed in touch with her family but did not return often to visit. Sue reported having had two major depressive episodes. She met current criteria for a major depressive disorder that had begun several months previously when her youngest child had married and moved away; her diagnosis was recurrent major depression with antecedent dysthymia (double depression).

The patient was neatly dressed for the screening interview. She apologized for bothering the clinical staff member by taking his time with her problems and when she was not able to answer every question. She was noticeably afraid that she would say something wrong, make a mistake, or behave inappropriately.

Significant Other List

Father, mother, sister, maternal grandmother, elementary school teacher, paternal grandfather.

Significant Other History and Causal Theory Conclusions (CTC)

1. *Father:* "Drank alcohol excessively throughout my childhood and adolescence. Became drunk several times a week, and his mood always changed to anger. During these episodes, he berated me and my siblings for every mistake we ever made and repeatedly reminded us that we were 'useless,' 'worthless,' and 'would never amount to anything.' We would run away and try to hide during these tirades. Even when he wasn't drunk and I would try to be nice to him, he would think of something I had done wrong and let me have it."

CTC: "I feel that I'm a worthless person and mess up everything I try to do."

2. *Mother:* "My mother was like a mouse. She would never stand up to my father when he would begin abusing us. She always left the room and went to the bedroom and cried. Every now and then he would hit her, and she would cower and move away. He did anything he wanted around her, and she never said a word. She was different with me. When he wasn't around, she was always on my case about something I'd done wrong. I didn't wash the dishes right, I didn't clean up right—it was always something. I got the same thing from her I got from him—I was a royal 'screw-up.'"

CTC: "I feel that being a woman makes me a mistake-prone loser."

3. *Sister:* "She gave me the only mothering I ever got. She sewed dresses for me to wear to school, and she would help me with my homework. I learned to be nice from watching her around other people."

CTC: "I try to be nice to others and that comes from my sister."

4. *Maternal grandmother:* "She is just like my mother and treats her the way my mother treats me. Nothing is ever good enough. She's always pointing out the things my mother does wrong. She does the same with me. Nothing is ever right."

CTC: "I feel now that nothing I do will be right."

5. *Elementary school teacher:* "We called her the 'screamer.' She screamed when anyone made a mistake—especially at me. In spite of all her screaming, I realized I understood what she was teaching. Most of the time the others didn't, but I did. I think she knew I did, but this just seemed to make her want me to be perfect. When I made mistakes, she would scream and scream at me for my stupidity."

CTC: "I know I'm smart, but I still mess things up."

6. *Paternal grandfather:* "He was an alcoholic and was drunk a lot of the time. He used to tell me, 'Honey, you're smart.' He seemed to recognize that I was different from the other children when it came to book learning."

CTC: "I feel that I'm smart and can understand things."

Major Interpersonal CTC Theme and the Transference Hypothesis

The salient "stamp" left on Sue by her significant others was her fear of failure due to the negative consequences she had experienced: "punishment; having my mistakes pointed out; being told I am stupid; being reminded that I've messed up again; being told that nothing I do will ever be right." Sue lived her life under the aegis of this punitive interpersonal theme. In spite of her intellectual prowess and obvious accomplishments, her successful marriage and work history, she'd never been able to overcome the sense that she was a mistake-prone loser who would always mess up because of her errors. The psychotherapist constructed the following transference hypothesis:

"If I make a mistake around Dr. Reston, then he will point out my errors and make be feel like a failure/loser (the way everyone else has)." [Failure of making mistakes TH area]

Patient: I forgot my appointment Monday.* I was so upset that I didn't have the courage to call you. I knew I would mess up this therapy with my mistakes. I always do this, you know.

        *[A *hot spot* moment has occurred, and the TH has been implicated.]

Dr. Reston: Always do what?
Patient: Always mess up anything I try to do. I don't think you'll want me to continue. I'll just pay you and leave (*begins to get up and walk toward the door*).
Dr. Reston: Hey, wait a minute! Don't leave! (*patient stops and turns around*)
Patient: What?
Dr. Reston: Please sit down and let's talk about what's happened. You haven't heard my side.
Patient: I know what you're going to say. I don't want to hear your side.
Dr. Reston: I don't think you have any idea what I'm going to say. Why don't you hang around and find out?
Patient: I know what happens when I screw up—I just don't want to listen to someone tell me what I know I've done.

Dr. Reston: You don't have any idea what's going on inside me right now. The very last thing I want to do is hassle you or punish you for forgetting the appointment. I'm very happy you came today—in fact, I'm delighted to see you.

Patient: I know what I've always heard from everyone else when I mess up.

Dr. Reston: I'm not everyone else. Will you wait for me to define myself? It may take more than a few minutes.

Patient: Yes, but I'm afraid of what you are going to say to me (*returns to her seat*).

Dr. Reston: I think I understand that. Let's go back to what happened last week. Tell me what happened. Let's reconstruct that situation. I think it will become clear in a moment *why* I'm asking you to do this.

Patient: Well, I forgot our Monday afternoon appointment. In the morning I was making out my day's work schedule, and I forgot to mark my appointment on the calendar. If I don't write something in, it's like it doesn't exist for that day. That's what happened.

Dr. Reston: Because this is the first time you and I have gone through this exercise, I must tell you that I'm going to ask you some questions about the missed appointment. It's important that you stay with me until we finish. At first, I don't think that what we are going to do will be easy or pleasant. But, at the end, I hope it will all make sense and I hope that you will feel better. Will you hang with me through this?

Patient: Yes, but I want to leave.

Dr. Reston: I'm aware of that. Now, I want you to think about when you first realized that you had forgotten the Monday appointment. When did you realize you had forgotten?

Patient: About an hour after the appointment. It just popped into my mind: "My God, I've forgotten my therapy appointment!"

Dr. Reston: Let me ask you this. What would your *father* have said or done, had you forgotten something the two of you agreed to do?

Patient: Oh, God! He would have glared at me, then burst out with his string of profanities about what a stupid bitch I was. How I never did anything right. His look always said to me I was the embodiment of stupidity (*begins to sob*). He would not have quit yelling until there was nothing else left to say. I would have gone away feeling that I was worthless and a loser—like I felt when I first came in here today.

Dr. Reston: How would your *mother* have reacted to this kind of forgetfulness?

Patient: She would have told me that I was "a loser." She would also remind me that she was embarrassed to have me for a daughter, that I'd never amount to anything because I was such a "screw-up." All I expect out of myself is to screw up. I can't do anything right. I mess up everything I try to do.

[The actual discrimination task begins here as the therapist directs the patient's attention to his behavior and contrasts his behavior to that of the two significant others, father and mother. Hopefully, the emotional distress will decrease as the patient associates his behavior with a facilitative positive response.]

Dr. Reston: Now, think about what *I* did when you first came in here today. What did *I* do and how did *I* respond to you?

Patient: I don't remember.

Dr. Reston: Try to remember what I said and did. It's very important that you do. Take your time and think about my personal responses to you.

Patient: Well, you didn't yell at me and tell me that I was stupid and a loser.

Dr. Reston: I certainly did not. What did I do?

Patient: You asked me not to leave when I was walking out the door.

Dr. Reston: Yes. What else?

Patient: You seemed relieved when I sat back down.

Dr. Reston: I was very relieved when you didn't leave. How did you know that? What did I do that gave you that impression?

Patient: It was in your face, your look, and you sighed like you were relieved. I was glad I didn't go. Then you said you were glad that I had come today. That really surprised me—I mean, what you said and how you said it.

Dr. Reston: How did I say it?

Patient: Like you really meant it. Then you asked me to go through this exercise with you. I'm still not sure what's going on here.

Dr. Reston: How was my behavior with you different from the reactions you would have gotten from your father and mother, had you forgotten something with them?

Patient: You didn't yell or call me "stupid" or tell me that I was "a loser."

Dr. Reston: Were there any other differences?

Patient: Somehow, I wasn't afraid anymore. I mean, when I thought about forgetting the appointment, I wasn't afraid of you and what you would say.

Dr. Reston: How is that possible? You forgot the appointment and yet you weren't afraid of my response. What made the difference? Something happened here between us that's new for you.

Patient: I can't explain it. I felt like you wouldn't punish me for screwing up.

Dr. Reston: Are you saying that I'm different compared to your father and mother? That you ended up feeling different with me, even after having made a mistake?

Patient: Yes, I do feel different and you're not like my parents. But I'm having trouble believing that you're being honest with me. I, uh, I'm sorta waiting for the other shoe to drop.

Dr. Reston: You mean, you clearly feel different right now, but you're not sure about me and whether or not my responses to you are honest.

Patient: Yes, I'm just not sure. I guess I don't trust you yet.

Dr. Reston: I'm sure you don't trust me after having gone through what you've been through. Please do me a favor. When you are able to trust that my responses are real, will you let me know? This will be an important milestone for us.

Patient: Yes.

Commentary

Dr. Reston exposed Sue to the "mismatching" perceptual demands of the IDE. The mismatching component of the IDE occurs when Sue is asked to describe the positive behavior of Dr. Reston, which requires a formal operational perspective—a perspective that was not easy for her to achieve. She had to be assisted to focus attention on the therapist rather than do what she usually did: that is, replay the learned punishment scenario in her head.

She associated being punished with making a mistake; there were no exceptions. Sue's interpersonal detachment from Dr. Reston is also apparent throughout the session. Walking out of Dr. Reston's office was appropriate behavior for Sue, given the fact that she was responding to *herself* and not to the therapist. Leaving the room meant that she could avoid the anticipated negative consequences. Figure 6.2 illustrates the cognitive–emotional–behavioral limits of the preoperational patient, which we see played out here. Sue's initial impulse to walk out the door is a clear example of a disengaged patient responding only to him- or herself. Dr. Reston, in successfully aborting the attempt to leave, enabled the two of them to walk through the IDE, a technique designed to help Sue encounter a different interpersonal consequence for making mistakes.

Articulating the behavioral differences between Dr. Reston and her father and mother in the making-a-mistake situation begins the discrimination training: *"Here is what happened when I made a mistake around my father and mother, versus what happened here when I made a mistake with Dr. Reston."* Two points are important: (1) a single discrimination trial was not sufficient to overthrow her fear of being punished for mistakes. Sue found it impossible to believe that Dr. Reston was being completely honest: "But I'm having trouble believing that you're being honest with me. I, uh, I'm sorta waiting for the other shoe to drop." Acquisition learning takes time, and repeated IDE trials will be required to penetrate Sue's self-contained preoperational world. (2) Even though Dr. Reston's positive behavior remained suspect, Sue verbalized a reduction in felt distress: "Somehow, I wasn't afraid anymore. I mean, when I thought about forgetting the appointment, I wasn't afraid of you and what you would say." Dr. Reston's personal response to Sue had broken into the orbit of her self-contained distress and reduced her felt discomfort. The negative reinforcement value of the therapist to decrease the patient's discomfort will increase in the future as his behavior acquires greater interpersonal credibility.

The reader may also wonder why Dr. Reston did not initiate the third step in IDE training, which is asking the patient to consider the interpersonal alternatives that are now possible if punishment for mistakes is absent. Because this was the first time that the IDE was administered and because the patient was not persuaded that Dr. Reston was being totally honest, Dr. Reston decided to omit this step. He felt that it was sufficient to open "a crack" in a perceptual door that had been shut for most of Sue's life—a door that leads from the world of significant others to the world of the psychotherapist. There would be sufficient time during future IDEs to explore the interpersonal possibilities. As noted in Chapter 5, use of a judicious strategy that maintains synchrony with the pace of the individual is a pedagogical hallmark of disciplined personal involvement with the chronically depressed adult.

Case Scenario 2

Peggy was 32 years old, married for 10 years with two children, a girl and boy who were 9 and 8 years of age. She worked periodically as a clerk in the parts department of a Ford dealership. She reported a history of double depression that began when she was a sophomore in high school. The patient grew up in a strict Catholic family and attended Mass several times a week and always on Sunday. She had an older brother who became a priest and a younger sister who lived in the same city and with whom she felt very close. Her father was a strict disciplinarian who felt that girls "should be submissive and compliant as well as seen and not heard." Peggy told the therapist that her father overheard a conversation years before that she had with a ninth-grade girlfriend. The friend betrayed her trust by disclosing one of Peggy's closely guarded secrets. Peggy screamed "you bitch" over the phone. The father made her terminate the call and grounded her to the house for a week; she could attend school but do nothing else. She reported several other instances in which the father had severely punished her for speaking up and making her views known. Her mother, a very religious woman who displayed a photograph of Mother Teresa prominently on the parents' bedroom wall, was "as strict about rules as Daddy." She kept tight reins on what Peggy wore to school and what she wore to parties and other social events. When she reached puberty, the clothing and social restrictions increased. For example, she was allowed to attend only those parties where the parents knew the chaperones. Peggy was asked out frequently but could not date until she was 17 years old.

She performed well in school and was popular with her peers. She confided that her strict Catholic parents put a real damper on her social life; however, she never protested and complied with her parents' wishes. She described herself as compliant, never questioning authority, and submissive and sweet. Peggy graduated from high school with high honors. She commented sarcastically that she'd been so sheltered that she had only kissed a boy one time. Her performance in school made it easy for her to be accepted to the state university. During her junior year, she met her future husband. They dated for 2 years and married a year after both had graduated. Her husband was also a strict Catholic, and, in many ways, Peggy continued to practice her religion the way she had done while living at home. During the early psychotherapy sessions, she was extremely compliant, even in situations where being compliant meant she was obviously inconvenienced.

The patient could not provide a reason for becoming depressed as an adolescent. She could only say that "I've been depressed for as long as I can remember." Prior to coming to therapy, she reported one major depressive episode following a severe conflict with the part's department boss. He had made several sexual advances toward her that she didn't know how to handle. In exasperation one day, Peggy screamed at him in the shop in front of a number of employees. The problem became public knowledge, and her boss was subsequently fired. The major depressive episode lasted 8 months and then the patient returned to her antecedent dysthymic baseline. Peggy had never sought treatment for her depression.

During the second session, her psychotherapist, Dr. Frederick, conducted a Significant Other History. Peggy listed six persons who had played major roles in her life: father, mother, maternal grandmother, older brother, younger sister, and her great aunt.

Significant Other History and Causal Theory Conclusions (CTC)

1. *Father:* "He was extremely rigid and authoritarian and imposed strict discipline on all the children. His punishment was excessive whenever I behaved in ways that he felt were 'unladylike.' One unladylike behavior was expressing any kind of hostility or saying off-color words. He demanded that I be compliant with everyone and never question authority; authority included parents, teachers, priests, nuns, and any adults who came to the house for meals or parties. He liked it best when I remained quiet and didn't enter into conversations. I never felt free to express myself around him. I usually remained quiet."

CTC: "I'm passive and compliant, I don't speak up, and above all, I do what I'm told."

2. *Mother:* "She was rigid and authoritarian, particularly when it came to religion and proper female behavior. She closely watched the way I dressed and who I socialized with. She was a 'stickler for the rules' and expected me to obey them without question. I don't remember her being warm or enjoying getting close to anyone. I don't remember her holding me. As long as I obeyed and did what I was told, she and I got along."

CTC: "I follow the rules without asking any questions; I'm a lady at all times."

3. *Maternal grandmother:* "I spent a lot of time with her growing up. She loved me and often told me so. She was warm, gentle, and kind. She used to say that my parents were too hard on me. It was the only time I ever heard anyone say that my parents were too strict."

CTC: "I know what it is like to be loved."

4. *Older brother:* "He always did the right thing and never gave my parents any trouble. He obeyed all the rules, and I used to think he was perfect. He spent a great deal of time at the church and finally decided to become a priest. He was nice to me, but we were never close. I could never be as good as him."

CTC: "I feel inferior around religious people."

5. *Younger sister:* "Growing up, she and I were not close, but we are very close now. She lives a few blocks away, and we talk almost daily. She and I spend a lot of time talking about our early homelife. She rebelled against all the family rules when she was a teenager. She would stay out late, and she probably slept with a lot of guys. My parents sort of gave up trying to control her."

CTC: "I can have a loving relationship with a woman."

6. *Great aunt:* "My maternal grandmother's sister was a nun and the family saint. Everyone looked up to her and told stories about how kind and good she was. She came to visit several times a year and would talk to me. She would ask how I was doing and if I was obeying my parents. I think she liked me, but I was never sure."

CTC: "I am not as good a person as she is."

Major Interpersonal CTC Theme and the Transference Hypothesis

The prominent theme running through the Significant Other History was being a "good person" and "doing the right thing." For Peggy, this meant being passive, following the rules, doing what she was told without protest or expressing what she wanted and, above all, respecting authority via compliance. The theme of compliance ran through her recalled experiences with her father, mother, older brother, and great aunt. Dr. Frederick constructed the following transference hypothesis:

"If I tell Dr. Frederick what I want/don't want (i.e. assert myself), *then he will reject me and punish me in some way."* [Disclosure of wants TH area]

Peggy brought in a Situation Analysis (SA) during the seventh session that exposed the transference hot spot. In response, the therapist administered the IDE. The SA scenario was as follows: Peggy went to her psychiatrist's office for a scheduled medication check. She waited 50 minutes and when the doctor came out, she told Peggy that the clinic always "double books" and that she could not be seen that day—someone else would be seen in her slot. She also asked Peggy to return the following week for an appointment. Peggy acquiesced without protest and agreed to reschedule. She left the office and cried all the way home. Her *desired outcome* in the SA was to tell the psychiatrist that "I want to be seen now. It's inconvenient for me to drive all the way back here next week for another appointment." During the remediation phase of SA, it became clear that if Peggy wanted to achieve her desired outcome, she would have to assert herself to the psychiatrist and tell the doctor what she wanted. Just talking about what she would have to do raised considerable anxiety in the patient. Adding the assertive behavior component in SA remediation also exposed the *hot spot* content of Dr. Frederick's transference hypothesis. Throughout the remediation phase, Dr. Frederick was supportive and helpful, knowing how difficult it was for Peggy to talk about standing up for herself and tell the doctor what she wanted. Several times he smiled at her and commented, "You've done excellent work in a very difficult situation." Peggy even remarked that his support made it easier for her to discuss asserting herself. When the SA was completed, Dr. Frederick again smiled at the patient, who looked at him and exhaled a sigh of relief.

Dr. Frederick: You looked uncomfortable when you talked about telling the doctor what you wanted.
Patient: I've never done anything like this before. I don't think I could do it. I feel it would be "unladylike."

Dr. Frederick: Let's focus on your telling the doctor what you wanted—that is, you wanted to be seen then. Had your *father* been in the room and heard you say this, what would be his reaction to you?

Patient: (*looking a little horrified*) He would have turned around after giving me one of his looks and walked out of the room. On the way out he might have said something like, "No daughter of mine would ever talk like that. I don't know who this woman is. She's not my daughter!" He can't punish me now like he used to, but he can give me that look or tell me that I've turned into a horrible person. It would take me a long time to get over his disgust and anger. I used to feel so guilty that I wouldn't be able to speak—just look down at the floor. I remember those feelings well. Just talking about this makes me feel that way now.

[The felt discomfort in the patient is desirable during the phase of IDE work in which she recalls the negative experiences with the father and mother.]

Dr. Frederick: Had your *mother* heard you assert yourself to the psychiatrist, what would have been her reaction?

Patient: Mother would have been incredulous. She wouldn't have believed what I said. Again, her looks would betray her feelings. She would have been angry and embarrassed over what I had done. When we left the psychiatrist's office, I would have had to listen to a stern lecture. Asserting myself would be totally unacceptable, and I would have had "hell to pay." At some point, my mother would have told me that I had sinned against God, that Mother Teresa would never have behaved this way. You see, in the world I grew up in, strict rules dictated everything. Doing what I was told was written in stone. I never thought I had any choices until I came to see you. I just thought that doing what I'm told is the way life is and the way it was meant to be. That's the Catholic way: You don't think, you just obey. Even now, the old feelings scream at me "No!" "No!" "No!" when I think about making choices and doing or saying what I want. It's these feelings that won't leave me alone. They're like barricades to my changing anything. I don't know how to feel any different. I'm stuck with punishment feelings rising up inside any time I try to do what I want. (*Peggy's felt despair is palpable and omnipresent in this moment.*)

[The interpersonal discrimination task really begins at this point. Peggy has described a preoperational emotional dilemma that has entrapped her and in which she is currently enmeshed. Dr. Frederick will administer a "mismatching" task by shifting the attentional focus of the patient, and in doing so, taking her out of the preoperational orbit and into the situational context—namely, the person of the therapist (see Figure 6.1). An optimal outcome would be a decrease in felt discomfort as Peggy attends to the positive behavior emitted by Dr. Frederick. The therapist's behavior remains anchored within the situational event, which is similar to those in which Peggy received punishment from both parents. The stage is set for the administration of negative reinforcement to strengthen assertive behavior.]

Dr. Frederick: Sitting with you as you recalled how your parents might react to your assertive behavior has been like sitting in a torture chamber. Now I want you to change your focus from your parents to me. Describe my reactions to you as you talked about asserting yourself to your psychiatrist and telling her what you wanted. How did I react?

Patient: I'm not really sure ... you didn't punish me or make me feel like I had done something wrong.

Dr. Frederick: Can you be more specific. What did I do?

Patient: Well, you were supportive and encouraging. You even complimented me for doing "excellent work in a very difficult situation." You smiled at me several times, as if you were pleased with me. But I wouldn't expect you to react like my parents—you're my therapist.

Dr. Frederick: That comment just neutralized my responses to you—made them sound sorta fake.

Patient: You do what therapists are supposed to do, don't you?

Dr. Frederick: You just took the wind out of my sails again and made my responses to you sound contrived, fabricated.

Patient: I can't believe anyone could really like what I did. I mean, I spent my entire life believing that I must be passive and compliant; that living this way is God's will. How can I experience your responses as genuine, much less right?

Dr. Frederick: What you're telling me is that my responses are so different from anything you've experienced up to now that you can't believe that they are real, genuine, or even okay.

Patient: The only thing I've ever known and believed is what my parents taught me. You don't realize how different you are. How did you learn to be this way? I mean, to be different than my parents?

Dr. Frederick: I grew up in a different world than you did. In my world, it was all right if people said what they wanted and asked to be treated fairly. These behaviors were severely punished and called sinful and wrong in your world. You've paid a high personal price for the way you were taught to live; your upbringing has left you in pain.

Patient: It's like looking at two ways to live. One way is to stay in the background and do what I'm told. The other way here is to let other people know what I want and don't want. I'm not sure I can be any other way than "a passive, compliant Peggy."

Dr. Frederick: You just were. You told me what's what about the two ways of living and then you said you're not sure you can be any other way than you've always been. That's putting yourself squarely on the line with me—haven't seen anyone do it any better.

Patient: Do you realize how different it is for me to talk this way with you?

Dr. Frederick: Yes. It's like night and day. Your old way is "night" and the new way is like stepping out into the sunlight. Where's all that uneasiness and discomfort you felt a few minutes ago? You look a little more relaxed than you did a few minutes ago.

Patient: I am a little more relaxed. Not totally, but I feel a little easier than I did a moment ago.

Dr. Frederick: Do you know why you feel easier and not so uncomfortable? Focus on what's been going on between the two of us in answering that question.

Patient: I don't think, I really don't believe, that you would punish me for speaking up for myself with that doctor.

Dr. Frederick: No, I wouldn't. I might clap though, or cheer.

Patient: This is very different for me. I'm going to have to think about all this for a while.

Dr. Frederick: Make sure when you think about what's happened here today that you focus on the two of us and especially how I've responded to your talking about asserting yourself.

Commentary

One IDE exercise certainly doesn't resolve the patient's preoperational emotional dilemma. CBASP is an acquisition learning model of psychotherapy in which the IDE exercise is used to reconnect the patient perceptually with the situational context (the person of the therapist). Repeated IDE trials will be necessary to fully achieve this goal. But movement toward this end has begun in the above scenario. In this mismatching exercise, Dr. Frederick pits himself against a herd of significant others who taught Peggy to remain passive and compliant and do what she is told, particularly around authority figures. In focusing attention on his contingent responses to her assertive behavior, a modicum of emotional relief was achieved. The critical motivational leverage of therapists is decreasing felt discomfort via adaptable behavior. The IDE is used to mollify patients' reactions to early emotional trauma, and any behavior that reduces pain is reinforced. Making it explicit to patients in a discrimination exercise that the therapist is qualitatively different from hurtful significant others opens possibilities for emotional relief that have not existed previously.

In this IDE, Dr. Frederick took Peggy into the lion's den of punishment with her father and mother while maintaining the situational focus: a situation in which Peggy discusses asserting herself to an authority figure and palpably experiences rejection, anxiety, shame, and guilt. Then he demonstrated a way to reduce the felt distress by shifting her attention to his positive personal responses (in the same situational context). The implicit message to the patient is the following: "*I'm not your mother or father. You've got a different interpersonal reality here with me! You can assert yourself without fear here.*"

The reader may be surprised that so much emotion can be generated in a hypothetical situation that has not yet occurred; Peggy has yet to assert herself intentionally to the doctor. By focusing the IDE solely on a particular *slice of time*, particularly a situation in which the patient easily recalls aversive memories (i.e., the parents' consequation history for any assertive behavior), felt distress can be potentiated. Such focusing also sets the stage for a therapist to *decrease* the patient's discomfort by associating the target behavior (e.g., assertion) with the therapist's positive contingent personal responses (support, encouragement, expressed pleasure). Over time, Peggy will come to perceive that indeed she does experience felt relief when she concentrates on Dr. Frederick's responses to her behavior. The reconnection process with the situational context (Dr. Frederick) will finally overthrow the preoperational emotional dilemma that maintains the chronic disorder. The final goal of treatment will be realized when these in-session gains are transferred to Peggy's interpersonal relationships with others.

Case Scenario 3

Gary was a 33-year-old male, chemical engineer, never married, who lived alone. He reported an early-onset history of recurrent major depressive episodes. The patient described numerous episodes of major depression beginning when he was 17 years of age, with no full recovery interepisode. The episodes followed breakups with girlfriends and several social conflicts with male friends. His family history was remarkable in regard to his role in the family. His parents always spent most of their time and energy on Gary's older brother and sister, who were both Phi Beta Kappa graduates of prominent East Coast universities. Gary, the youngest child and "an accident," entered the family when the older siblings were in high school. The parents were in their early 50s and were not prepared, or willing, to begin the childrearing process again. The upshot of his birth in the family, he said, was that "I was pretty much left to fend for myself." No one attended his ball games or the plays he participated in during elementary and middle school. His parents did not compliment him when he did well in school or when he achieved recognition for scholastic honors, such as being tapped for the National Honor Society his junior year in high school. His father was a CEO with a large manufacturing corporation, and his mother was a CPA who did freelance accounting work for a number of local firms. Gary could never remember a time when he and his father had had a serious conversation, nor did he recall a time when his mother had sought him out with hugs or other types of physical contact. She was not a particularly emotional person.

Gary said that his older brother and sister were always studying or busy with school and their social activities. He read a lot, had a few friends during high school, but mostly stayed by himself. He began dating during early high school and fell in love with a classmate during his junior year. The couple broke up 2 months prior to graduation. The breakup was followed by Gary's first major depressive episode. He attended the graduation ceremony (his parents were out of town, but Annie, the family maid, was there), came home, and drank a fifth of bourbon. He passed out and remained in his room for almost 2 days. No one ever checked on him.

Gary evinced good social skills during the screening interview and showed that he had learned to interact socially in appropriate ways. He personified loneliness and appeared to expect little or nothing from anyone. He was surprised when the clinician asked when he would like to come back and begin treatment. He remarked that he didn't even think about coming back. He just came to the clinic to talk about himself. As noted above, Gary was diagnosed with major depression, recurrent, without full interepisode recovery, and began CBASP treatment 2 weeks later. He was referred to a psychiatrist for antidepressant medication. In discussing the case at an intake conference the day after the screening interview, the social worker described Gary as "a man whom life has left alone." His presenting BDI-II score was 39, indicating severe depression.

Gary was referred to Dr. Martelli for psychotherapy. During the second interview, Dr. Martelli administered the Significant Other History. The patient listed six significant others: mother, father, older brother, sister, Annie, and a college roommate.

Significant Other History and Causal Theory Conclusions (CTC)

1. *Mother:* "She was an 'executive' type woman. She was a good accountant and made a lot of money. She worked most of the time. She was nice to me, saw that I had clothes and food, but that was about it. I never felt that I played an important role in her life other than she had to make sure I was taken care of. We always had maids to take care of the house and to cook the meals. I don't even know if she and my father had a good marriage. They were always quite businesslike around us children. Mom never punished me or spent any time with me. She always seemed to be too busy, going on to the next business assignment. She surely loved her work. I'm not sure how she felt about anything else, though I heard her remark once that she was proud of my older brother and sister."

CTC: "I feel that a woman couldn't really care for me."

2. *Father:* "My father was a hard worker and was gone a lot. When he was at home, he seemed to stay on the phone a lot talking to his business associates. He made a lot of money, and we lived in a large home, belonged to the country club, and socialized with important people in our town. The mayor came to dinner frequently, and the conversation usually centered on politics. In many ways, my relationship with my father was similar to that of my mother. I stayed in the background, and he pretty much left me alone. I don't think I played an important part in his life, though he was not mean to me or unfair in what he asked me to do. Looking back on it now, I felt like I was sort of a 'fixture' in his life—like something on his desktop computer screen that he didn't look at very much."

CTC: "Stay in the background; Others don't want me around."

3. *Older brother:* "Very independent person. I don't think he ever needed anyone. He seemed to get along well with people and appeared to be popular with the crowd he ran with. He and I were never close. Every now and then he and I would go to a movie together. I used to look forward to those times. I wish I could let things roll off my back the way he does—things never seemed to bother him."

CTC: "I can't be nonchalant like my brother."

4. *Sister:* "She was like my mother—a 'driven' person. She was very ambitious, always made excellent grades, and graduated *cum laude* from her university. She went to graduate school and got a Ph.D. in social psychology. She teaches at the state university and loves to do research. I think she's published a lot of journal

articles and even written a book. She never married—never stopped long enough to have a relationship."

CTC: "I feel that women are more concerned about work than relationships."

5. *Annie:* "Annie is the one who really raised me. She was our maid for over 20 years. She began working for the family shortly before I was born. I guess she was the only mother I ever had. I loved her, and we spent a lot of time together before I went to school. I always felt she loved me. She used to bring me little toys that she made, and we'd play with them together. Annie told me stories, and I can remember sitting on her lap and feeling warm and safe. When I was in college, Annie would write me letters and tell me that she missed me and hoped I was doing fine. She died several years ago. I went to her funeral. No one else in the family attended. I must have cried for a week. I miss her so much, even now."

CTC: "I know what it's like to love someone."

6. *College roommate:* "Bill and I roomed together for 3 years. He and I have been close friends since our college days. We write each other periodically. He's been a successful salesman and seems to have a happy family. He and his wife have three children. Wish we lived in the same town. I would like to be with him more."

CTC: "Bill taught me how to be a friend."

Major Interpersonal CTC Theme and the Transference Hypothesis

The first four major players on Gary's list (mother, father, older brother, sister) all treated him like a "family appendage." He was raised in an emotionally deprived environment where basic, affective nurturance was absent. Annie, the family maid, was a source of refreshing warmth and care in an otherwise arid developmental environment. His attachment to Annie was a godsend and probably saved him from psychological disaster. From her he experienced giving and receiving love. Bill, the college roommate, was also another source of nurture who taught Gary the parameters of friendship. These latter two relationships, although salubrious in many ways, couldn't neutralize or overcome the early emotional deprivation and the concomitant interpersonal expectations that derive from such sterile home environments.
    Dr. Martelli constructed the following TH:

"If I have a relationship with Dr. Martelli, then he will react as if I'm unimportant and not worthy of his time (like my mother, father, older brother, and sister). [Interpersonal intimacy TH area]

Gary brought in a Situational Analysis during the ninth session that had a successful outcome—he produced his desired outcome. He and a colleague were discussing safety measures for employees who worked in a highly toxic chemical production section of the plant. The patient wanted greater safety precautions taken, whereas his colleague was rather blasé about the safety problem. Gary felt so strongly about the matter that he took his proposal to the plant manager, who, when he understood the risks, supported instituting the plan immediately. The plan was put into effect the next day. No one mentioned Gary's success or the fact that he had, by himself, implemented procedures that might save lives or at least prevent serious injury. Dr. Martelli was duly impressed by Gary's concern for his fellow workers and for the accomplishment he alone had achieved. He remarked several times that he thought Gary had accomplished a very significant achievement. After the SA work was completed, Gary said, "In the company, it's like nothing has happened. No one cares. It's the story of my life. Nothing I do makes any difference to anyone." Gary had totally overlooked the comments and behavior of his therapist, whose very positive personal responses were lost amid his despair.

Dr. Martelli did something that was highly unusual for him. He stood up in front of his chair and began to clap. He clapped and clapped and clapped, all the while never taking his eyes off Gary, who remained seated, looking astonished at what was taking place. During the clapping, Martelli began to yell in a loud voice, "Bravo, Gary! Bravo, Gary! I don't give a damn if no one else in the world responds to what you've done. I think you've done one of the noblest deeds I've ever heard of! Bravo, Gary!" As Martelli continued to clap, the patient's eyes began to well up with tears, and he put his head in his hands and sobbed. The doctor waited until an appropriate time, then walked over and asked Gary to stand up, saying he wanted to shake his hand. Gary stood up, and they shook hands and looked at each other. The patient reached out and hugged his therapist for a long time. When Martelli returned to his chair, he took out a handkerchief and wiped his eyes. Then, because the moment had involved the TH *hot spot*, he administered the IDE.

Dr. Martelli: Whew! Pretty intense moment we just had, eh?

Patient: Yes (*still sniffling*). I've never had anyone respond to me like this. I don't know what to say.

Dr. Martelli: I think what's just happened between us is very significant. I want to take some time and examine it from several angles. Then we can discuss the implications for both of us. This is not going to be easy for you, but stick with me as we go through this. You just did something that I think was terrific. If your *mother* hears of what you have accomplished at the plant, how will she react?

Patient: The best she would do would be to say, "That's nice." She'd never ask me to explain the significance of the safety measures we put in. She probably wouldn't say anything. She never said anything when I made the honor roll or did something playing football that was reported in the newspaper. I really never thought that she cared what I did.

Dr. Martelli: How will your *father* react when he hears about your accomplishment at the plant?

Patient: If I try to tell him what I've done, he'll be too busy to take notice. He'll get a phone call, and we'll never talk about it again. He'd never bring it up and continue the conversation.

Dr. Martelli: How about your *brother*? What would he say?

Patient: I honestly don't know. He never said anything to me about anything I ever did. I just don't know—probably something like "that's nice."

Dr. Martelli: And your sister? How would she react?

Patient: My sister wouldn't care one way or the other. She's too focused on herself and her work. She doesn't care about anyone in the family. Rarely visits the parents or communicates with them.

Dr. Martelli: Any idea what my response is to these four individuals you've just described?

Patient: No, what?

Dr. Martelli: Their behavior toward you makes me angry. They're all a self-centered bunch of people who don't know how to think of anyone else but themselves—especially when it comes to you.

[Dr. Martelli deliberately makes a disparaging comment about Gary's nuclear family. He's trying to align himself totally with the patient and disassociate himself from these four significant others. His goal here is to try to potentiate the impact of the pending discrimination task.]

Patient: They've surely ignored me for as long as I can remember.

Dr. Martelli: You've described your entire family's probable reactions to the noble deed you've done. Let's shift gears now and focus on my responses to what you did. First, tell me what safety measures you had installed and why.

Patient: The toxic chemicals involve the manufacture of a type of cleaning fluid for oil leakages that come from heavy machinery. If the fluid splashes on bare skin, it burns and destroys the skin. The burns can be very serious. If the mixture splashes in the eye, the eye is lost. This stuff is highly dangerous, and our employees have been working with it in coveralls and with no protective clothing. I was down in the pits where this stuff is made last week and when I left I was frightened by the safety hazards. I almost halted production then until I could get something done. What I've done is put protective suits and shoes on the workers, protective gloves must be worn when handling the containers, and plexiglass face masks must be worn in the manufacturing area at all times. Now the employees are safe from injury in case of spills or splashes. I feel much better now. What I've done ought to have been done a long time ago. This company is lucky no one has been hurt.

Dr. Martelli: You mentioned that this procedure should have been implemented a long time ago. Why wasn't it done?

Patient: Because no one either thought about it or cared enough about the workers to do it.

Dr. Martelli: Nothing was done until you did it, right?

Patient: Right. Why would you care about what I did?

Dr. Martelli: You tell me, why should I care what you did?

Patient: I'm not sure. No one else ever has.

Dr. Martelli: I'm not "no one else." You didn't answer my question. Why should I care what you did?

Patient: I'm really not sure. I don't know.

Dr. Martelli: Because what you do and what happens to you matters to me. I'm not sure why, it just does. Your genuineness is easy to admire and like.

Patient: Talking about all this with you is a different experience. You seem interested in me and what I've done.

Dr. Martelli: I am. What have I done that's given you that idea?

Patient: I don't remember it happening to me before.

Dr. Martelli: What have I done that makes you feel that I'm interested in you?

Patient: You stood up and clapped, you yelled "Bravo, Gary!" You walked over and shook my hand. Everything you did said that you are interested in me. I think you would have a hard time bullshitting me for that long if you really didn't feel that way.

Dr. Martelli: I don't bullshit about things like this.

Patient: It's just very new. I've never experienced this kind of recognition before from anyone. I've always felt that what I did didn't matter. You act like it matters.

Dr. Martelli: It does.

Patient: So, what do I do now? I mean, what's next?

Dr. Martelli: Just enjoy it. Let yourself enjoy what you've experienced with me. It's different, man, different from the desert you grew up in.

Commentary

Dr. Martelli mismatched the usual preoperational cognitive–emotional style of the patient by administering the IDE. The goal was to attempt to connect the perceptual outlook of the patient with the situational context (viz., the therapist). He did this by engaging in poignant and intimate interpersonal behavior that he thought would be difficult for Gary to overlook. Indeed, the patient was astonished by the therapist's behavior. Chronic emotional deprivation and the cognitive wasteland resulting from this type of interpersonal learning history require strong interpersonal intervention—and that's exactly what Gary received. The interpersonal message Dr. Martelli sent was *take a good look at who's with you and what I'm doing in this moment!*

Gary represents a type of chronically depressed patient who has a history of deprivation, a lifetime of being left alone. The therapeutic goal in this instance is to inject salubrious positive attention into the perceptual interpersonal desert and to help this individual become aware of "company" instead of being left alone. In Gary's case, this meant exposing him to positive interpersonal attention in a situation in which he had never before received attention. Other types of exposure in the psychological literature, particularly in the treatment of PTSD, often make us think of "something being taken away" (Foa, Dancu, Hembree, Jaycox, Meadows, & Street, 1999; Hembree, Rausch, & Foa, 2003) or "activating the trauma memories in order to modify pathological aspects of these memories" (Foa & Rothbaum, 1998, p. 51)—that is, breaking up, removing, or at least mitigating the associations between the recalled memories and the adverse affect. With Gary, the goal was not to take something away; rather, the goal was to insert something that had not been present before. The novel interpersonal experiences included positive attention (clapping, verbal accolades) for his behavior; tactile encounters (a handshake, a hug) expressing pleasure over what he had accomplished; and the clinician's time and attention, which enabled Gary to talk about his accomplishments with a highly interested participant. All of these consequences were new.

Such consequences for laudatory behavior are so basic to most people that clinicians easily overlook their absence in patients who never received them. The TH sensitized Dr. Martelli to their absence, and when Gary protested that "In the company, it's like nothing has happened. No one cares. It's the story of my life. Nothing I do makes any difference to anyone," the transference *hot spot* was apparent to Dr. Martelli. He then behaved in ways that were diametrically opposed to the behavior of Gary's four significant others in order to introduce the novel learning situation. The way Dr. Martelli behaved made it impossible for Gary to overlook what the therapist was doing. Gary unavoidably made contact with the situational context (the therapist) in the session (see Figure 6.1) and, in doing so, transcended the chronic egocentrism of his cognitive–emotional response style (see Figure 6.2). In the final steps of the IDE, Dr. Martelli made explicit what had just taken place and compared and contrasted it with Gary's previous history. Then the two talked about the implications of the dyadic encounter and what it might mean for Gary.

Such encounters between therapist and patient will have to be repeated during treatment. The habitual and protracted learning experiences of these patients require repeated interpersonal exposure and practice with therapists who personify a new interpersonal reality.

Case Scenario 4

Heidi was 48 years old when she came to the clinic. Describing a chronic course of depression, the patient said that she had been "depressed for as long as I can remember." Heidi was born in Dresden in 1954 during the height of Communist rule in East Germany. She and her family had lived in a large, four-story apartment complex where all families were allotted the same amount of square footage and lived in drab surroundings. She was the oldest of four children. Her mother and father worked in a nearby factory, trying to earn enough money to feed their large family. At an early age, Heidi was given the responsibility of taking care of her two sisters and younger brother. She washed, cooked, cleaned the house, and watched them while they played in a nearby park. She prepared their lunches when they went to school, saw that they had the right clothes to wear, and then went to school herself after the last one left. When Heidi was 12, her father disappeared and she never saw him again. She found out later that he had escaped to West Germany with several men in the factory. No one in the family, including his wife, knew that he was leaving. Heidi's mother became angry and bitter over her fate and became more and more difficult to live with. Heidi continued to care for her siblings and ended up trying to protect them from the wrath of the mother, whose increasing anger took the form of severe spankings and verbal tirades whenever the children misbehaved. Heidi described her life as "a thankless Cinderella without a Prince Charming to rescue me." She told the social worker that her adolescent years were a time during which she felt abandoned, alone, and hopeless. Her school attendance became increasingly sporadic because of the responsibilities at home, particularly after her father left the family. Talking about this period in her life led to bouts of crying.

Heidi left home when she was 19 years old (1973) and worked as a waitress and housekeeper (and any other jobs she could find) in the nearby town of Moritzburg. Her mother had become severely ill with emphysema, and the younger children had gone to live with the maternal grandparents. Heidi began to date a man 10 years older and finally married him when she was 24. They had a stable marriage for 4 years, until he had an affair and left the marriage. She obtained a divorce in 1982. The couple never had children. Heidi continued to live and work in Moritzburg and save as much money as she could. When the Berlin Wall came down in 1989 and traffic between East and West Germany opened, Heidi moved to West Berlin and began schooling to prepare for obtaining a degree in accounting at the university. Her teachers saw intellectual promise in her and encouraged her to leave Germany and go to New York to complete her schooling. In 1994, she flew to New York, rented an apartment in Brooklyn, and attended a college in the city. She graduated with honors and obtained her CPA certificate a year later.

She had been working as an accountant at an investment firm for 5 years when she came to the clinic. Heidi had never sought mental health treatment before, but a breakup of a love affair had thrust her into a major depressive episode. She was diagnosed with a single episode of major depression with antecedent, early-onset dysthymia.

The social worker who conducted the intake found her friendly and attractive, neatly dressed, cooperative, and severely depressed (BDI-II of 41). Heidi admitted that "I don't think anything will help me get over my depression, but I'm very tired of feeling this way." Her English was very good. She had been speaking English for many years and obviously had mastered the language.

Significant Other List: mother, father, maternal grandmother, maternal grandfather, husband, and younger sister.

Significant Other History and Causal Theory Conclusions (CTC)

1. *Mother:* "Hard worker. Never quit going to work regardless of the difficulties. I don't believe she ever missed a day of work in her life. She cared for me when I was little, but when I was around 8, I had to take over the household duties and raise my sisters and brother from then on. Mom had to work to keep enough money coming in to clothe and feed us. I don't remember her as being a very warm type of individual. She was mostly 'strictly business.' I learned early that if I messed up and didn't do what I was supposed to do, I would pay the price of a severe tongue lashing. She never physically spanked me—that was to come later, after my father abandoned the family. When I was about 12, my father left and Mother turned sullen, angry, and inconsolable. She took her anger out on my sisters and

brother. I tried as best I could to protect them from her rages. Sometimes it worked and sometimes it didn't. I left at 19 years of age when Momma became ill because she smoked all the time. She was hospitalized for emphysema and could no longer work. My sister and brother went to live with my grandparents, where they stayed until they went to work."

CTC: "I work hard regardless of the circumstances."

2. *Father:* "I remember my father as a kind man. He used to take me and my sisters and brother to the park and watch us play. He was strict but fair. Daddy never spanked any of us, but somehow I knew that when he said something he meant business—I always took what he said seriously and never questioned him. I guess his 'word was law' around the house. He loved good music. We had an old phonograph player and he used to listen to Mozart and Bach. I remember sitting on his lap while he hummed the melodies. I liked those times. Then one day he never came home from work—without any warning he was gone. Gone! He left without saying goodbye. I never understood that. I never understood how someone could abandon his loved ones the way he did. He just vanished, and I never saw him again. I never knew what happened to him. I still don't, and it's been 36 years. Looking back on it, I don't think I ever really knew much about him. My mother has never told me a lot about him or what he did before they married. I never knew his parents, and he never talked about them. I think he had a brother, but I'm not sure."

CTC: "I feel that men can't be trusted."

3. *Maternal grandmother:* "She helped me with my chores around the house. She and Grandpa lived close by. She would take washing home and bring it back, clean and folded. Grandma never talked very much, and she wasn't a very warm person. But she was kind and would do anything I asked her. She didn't have much money, but she did have time, and she shared it with me and my sisters and brother. I loved her and appreciated what she did for me. Her help probably kept me afloat when the kids were very young."

CTC: "I learned that I could count on someone for help."

4. *Maternal grandfather:* "Grandpa was always around. He used to smoke huge cigars. He smelled, but he was a kind and funny man. I remember his anger at my father when he abandoned us. He would rage for hours around the house. He never forgave my father for what he did to us. Then he got sick and died when I was 15 years old. It was sudden. I really missed him and even used to get mad at him for leaving us. He couldn't help dying, but I was mad at him for leaving us all alone."

CTC: "You just cannot count on a man to hang around—he always leaves."

5. *Husband:* "I married Hans when I was 24. He was 10 years older and owned a small farm outside of Moritzburg. Hans had moved from Frankfurt to Moritzburg several years before. He'd been in the army, and I never met his family. I think they lived in Frankfurt, but I'm not sure. I married him and didn't know a whole

lot about his past. Regardless, we were very much in love and spent long hours together taking walks in the countryside. We both had bikes and loved to ride across the fields. Hans always liked to spend time at home. I used to get angry with myself for feeling depressed when I was around him. I felt it was unfair to him. But I have to say that I felt genuine happiness when I was with him. We tried to have children, but I never got pregnant. During the last 2 years of the marriage, he began to drink a lot and frequently came home drunk after spending the evening at the tavern. I started fussing about his drinking, and our relationship began to sour. I felt there was nothing I could do to make things right. Then I found out from some townspeople that Hans was having an affair. I finally asked him to leave, and we got a divorce in 1982. My world came crashing down. I finally realized that I had to learn a trade, so I went back to school."

CTC: "I can't trust a man."

6. *Younger sister:* "We email each other every day. I haven't seen her in years; she's married and has several children. She and her husband still live in Moritzburg. She has always appreciated the things I did for her when she was small. Sometimes she even calls me 'Mom.' In many ways, I have been her mother and I still am. She tells me how proud of me she is, and we exchange pictures of each other over email."

CTC: "I can be close to women; they don't abandon the relationship."

Major Interpersonal CTC Theme and the Transference Hypothesis

The salient theme Heidi describes with her father, maternal grandfather, and husband is one of abandonment. From her mother she learned to work hard—a learning followed by the same abandonment with her mother's illness and the subsequent breakup of the family. The only stable persons in her life were her grandmother and her younger sister. She began to see Dr. Reynolds (a male) for psychotherapy shortly after coming to the clinic. After conducting the Significant Other History during the second session, Dr. Reynolds constructed the following TH:

"If I get close to Dr. Reynolds, then he will abandon me or withdraw from me in some way." [Interpersonal intimacy TH area]

A transference *hot spot* arose between them during the eighth and ninth sessions. Dr. Reynolds was summoned to court to testify on behalf of one of his patients. The court date fell on the same afternoon that Heidi's appointment was scheduled. Afraid that he would not be back in time to see Heidi, Dr. Reynolds asked his secretary to cancel the appointment and reschedule one for the same time the following week. Heidi did not call to cancel, nor did she come to the next session. Dr. Reynolds called Heidi to talk about why she had missed the appointment. During the conversation, the reason became apparent. Heidi said, "I figured, here we go again. Dr. Reynolds has something else to do, so there's no reason for me to go back." The clinician knew immediately what had happened. His TH should have alerted him to the likelihood that the abandonment issue would be evoked in any cancellation with Heidi, but he'd been so busy that he hadn't thought about the implications. He told her the circumstances for the cancellation and apologized for not calling her himself. He asked Heidi if she had time to see him the next morning, and the patient agreed to come in. The IDE was administered during this session.

Dr. Reynolds: I'm really glad you came in.

Patient: I almost didn't. It was too painful to think about losing someone else.

Dr. Reynolds: My secretary's call dug up a bushel load of bad feelings and memories.

Patient: It didn't at first. Then I began to think about it, and that's when it all hit me—here's another person leaving me to do something else.

Dr. Reynolds: I'm sorry that I didn't call you and tell you why I had to cancel our appointment. Had I called, would that have made any difference?

Patient: I don't know. I know all this must seem crazy to you—I mean, that I would react this strongly to your canceling an appointment. These things happen all the time to professional people.

Dr. Reynolds: Okay, it happens all the time to people. So why did it hit you like a tidal wave? What's the big deal for you about cancellation? [Dr. Reynolds already knows the answer but asks to set the stage for the IDE]

Patient: Because it's always what happens to me anytime I get involved with a man. I expect it, and it always happens. It's just the way my life has been. Always! That's why it's such a big deal!

Dr. Reynolds: The look on your face—shock, fear, and sadness. I can't change what I did, but I feel so badly that I didn't cancel with you while we were sitting like this and talking.

Patient: (*sitting silent for a long time*) Has anyone ever left you before? Abandoned you when you thought things were going all right?

Dr. Reynolds: Yes. [Following the patient's lead here]

Patient: They have?

Dr. Reynolds: Fifteen years ago.

Patient: Who left you?

Dr. Reynolds: My first wife did. She said all I did was work, and she was tired of being by herself. Looking back now, I think she was right. I worked all the time.

Patient: Did she give you a chance to change?

Dr. Reynolds: No, she left and filed for a divorce, and that was it.

Patient: What did you do?

Dr. Reynolds: Hurt, just like you have.

Patient: But my stuff is different. [Attempted deflection]

Dr. Reynolds: You asked me if I'd ever been abandoned, and I told you I had.

Patient: You must have known it was coming.

Dr. Reynolds: Stupid me, I didn't have a clue until it was too late. Now let's talk about your experiences with abandonment and see how different your experiences were compared to mine. When was the first time for you?

Patient: When my father left the family when I was 12.

Dr. Reynolds: How did you react?

Patient: I felt hopeless and scared. I think I somehow blamed myself for his leaving. That doesn't make sense, does it?

Dr. Reynolds: I'm not sure about how you were to blame. But I know that I felt hopeless, scared, and that it was my fault that my wife left. What was the next time you felt abandoned?

Patient: Well, when Grandpa died, but the real painful one was when my husband had an affair and left me. You remember, I was living in Germany at the time.

Dr. Reynolds: How did you react to that loss?

Patient: Pretty much the same way. I felt hopeless and scared and very alone. I also felt that it was my fault and that I was no good and had been a bad wife. But to this day I can't tell you what I did wrong. The marriage was just over.

Dr. Reynolds: Again, I felt the same way, except I knew I was a bad husband. Turn your attention to our relationship. How did you react when my secretary cancelled the session?

Patient: Pretty much the same way—hopeless, scared, and alone. But why should I have reacted that strongly over a canceled appointment with you?

Dr. Reynolds: Let's see if we can make sense out of it. Compare my responses to you following my cancellation to those of your father and husband when they abandoned you.

[The discrimination exercise begins now. Dr. Reynolds will compare and contrast his responses to her reactions to his cancellation (with its abandonment connotations) to those of the father and husband, who abandoned the patient in a fait accompli fashion. The interpersonal discrimination will be made to illustrate that the therapist's behavior, compared to that of the other two significant others, was qualitatively different.]

Patient: I haven't thought about this until now. Somehow it seems different, but I'm not sure how.

Dr. Reynolds: What did I do after you missed your last appointment?

Patient: You called me and explained what had happened. You also apologized for canceling and for not calling me yourself.

Dr. Reynolds: Is that the way your father and husband behaved after leaving you?

Patient: Of course, not. They just left. They never looked back to tell me what was going on.

Dr. Reynolds: That's one difference. Any others?

Patient: You apologized and said you were sorry—you even acted like you were sorry.

Dr. Reynolds: That's two. Any more?

Patient: Well, I'm not sure about this one, but we're sitting here talking about what happened. This certainly never happened before.

Dr. Reynolds: This is a huge difference. Does this difference suggest anything to you?

Patient: (*long silence*) Yes (*another long silence*). You're not like them. I mean, you act differently. Maybe our relationship will be different. I'm not completely sure, but maybe it will.

Dr. Reynolds: I don't want to be like them. I don't want to be anything like them. I'd never try to do anything to hurt you. This is the last thing I would want to do. You've been hurt enough. You wondered a moment ago why you reacted so strongly to my canceling our appointment. Do you have any better idea now after discussing this abandonment issue?

Patient: I wanted to believe you were different. After the cancellation, I thought you were just more of the same.

Dr. Reynolds: So why did you have such a strong reaction?

Patient: I've just realized that this relationship is a lot more important to me than I thought. That's why I reacted the way I did. I think I feel safer than I have in a long time.

Dr. Reynolds: Our relationship is very important to me too.

Commentary

Dr. Reynolds almost lost the patient by not taking his transference hypothesis seriously enough. He obtained the right information in the Significant Other History, and the transference hypothesis was valid. However, he was very busy, as all of us are, and he somehow overlooked the fact that the success of this case was contingent upon him *being different from the other significant males in Heidi's life.* Cancellation situations with patients such as Heidi will always remain high-risk events.

Once again in this scenario, the patient's preoperational worldview was mismatched in a systematic way. Dr. Reynolds helped Heidi see how the earlier abandonment experiences were not synonymous with the current cancellation situation. Her emotional reactions to Dr. Reynolds, to her father, and to her husband were all similar until she recognized the situational differences. Then an emotional shift occurred in Heidi (from feeling hopeless, fearful, and isolated with all three individuals to feeling safe with the therapist) when she made connection with the situational context (Dr. Reynolds).

Finally, practitioners do not have to experience the same problems chronically depressed patients bring to therapy in order to help them. It just so happened that Dr. Reynolds felt abandoned in his first marriage and by disclosing the experience at this time, he used it in an effective way. It's hard for patients to dismiss or discount someone who has traveled the same path and lived to tell about it. The IDE made explicit that Dr. Reynolds' behavior was qualitatively different from Heidi's father and husband, regardless of his abandonment experiences. I feel strongly that it is the interpersonal differences between the therapists and the significant others that are the crucial mediating variables in the IDE change process.

Conclusions

In this chapter I discussed the rationale underlying the IDE and illustrated how disciplined personal involvement is integrated in the IDE and used to heal developmental trauma.

CBASP therapists, by highlighting their salubrious strivings with patients in IDE work, expose patients to positive interpersonal experiences that contrast sharply with learning experiences many report having had with significant others. Over time, four goals are realized as a function of IDE work: (1) patients acquire the ability to discriminate between the therapist and maltreating significant others; (2) new positive emotional bonds are strengthened between clinician and patient; (3) the perceived connection between the patient and the *situational context* (represented by the therapist) helps to overthrow the preoperational dilemma, as new emotional responses now become available; and (4) the transfer of these new perceptual cognitive–emotional skills as well as novel behavioral skills to relationships on the outside offers additional interpersonal opportunities that have not previously existed.

Afterword

I have tried to demonstrate why I feel that disciplined personal involvement is necessary in the treatment of the chronically depressed adult. Because the entire subject of therapist nonneutrality, or disciplined personal involvement with patients, has been so anathema in our field, I am also hopeful that my comments will open the subject for serious discussion among mental health professionals and, more importantly, result in serious research investigation. I realized early in my training of CBASP therapists that I was encouraging colleagues to become personally involved with patients; the trainees responded in various ways to my admonitions and their reactions ranged from outright opposition, hesitant compliance, to enthusiastic endorsement. The first training barrier I encountered was the inculcated and universal proscription against any and all types of nonneutral involvement with patients.

These professional barriers prohibiting personal involvement were not easily overcome. I realized then that this book was necessary. I had to make a formal case for therapist nonneutrality vis-à-vis the needs of the chronically depressed patient. In my mind, there is no other justifying rationale for personal involvement.

Finally, the longstanding proscription against nonneutrality has served our profession well, and there is wisdom in prohibiting clinicians from moving into this interpersonal domain. The most notable one is preventing psychopathological clinicians from abusing the therapist–patient relationship in deference to their own needs. I have never known a CBASP psychotherapist to abuse a patient with disciplined personal involvement. I hope this situation never occurs. Rather, I have seen many instances where substantive change has been the result of the personal involvement tactics of CBASP therapists. In the hands of mature clinicians, personal involvement offers many salubrious opportunities for healing. It is from the perspective of its healing potential for the patient and in the hope of its responsible usage that I offer this book to the field.

Appendix
Research Investigations to Determine How CBASP Works

What treatment, by whom, is most effective for this individual with that specific problem, under which set of circumstances?

—G.L. Paul (1967, p. 111)

How do our treatments, including psychotherapy, work?

—S.E. Hyman (2000, p. 88)

The content of the appendix is directed to research-oriented readers who want to pursue empirical means to assess the efficacy of disciplined personal involvement. I propose two ways to measure patient behavior change following the administration of disciplined personal involvement. Then I describe a third measurement procedure to assess what role the personal involvement techniques play in treatment outcome.

Some may wonder why I would close a therapy technique text with an appendix on research. There are four reasons for this appendix: (1) I've never felt comfortable practicing psychotherapy without concomitantly evaluating its effects. To me, practice and research are two sides of the same coin, with each side actively informing the other. Having been schooled in an operant single-case tradition, the integration of practice and research seems natural. CBASP developed out of single-case research (e.g., McCullough, 1984a,b,c, 1991), and this final section reflects my desire to make the practice of CBASP easily accessible to empirical investigation. (2) The second reason I end the book on a research note stems from concerns that I have today for my profession. Clinical psychology, like it or not, is in competition with strong professions in the contemporary health care system (e.g., the pharmaceutical industry, physical medicine, psychiatry, social work; Barlow, 2004). We, as mental health professionals, risk losing identify and status if we relinquish our dependence on applied research. Consistent with this reality is my determination to keep CBASP, and more specifically, the techniques involved in disciplined personal involvement, on solid empirical ground.

(3) I've also included this research appendix because there are questions that remain unanswered in the CBASP model. For example, does *disciplined personal involvement,* when combined with *Situational Analysis,* contribute to outcome efficacy? And if it does, is/are the active ingredient(s) the *interpersonal discrimination*

exercise or *contingent personal responsivity?* Or both? (4) My final reason for adding the appendix is because several types of chronically depressed patients don't seem to respond to CBASP. The potential moderator variables and the negative effects they impose on treatment outcome must be clarified.

Having demonstrated the general efficacy of CBASP in a recent national study (Keller et al., 2000), it is now time to answer the following question: *How does CBASP work and for what type of chronically depressed patient?*

Two Types of Dependent Variables

Two types of dependent variables (DVs) are described below: (1) Because CBASP is an acquisition learning model of psychotherapy, the first type of dependent variable examines how much learning is acquired over the course of treatment. Stated from a treatment outcome perspective, the issue here concerns the mediating effects (Kraemer, Wilson, Fairburn, & Agras, 2002) of in-session learning on the process and outcome change indices. Two measures are described that determine how much learning occurs through *Situational Analysis* (SA) administration. One illustrates the patient's ability to identify the interpersonal consequences of his or her behavior, and a second evaluates patient performance in self-administering SA. A third measure is used to assess behavioral change in the session following the administration of *contingent personal responsivity* (CPR); a fourth is associated with the *Interpersonal Discrimination Exercise* (IDE) and illustrates the extent to which the patient learns to discriminate the person of the therapist from maltreating significant others.

(2) A second type of DV in the model is *generalized treatment effects* (GTEs). GTEs are the traditional process and outcome indices of behavioral change that illustrate the symptom reduction and psychosocial gains (or lack thereof) made by patients as a function of treatment. As noted above, determining the mediating effects of in-session learning on the GTEs may help us to understand better *how* the model works (Hyman, 2000). One example of a GTE is depression intensity level, as reflected through Beck Depression Inventory-II (Beck, 1996); a second example would be DSM-IV (American Psychiatric Association, 1994) diagnostic shifts from baseline, such as when a patient moves from disorder to remission status; improvement in the quality of the marriage relationship as shown in Dyadic Adjustment Scale scores (DAS: Spanier, 1976), would be a third; and a fourth example would be comparative changes in the outcome scores reported on an end-of-treatment Minnesota Multiphasic Personality Inventory-I (MMPI) profile (Hathaway & McKinley, 1943).

It should be noted that psychotherapy does not operate directly on the symptoms of a disorder (e.g., low energy or fatigue, low self-esteem, feelings of hopelessness), on a patient's diagnostic status, or on the qualitative characteristics of the marriage dyad. Neither does therapy directly manipulate the psychasthenia (Pt) scale on the MMPI-I, which denotes a symptom configuration (self-doubt, obsessive preoccupations, and compulsive urges and acts). However, psychotherapy does inform, in a mediating way, the symptoms, diagnostic status, marital quality, and MMPI scores; its influence on the patient is seen in the main and interaction effects reflected by the GTEs when they are analyzed over the process of treatment and at outcome.

Needed Stage II CBASP Research

In the following material, I discuss several future directions for CBASP research. My proposals are somewhat similar to the stage model approach to research proposed by Rounsaville, Carroll, and Onken (2001). The stage approach begins with small n pilot studies (Stage I), moves to Stage II randomized clinical trials (RCTs), then transports and generalizes the empirical findings in Stage II to the clinical setting (Stage III). The overriding goal of the stage model is to develop treatment modalities that can be tested in actual clinic environments (Kazdin, 2001). To date, CBASP research has completed the Rounsaville et al. (2001) Stage I requirements (i.e., a CBASP manual with theoretical underpinnings has been developed; small n pilot studies with the target population have been successfully conducted; proven therapist-training routines are in place and have been tested; and successful therapist adherence and integrity trials have been completed). A Stage II project has been run with favorable outcome results (Keller et al., 2000: $n = 681$ outpatients), and a second Stage II RCT is now in progress (Kocsis, 2002: $n = 910$ outpatients) comparing CBASP to a type of "nondirective psychotherapy" known as brief supportive psychotherapy (BSP: Markowitz, 2002). CBASP research has moved rapidly from small n Stage I pilot studies (e.g., McCullough, 1984a,b,c, 1991) to two very large Stage II RCTs. There are strong pressures now from the National Institute of Mental Health and other funding agencies to move toward Stage III research, but I still feel strongly that Stage II mediating variable questions, as well as several moderator variable questions (Kraemer et al., 2002) associated with patient pretreatment status, should also be investigated.

For example, we reported on the mediating effects of SA learning (Manber et al., 2003; Manber & McCullough, 2000), such that patients who learned SA significantly better than others produced better treatment outcomes. Beyond this general finding, we cannot pinpoint the moderating patient variables that facilitate or inhibit SA learning, nor are we able to identify the relevant therapist variables that moderate effective SA teaching.

Specific CBASP Issues That Need Study

1. One outcome issue concerns the role disciplined personal involvement plays in patient change. It must be determined if *disciplined personal involvement* (CPR and the IDE used separately or in combination), when administered with SA (the major treatment technique of CBASP), contributes a mediating effect on treatment outcome.

2. In addition to studying the mediating effects of disciplined personal involvement, the *patient variables* that preclude response to treatment must be identified.

Contrasted to the nonresponder, the responding CBASP patient learns what is taught in therapy and generalizes in-session learning to daily living. By the end of treatment, the psychosocial functioning of the responding patient takes on this complexion: (a) the individual is adaptively informed by the interpersonal consequences of his or her behavior; (b) interpersonal problem solving is made easier because of criterion SA self-administration performance; (c) adaptive interpersonal skills are acquired and make interpersonal encounters more satisfying; and finally, (d) the person is emotionally disengaged from maltreating significant others and no longer views emotional encounters from a preoperational perspective. The sad truth is that not all patients fully respond; there are significant numbers who respond only to a moderate degree, whereas others don't respond at all.

My supervisory experiences in two national CBASP studies (Keller et al. 2000; Kocsis, 2002) involving 1,591 chronically depressed outpatients indicate that many patients at outcome fall short of optimal levels of functioning. It is generally assumed that combining psychotherapy with medication is the treatment of choice for chronically depressed outpatients. Nevertheless, based on the Keller et al. (2000) paper, 57 patients (25%) in the intent-to-treat combination group were classified as "nonresponders."

In numerous CBASP supervisor and psychotherapist teleconference calls between 1995 and the present time, the nonresponding patient remains the salient issue. Our discussions consistently place these individuals in one of four groups. For example, (1) nonresponders are unable to master the learning–performance demands of CBASP therapy; (2) they bring few social skills to treatment and appear unable to form interpersonal attachments; (3) they frequently evince chronic and severe (debilitating) economic stress and longstanding work-failure histories (i.e., many nonresponders are "poverty-line" individuals); and, finally, (4) these patients often present with chronic and severe Axis III illnesses (e.g., gross obesity, unmanageable asthma, chronic and severe pain, terminal illness). There are probably other patient characteristics that preclude response to treatment, but these are some of the more obvious ones. The possible moderating effect of these four patient characteristics needs to be determined. It remains to be demonstrated if our anecdotal observations have actually identified valid moderator response inhibitors.

Before suggesting several ways to disassemble or dismantle CBASP in future Stage II RCT investigations, I present and describe several instruments and methods that can be used to evaluate in-session acquisition learning, the first type of DV described above.

Performance Measures Reflecting In-Session Acquisition Learning

Situational Analysis

One of the goals of SA training is to demonstrate to patients the consequences of their behavior. I have noted in earlier chapters and elsewhere that learning to identify one's *stimulus value* and recognizing the effect one has on others—a perceptual set labeled *perceived functionality* (McCullough, 2000)—is the beginning of cure. The degree to which patients learn to recognize the interpersonal consequences of their behavior is assessed by the *Personal Questionnaire* (PQ).

The PQ is a data-gathering methodology developed by M.B. Shapiro (McCullough & Kasnetz, 1982; Shapiro, 1961, 1964; Shapiro, Litman, Nias, & Hendry, 1973); it is a self-report process-and-outcome procedure that is highly adaptable to many types of patient situations. As noted, rather than being a formal instrument, the PQ is a *patient self-report methodology* that can be used to rate the extent to which the patient(1) is able to recognize the interpersonal consequences of his or her behavior, or (2) is perceptually able to discriminate the person of the therapist from maltreating significant others. The PQ methodology, administration, and scoring rules used in CBASP are detailed in the following material.

STEP ONE. Three sentences reflecting a designated target behavior and, in this instance, degree of consequence recognition are constructed in the PQ: The statements denote *illness-level functioning* at baseline; *improvement-level functioning* during the process of therapy; and *recovery-level functioning* during the process of therapy. Each sentence is written on a 3 × 5 card, and the three cards are handed to the patient for a paired comparison rating task. The sentences used for consequence recognition are the following:

a. Card 1: an *illness-level sentence having very unpleasant implications:*

"Very rarely or never do I recognize the interpersonal effects I have on others."

b. Card 2: an *improvement-level sentence having moderately or slightly unpleasant implications:*

"Sometimes I recognize the interpersonal effects I have on others."

c. Card 3: a *recovery-level sentence having slightly or moderately pleasant implications:*

"Most of the time (more often than not) I recognize the interpersonal effects I have on others."

STEP TWO. Before the patient leaves the office following the third session, the secretary/research assistant will teach the individual how to make the paired comparison choices. The individual will be told that his or her therapist will NOT see the ratings until therapy ends. In addition, specific paired comparison rating instructions will be boldly written on the *PQ Patient Scoring Worksheet* (see Figure A.1) and the patient will be asked to read the instructions out loud. The secretary/research assistant will also explain that the paired comparison exercise *requires that the ratings must be based on how the patient is actually behaving right now and not on how he or she would like to behave*. The patient is then given the three cards (sorted randomly) and asked to compare each pair by selecting the card that best describes his or her behavior *right now*. The secretary/research assistant scores and records the paired comparisons. If "internally inconsistent" rating patterns occur, further instruction on completing the task is provided the next time the rating exercise is administered.

Patient: _____
                           (Print name)

Date/Session: _____

Examiner: _____
                         (Print name)

Instructions: Compare each 3 × 5 card one at a time with the other two cards. With each paired comparison, *circle* the card number below that best describes your behavior RIGHT NOW. Do <u>not</u> answer based on how you would like to behave but based on how you see yourself behaving RIGHT NOW.

Circle only one *card number* with each paired comparison:

CARD 1   versus   CARD 2
CARD 1   versus   CARD 3
CARD 2   versus   CARD 3

Figure A.1. Personal Questionnaire Scoring Worksheet.

Paired Comparison Procedures: The patient selects the sentence that is most descriptive of his or her behavior *right now* when Card 1 is compared to Card 2, Card 2 to 3, and when Card 1 is compared to Card 3. The PQ is administered at the end of the third session (sessions 1 and 2 are used for diagnosis and the Significant Other History exercise) and every third session thereafter (i.e., sessions 6, 9, 12, 15, 18, and so on).

STEP THREE. *Scoring Procedures:* There are four possible *internally consistent* rating patterns and four possible *internally inconsistent* patterns (Shapiro, 1961):

Internally Consistent Rating Patterns:
    Category I: Card 1 (*illness*) selected over 2 (*improvement*); Card 1 over 3 (*recovery*); Card 2 over 3 [weighted score = 4.0] = *illness*
    Category II: Card 2 over 1; Card 1 over 3; Card 2 over 3 [weighted score = 3.0] = *minimal improvement*
    Category III: Card 2 over 1; Card 3 over 1; Card 2 over 3 [weighted score = 2.0] = *significant improvement*
    Category IV: Card 2 over 1; Card 3 over 1; Card 3 over 2 [weighted score = 1.0] = *recovery*

PQ Summary Data Sheet

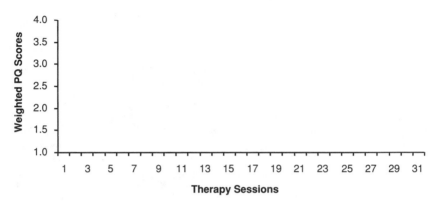

FIGURE A.2. Personal Questionnaire summary date sheet.

Internally Inconsistent Rating Patterns:

Category *V*: Card 1 *(illness)* over 2; *Card 3 *(recovery)* over 1; Card 2 *(improvement)* over 3 [weighted score = 2.5]

Category *VI*: Card 2 over 1; Card 1 over 3; *Card 3 over 2 [weighted score = 2.5]

Category *VII*: Card 1 over 2; Card 1 over 3; *Card 3 over 2 [weighted score = 3.5]

Category *VIII*: *Card 1 over 2; Card 3 over 1; Card 3 over 2 [weighted score = 1.5]

STEP FOUR. The weighted scores are plotted across sessions on the PQ Summary Data Sheet along with an *asterisk* used to indicate those sessions when the SA was administered. The *PQ Summary Data Sheet* is shown in Figure A.2.

STEP FIVE. A reliability estimate of the rating performance of each patient is obtained by dividing the number of *internally inconsistent* rating patterns by the total number of rating comparisons administered. The estimate is called the *grand reliability estimate* (Shapiro, 1961). For example, if 10 paired comparisons are administered over the course of therapy and 9 of 10 reflect internally consistent patterns, the grand reliability estimate = .90; 10 of 10 = 1.0, and so on.

Figure A.3 illustrates an example of a 24-session case in which the PQ ratings and the grand reliability estimate are shown.

Commentary: Pat completed the PQ every third session (from session 3 on) indicating his estimate of how well he was able to recognize the interpersonal effects of his behavior. It wasn't until the ninth session that he reported that "sometimes" he was able to identify the interpersonal consequences of his behavior. From that point on, Sam's recognition ratings improved. By the fifteenth session, the patient was recognizing the effects he was having on others "most of the time," suggesting

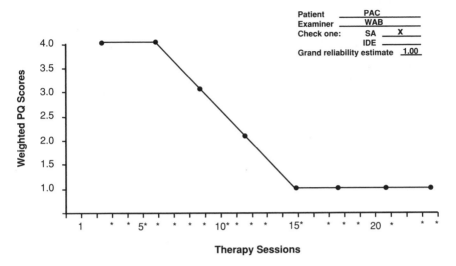

FIGURE A.3. Weighted PQ patient ratings across sessions showing the ability to recognize the interpersonal consequences of behavior. (Sessions when the SA was administered are indicated by an *asterisk*.)

that the acquisition of *perceived functionality*—a cognitive learning perspective denoting that a person is able to identify the interpersonal consequences he or she produces—was now in the learning repertoire. The PQ grand reliability estimate was 1.00, indicating that the patient's ratings had an excellent internal consistency. SA had been administered during most sessions, as indicated by the *asterisks* placed under the session numbers.

A second process measure illustrating how well patients learn to self-administer SA without therapist assistance is the Patient Performance Rating Scale (PPRF); construction of the scale, rater reliability estimates, and case examples are presented in Chapter 9 of McCullough (2000) and are not described here. As noted above, PPRF scores were found to be related to levels of therapeutic outcome (Manber et al., 2003; Manber & McCullough, 2000).

Contingent Personal Responsivity

The goals of CPR are (1) to modify maladaptive interpersonal behavior and (2) to demonstrate to patients that their verbal and nonverbal behaviors have specific interpersonal consequences on the clinician. The clinician makes explicit the patient's inextricable connection to the environment by consequating in-session behavior. There are many types of in-session maladaptive interpersonal behavior. The more familiar ones are listed below:

• Reflexive refusal to take seriously the consequation disclosures of the therapist (e.g., the patient reflexively says, "I'm sorry, I didn't mean to do that," and then emits the target behavior again; makes statements such as, "Surely you've been trained to deal with this"; "You surely are thin-skinned"; "See, I've just hurt you the way I hurt everyone else—I'm just worthless").

- Hostile and demeaning interpersonal comments directed toward the clinician (e.g., "You don't know how to help me"; "You don't know what you're doing"; "You're too young to know how to deal with problems like mine").
- Negative self-statements that interfere with the work of therapy (e.g., "I'll never be able to do that because I'm too *inadequate* "; "I'm a *nothing* of a person"; "Others have good reason to detest me—I'm *trash* "; "I'm *too guilty* to deserve anything good").
- Extreme passivity inhibiting the patient from taking any initiative (e.g., always sits quietly and waits for the therapist to take the lead).
- Active verbal avoidance designed to keep the therapist from addressing stressful topics (e.g., changing the subject, cracking jokes).
- Refusal to make eye contact with the clinician (e.g., keeps long hair in the face; sits facing away from the clinician; continues to look at the floor or the ceiling).
- Talks over the clinician and continues to talk regardless of what the clinician says or asks (e.g., inability to listen to anything the therapist says; continues to talk about the same subject, even when asked a question; pressured and monologic speech).
- Angry and exhibitionistic tirades expressed toward others that fill up the therapy hour (e.g., toward children, colleagues, spouse).
- Extreme verbal and nonverbal *friendly* compliance that doesn't lead to behavior change (e.g., always smiling; always nodding the head in agreement with therapist comments; completes homework perfectly but remains depressed).
- Refusal to complete homework or "extra-session" assignments.
- Habitual crying whenever life stress situations are addressed.
- Habitual lateness or missing of appointments.
- Active attempts to nurture/take care of the therapist (e.g., overly solicitous behavior; concerned that the therapist may be late for the next appointment or late getting home).
- Pervasive and frequently verbalized hopelessness that interferes with the work of therapy (e.g., "Nothing will ever be different"; "Nothing can work out for me").
- Beliefs about the therapist that are patently wrong but frequently articulated (e.g., "You could never care for me"; "We cannot have an authentic relationship because you are a professional"; "If I harmed myself, you'd get over it quickly").
- Excessive verbal and nonverbal self-pity (e.g., the extreme "poor me" reaction) that often follows real-world disappointments.
- Extreme withdrawal and social isolation (i.e., these patients are usually unmarried, live alone, are unemployed, and rarely leave their house or apartment).

These chronic patterns, when acted out in the session, significantly interfere with therapy progress. The effects of CPR administration are assessed in this manner:

STEP ONE. The patient's interpersonal pathological behavior is targeted and operationalized. For example, if a patient continues to make hostile-demeaning comments to the therapist, the comments are carefully pinpointed and defined as the *behavioral target* (e.g., patient statements that question the clinician's competence or that insinuate that the clinician doesn't know what he or she is doing). Target behavior occurrence is then recorded as either *frequency data* (e.g., number of hostile comments made during a taped segment) or as a *time-duration variable* (e.g., length of time patient cried during a videotaped segment or refused to make eye contact).

STEP TWO. Randomly select a 10-minute videotaped segment during session 1 and every fourth session thereafter and record the *frequency* or *duration* of the target behavior occurrence.

STEP THREE. The therapist's *consequation responses* are operationalized as follows: The response must label the patient's behavior or refer directly to it and include a personal response to the target behavior (e.g., "The comment you just made about my competence really hurt. Why do you want to treat me like this?" or, "Your crying makes me feel helpless—makes me feel that I cannot help you regardless of what I do").

STEP FOUR. A graph is plotted to illustrate the two sets of data: (a) the *frequency* or *duration* of the target behavior occurrence per videotaped segment; and (b) the *frequency* of therapist consequation responses during the segment. The rater also indicates if the therapist made a consequation response during the taped segment.

Two graphs are shown below that illustrate the change process results of CPR administered to two chronically depressed adults. One graph presents frequency data (Figure A.4) and the other (Figure A.5), duration data.

Commentary. Andrea, whose progress is graphed in Figure A.4, began therapy making frequent hostile–dominant statements to her therapist. She accused the

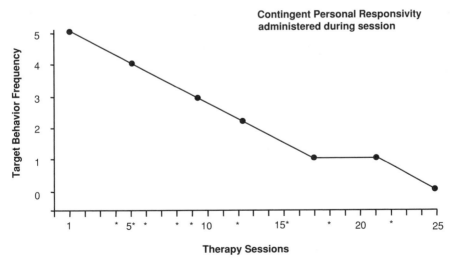

FIGURE A.4. Target behavior frequency occurring during 10-minute randomly selected video segments rated every fourth session. (Sessions when CPR was administered are indicated by an *asterisk*.)

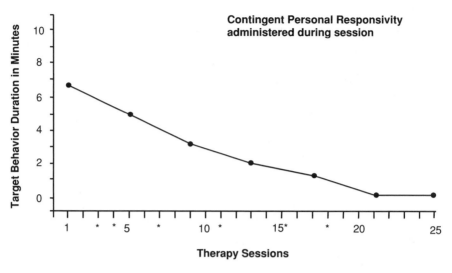

FIGURE A.5. Target behavior duration in minutes during 10-minute randomly selected video segments rated every fourth session. (Sessions when CPR was administered are indicated by an *asterisk*.)

clinical psychology practicum trainee of not knowing what she was doing, of being incompetent and ill-prepared to treat such a serious case. The patient set the hostile tone in the first session (verbal hostility defined as, " *Stay away from me!*") wherein five such statements were recorded on the taped segment. After watching the tape, operationalizing the hostile–dominant statements as the *behavioral target*, and then coding the frequency of the behavior during a 10-minute segment, the supervisor and student discussed the best way to consequate Andrea's behavior. The clinical student agreed that after the target behavior occurred, whenever appropriate, she would deliver a CPR by saying something like this:

"The comment you just made about my competency hurt—it stung me. The effect you have on me when you say such things is that it makes me want to keep my distance from you—to back off. Why do you want to keep me at a distance?"

From time to time, the therapist varied the actual wording of the CPR, but the consequation content of the message (i.e., "You just pushed me away by your comment") remained the same. The clinical student delivered CPR during sessions 4, 5, 6, 8, 9, 12, 15, 18, and 22, as indicated by the asterisks in Figure A.4, which shows a progressive decrease in the target behavior over time. The therapist successfully managed a very disruptive in-session behavior by using CPR to gain control over it.

Commentary. Hannah, whose progress is graphed in Figure A.5, cried throughout most of the early sessions. Her tears and sobs precluded serious discussion of any life issues. After the first session ended, the practitioner viewed the videotape and operationalized the *behavioral target* as "crying, wiping tears from the eyes, and/or sobbing sounds." He then randomly selected a 10-minute segment and recorded $6\frac{1}{2}$ minutes of crying. It was clear that the "duration of the target behavior" rather than its frequency, provided the best means to monitor change. The next step was deciding how he would administer CPR. He decided to make a statement like the following whenever the patient stopped crying and was able to attend:

"Your crying makes it impossible for the two of us to talk. I'm not able to talk while you are crying and we really need to discuss some serious things going on in your life. I'll wait until you stop crying and then we'll talk together."

CPR was delivered during sessions 3, 4, 7, 11, 15, and 18, as indicated by the asterisks. Taped segments were duration-coded every fourth session, and Figure A.5 illustrates that the patient's crying behavior gradually diminished over time. By session 21, the crying had stopped.

Interpersonal Discrimination Exercise

The goal of the IDE is to enable patients to make clear emotional discriminations between maltreating significant others and the psychotherapist.

The IDE, as described in Chapter 6, thrusts the therapist into a perceptual emotional arena involving the patient and significant others. Over time, the technique loosens the emotional connection between the patient and significant others and finally modifies the debilitating connections, replacing them with salubrious emotional connection to the clinician. I hypothesized that this process is accomplished when patients learn to emotionally discriminate the therapist from his or her maltreating significant others (McCullough, 2000).

Measuring emotional discrimination learning can be done using the *Personal Questionnaire* (PQ).

STEP ONE. Following session 2, the therapist, using the causal theory conclusions obtained during the Significant Other History, constructs one transference hypothesis. The transference hypothesis implicates one interpersonal domain (i.e. intimacy; personal disclosure of wants, needs or problems; making mistakes; expressing negative affect) as well as one or more maltreating significant others.

STEP TWO. Three statements, all reflecting levels of discrimination functioning in the transference hypothesis domain, are constructed in the PQ: an *illness-level* sentence; an *improvement-level* sentence; and a *recovery-level* sentence. Each sentence is written on a 3 × 5 card, and the three cards are handed to the patient for the paired comparison rating task.

a. Card 1: an *illness-level sentence having very unpleasant implications:*

"I feel that my therapist will end up being like, or behaving toward me like, my _____, _____, _____, _____" [significant others].

b. Card 2: an *improvement-level sentence having moderately or slightly unpleas-ant implications:*

"I feel that there is a possibility that my therapist will not end up being like, or behaving toward me like, my _____, _____, _____, _____" [significant others].

c. Card 3: a *recovery-level sentence having slightly or moderately pleasant impli-cations:*

"I feel that my therapist will not end up being like, or behaving toward me like, my _____, _____, _____, _____" [significant others].

STEP THREE. As noted, before the patient leaves the office following the third session, the secretary/research assistant teaches the individual how to make paired comparison ratings. The individual will be told that his or her therapist will *not* see the ratings until therapy ends. In addition, specific paired comparison rating instructions are written on the *PQ Scoring Worksheet* (see Figure A.1), and the patient is asked to read the instructions out loud. The secretary/research assistant will also explain that the paired comparisons require *"emotional comparisons"* to be made; that is, the comparisons must be based on how the patient actually feels about the therapist RIGHT NOW and not on how the patient would like to feel about the therapist. The patient will then be given the three cards (sorted randomly) and asked to compare each pair by selecting the card that reflects how he or she feels RIGHT NOW. The secretary/research assistant will score and record the paired comparisons. If *internally inconsistent* rating patterns are found, further instruction is provided the following week on the correct way to make the ratings. The sessions during which the IDE is administered are noted by an asterisk on the *PQ Summary Data Sheet.* The PQ is administered at the end of the third session and every third session thereafter (i.e., sessions 6, 9, 12, 15, 18, and so on; see Figure A.2).

STEP FOUR. A reliability estimate (the grand reliability estimate; Shapiro, 1961) of the rating performance of each patient is obtained by dividing the number of *internally inconsistent* rating patterns by the total number of rating comparisons administered.

Commentary. Larry, whose progress is graphed in Figure A.6, was administered the PQ at session 3 and every third session thereafter. One of the goals of the IDE is to help patients perceptually discriminate the person of the therapist from maltreating significant others. The PQ is used here as a self-estimate signifying the patient's degree of certainty in making the interpersonal discrimination.

The Significant Other History revealed that Larry had had a highly abusive developmental history, wherein he had been severely and verbally punished by his parents for any mistake. Mistakes he made around the home, from forgetting his chores to failure to "cut the grass perfectly," as well as mistakes in school performance led to severe parental verbal punishment. The clinician derived a

PQ Summary Data Sheet

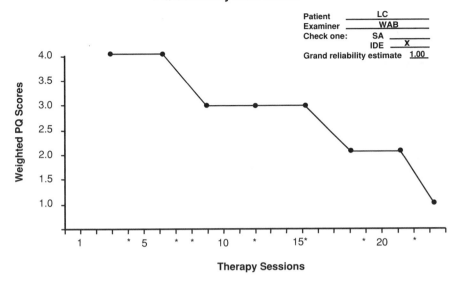

FIGURE A.6. Weighted PQ patient ratings across sessions showing the patient's ability to discriminate the therapist from maltreating significant others. (Sessions when the IDE was administered are indicated by an *asterisk*.)

transference hypothesis from Larry's causal theory conclusions: *"If I make a mistake around Dr. Roberts, then I will be severely criticized and reminded of what a screw-up I am."* Mistake events that occurred during treatment (e.g., a missed appointment, SA homework done inappropriately or that contained obvious mistakes) became "hot spot" situations that resulted in the therapist's administering the IDE.

Figure A.6 graphs Larry's difficulty in perceptually differentiating the person of the therapist from his significant others. It took 18 sessions before he began to gain a moderate degree of certainty that his therapist would not turn out to be like his parents. Certainty was realized during the final PQ administration when he achieved a PQ rating of 1.0 ("I feel that my therapist will not end up being like, or behaving toward me like, my parents."). The asterisks denote that the IDE was administered during sessions 4, 7, 8, 12, 15, 19, and 22. The grand reliability estimate over multiple PQ administrations achieved strong reliability (1.00).

GTE Measures That Can Be Used in Future Stage II Trials

CBASP researchers seeking to answer questions pertaining to the mediating effects of disciplined personal involvement or pretreatment patient characteristics that may inform outcome can utilize many of the GTE measures employed in previous CBASP studies. Suggested measures are listed below.

Suggested GTE Instruments Assessing Treatment Outcome:

1. Comorbid Axis I (SCID-P; First, Spitzer, Gibbon, & Williams, 1995) and Axis II diagnostic status at baseline and outcome (SCID-II; First, Spitzer, Gibbon, Williams, & Benjamin, 1994)
2. Process and outcome depression intensity levels assessed by the self-report Beck Depression Inventory-II (BDI-II: Beck, 1996) and/or by the rater-administered HAM-D-24 (24-item Hamilton Depression Rating Scale; Hamilton, 1967; Keller et al., 1998; Keller et al., 2000)
3. Baseline and outcome work status and satisfaction assessed by the Longitudinal Interval Follow-up Evaluation (LIFE; Keller et al., 1987)
4. Patient interpersonal style changes reflected in the IMI (Kiesler & Schmidt, 1993)
5. Changes in the quality of the marital relationship measured by the Dyadic Adjustment Scale (DAS; Spanier, 1976)
6. Baseline and outcome patient quality-of-life assessed by the Quality of Life Enjoyment and Satisfaction Questionnaire (Q-LES-Q; Endicott, Nee, Harrison, & Blumenthal, 1993).

Suggested Moderator Variable Measures:

1. Patient demographic characteristics
2. Economic status assessed by the Hollingshead Index (Hollingshead, 1975)
3. Available social support network estimated by the Interpersonal Support Evaluation List (ISEL; Cohen, Mermelstein, Kamarck, & Hoberman, 1985)
4. Current psychosocial functioning level determined by the Global Assessment of Functioning Scale—Revised (GAF-R; McCullough, 1996) and the LIFE (Keller et al., 1987)
5. Present DSM-IV (American Psychiatric Association, 1994) Axis III health status (SF-36: Medical Outcomes Study 36 Item Short-Form Health Survey; Ware & Sherbourne, 1992)
6. Clinician interpersonal style as measured by the IMI (Kiesler & Schmidt, 1993)
7. Quality of the therapeutic alliance assessed by the Working Alliance Inventory (WAI; Horvath and Greenberg, 1989; Tracey & Kokotovic, 1989).

Summary of Remaining Stage II Research Questions

In summary, four questions remain to be answered in future CBASP Stage II research trials:

1. What *pretreatment characteristics* of chronically depressed outpatients may moderate (inhibit) response to treatment?
2. When *disciplined personal involvement* is administered with *Situational Analysis* (the basic CBASP technique), does disciplined personal involvement have a mediating effect on treatment outcome?

A *dismantling design* comparing three conditions could be employed to answer this question: (a) CBASP with SA *and* disciplined personal involvement *versus* (b) CBASP with SA (*no* disciplined personal involvement) *versus* (c) CBASP with disciplined personal involvement (*no* SA).

3. If disciplined personal involvement is found to be a significant mediating variable, is *contingent personal responsivity* or the *Interpersonal Discrimination Exercise* the active ingredient?

4. Do the two measures associated with Situational Analysis (viz., the PPRF and the PQ) and the PQ measure associated with the Interpersonal Discrimination Exercise predict treatment outcome when administered at therapy midpoint?

References

Ahern, S., & Bailey, K.G. (1997). *Families-by-choice: Finding families in a world of strangers*. Minneapolis: Fairview Press.

Ainsworth, M.D.S., Blehar, M.C., Waters, E., & Wall, S. (1978). *Patterns of attachment: A psychological study of the Strange Situation*. Hillsdale, NJ: Erlbaum.

Akiskal, H.S., & McKinney, W.T. (1973). Depressive disorders: Toward a unified hypothesis. *Science, 182*, 20–28.

Akiskal, H.S., & McKinney, W.T. (1975). Overview of recent research in depression: Integration of ten conceptual models into a comprehensive clinical picture. *Archives of General Psychiatry, 32*, 285–305.

American Psychiatric Association. (1994). *Diagnostic and statistical manual of mental disorders* (4th ed.). Washington, DC: Author.

American Psychological Association. (2002). *Ethical principles of psychologists and code of Conduct*. Washington, DC: Author.

Anchin, J.C., & Kiesler, D.J. (1982). *Handbook of interpersonal psychotherapy*. Elmsford, NY: Pergamon.

Aron, L. (1996). *A meeting of minds: mutuality in psychoanalysis*. Hillsdale, NJ: Analytic Press.

Ayllon, T., & Azrin, N.H. (1968). *The token economy: A motivational system for therapy and rehabilitation*. New York: Appleton-Century-Crofts.

Bailey, K.G. (1987). *Human paleopsychology: Applications to aggression and pathological processes*. Hillsdale, NJ: Erlbaum.

Bailey, K.G. (1988). Psychological kinship: Implications for the helping professions. *Psychotherapy, 25*, 132–142.

Bailey, K.G. (1997, September). *Evolutionary kinship theory: Merging integrative psychotherapy with the new kinship psychotherapy*. Paper presented at the annual meeting of the Across-Species Comparisons and Psychopathology (ASCAP) Society, Tucson, AZ.

Bailey, K.G. (2000). Evolution, kinship, and psychotherapy: Promoting psychological health through human relationships. In P. Gilbert & K.G. Bailey (Eds.), *Genes on the couch: Explorations in evolutional psychotherapy* (pp. 42–67). Philadelphia: Taylor & Francis.

Bailey, K.G. (2002). Recognizing, assessing, and classifiying others: Cognitive bases of evolutionary kinship therapy. *Journal of Cognitive Therapy: An International Quarterly, 16*, 367–383.

Bailey, K.G., & Wood, H.E. (1998). Evolutionary kinship theory: Basic principles and treatment implications. *British Journal of Medical Psychology, 71*, 509–523.

Bailey, K.G., Wood, H.E., & Nava, G.R. (1992). What do clients want? Role of psychological kinship in professional helping. *Journal of Psychotherapy Integration*, 2, 125–147.

Balint, M. (1968). *The basic fault*. London: Tavistock.

Bandura, A. (1961). Psychotherapy as a learning process. *Psychological Bulletin*, 58, 143–159.

Bandura, A. (1969). *Principles of behavior modification*. New York: Holt, Rinehart & Winston.

Bandura, A. (1976). Effecting change through participant modeling. In J.D. Krumboltz & C.E. Thoresen (Eds.), *Counseling methods* (pp. 248–265). New York: Holt, Rinehart & Winston.

Bandura, A. (1977). *Social learning theory*. Englewood Cliffs, NJ: Prentice-Hall.

Bandura, A., Lipsher, D.H., & Miller, P.E. (1960). Psychotherapists' approach–avoidance reactions to patient's expressions of hostility. *Journal of Consulting Psychology*, 24, 1–18.

Bandura, A., & Walters, R.H. (1964). *Social learning and personality development*. New York: Holt, Rinehart & Winston.

Barber, J.P., Luborsky, L., Crits-Cristoph, P., et al. (1999). Therapeutic alliance as a predictor of outcome in treatment of cocaine dependence. *Psychotherapy Research*, 9, 54–73.

Barlow, D.H. (2004). Psychological treatments. *American Psychologist*, 59, 869–878.

Barlow, D.H., & Durand, V.M. (1999). *Abnormal psychology* (2nd ed.). Pacific Grove, CA: Brooks/Cole.

Barrett, M.S., & Berman, J.S. (2001). Is psychotherapy more effective when therapists disclose information about themselves? *Journal of Consulting and Clinical Psychology*, 69, 597–603.

Beck, A.T. (1996). *Beck Depression Inventory–II*. San Antonia: Psychological Corporation.

Beck, A.T., Rush, A.J., Shaw, B.F., & Emery, G. (1979). *Cognitive therapy of depression*. New York: Guilford Press.

Beier, E.G. (1966). *The silent language of psychotherapy*. Chicago: Aldine.

Blanchard, E.B. (1977). Behavioral medicine: A perspective. In R.B. Williams & W.D. Gentry (Eds.), *Behavioral approaches to medical treatment* (pp. 1–13). Cambridge, MA: Ballinger.

Bleuler, M. (1991). The concept of schizophrenia in Europe during the past one-hundred years. In W.F. Flack, D.R. Miller, & M. Wiener (Eds.), *What is schizophrenia?* (pp. 1–15). New York: Springer-Verlag.

Bordin, E. (1979). The generalizability of the psychoanalytic concept of the working alliance. *Psychotherapy: Theory, Research, and Practice*, 16, 252–260.

Bordin, E. (1994). Theory and research in the therapeutic working alliance: New directions. In A.O. Horvath & L.S. Greenberg (Eds.), *The working alliance: Theory, research, and practice* (pp. 13–37). New York: Wiley.

Borys, D., & Pope, K.S. (1989). Dual relationships between therapist and client: A national study of psychologists, psychiatrists, and social workers. *Professional Psychology: Research and Practice*, 20, 283–293.

Bowlby, J. (1982). *Attachment and loss: Vol. I. Attachment*. New York: Basic Books. (Original work published 1969).

Bowlby, J. (1973). *Attachment and loss: Vol. II. Separation, anxiety and fear*. New York: Basic Books.

Bowlby, J. (1980). *Attachment and loss: Vol. III. Loss: Sadness and depression*. New York: Basic Books.

Bridges, N.A. (2001). Therapist's self-disclosure: Expanding the comfort zone. *Psychotherapy: Theory, Research, Practice, Training, 38*, 21–30.

Brown, G.W., & Moran, P. (1994). Clinical and psychosocial origins of chronic depressive episodes: I. A community survey. *British Journal of Psychiatry, 165*, 447–456.

Browning, R.M., & Stover, D.O. (1971). *Behavior modification in child treatment: An experimental and clinical approach.* New York: Aldine-Atherton.

Cashdan, S. (1973). *Interactional psychotherapy: Stages and strategies in behavioral change.* New York: Grune & Stratton.

Chambless, D.L. (2002). Beware of the dodo bird: The dangers of overgeneralization. *Clinical Psychology: Science and Practice, 9*, 13–16.

Cicchetti, D., Ackerman, B.P., & Izard, C.E. (1995). Emotions and emotion regulation in developmental psychopathology. *Development and Psychopathology, 7*, 1–10.

Cicchetti, D., & Barnett, D. (1991). Attachment organization in maltreatred preschoolers. *Development and Psychopathology, 3*, 397–411.

Cicchetti, D., & Toth, S.L. (1998). The development of depression in children and adolescents. *American Psychologist, 53*, 221–241.

Cicchetti, D., & White, J. (1988). Emotional development and the affective disorders. In W. Damon (Ed.), *Child development: Today and tomorrow* (pp. 172–193). San Francisco: Jossey-Bass.

Cohen, S., Mermelstein, R., Kamarck, T., & Hoberman, H. (1985). Measuring the functional components of social support. In I. G. Sarason & B.R. Sarason (Eds.), *Social support: Theory, research, and applications.* pp. 73–94. Boston: Martinus Nijhoff.

Constantino, M.J., Castonguay, L.G., & Schut, A.J. (2002). The working alliance: A flagship for the "scientist-practitioner" model in psychotherapy. In G. Tryon (Ed.), *Counseling based on process research* (pp. 81–131). New York: Allyn & Bacon.

Conway, J.B. (1987). *A clinical interpersonal perspective for personality and psychotherapy: Some research examples.* Paper presented to the Department of Psychology, University of British Columbia, Vancouver, British Columbia, Canada.

Cowan, P.A. (1978). *Piaget with feeling: Cognitive, social, and emotional dimensions.* New York: Holt, Rinehart & Winston.

Davidson, R. (1991). Cerebral asymmetry and affective disorders: A developmental perspective. In D. Cicchetti & L.S. Toth (Eds.), *Rochester symposium on developmental psychopathology: Vol. 2. Internalizing and externalizing Expressions of dysfunction* (pp. 123–154). Hillsdale, NJ: Erlbaum.

Dewey, J. (1997). *Democracy and education: An introduction to the philosophy of education.* New York: Free Press. (Original work published 1916)

DiSalvo, C., & McCullough, J.P., Jr. (2002). Treating a chronically depressed adolescent female using the Cognitive Behavioral Analysis System of Psychotherapy. *Journal of Contemporary Psychology, 32*, 273–280.

Drotar, D., & Sturm, L. (1991). Psychosocial influences in the etiology, diagnosis, and prognosis of nonorganic failure to thrive. In H.E. Fitzgerald, B.M. Lester, & M.W. Yogman (Eds.), *Theory and research in behavioral pediatrics* (pp. 19–59). New York: Plenum press.

Durbin, C.E., Klein, D.N., & Schwartz, J.E. (2000). Predicting the $2^1/_2$-year outcome of dysthymic disorder: The roles of childhood adversity and family history of psychopathology. *Journal of Consulting and Clinical Psychology, 68*, 57–63.

Endicott, J., Nee, J., Harrison, W., & Blumenthal, R. (1993). Quality of Life Enjoyment and Satisfaction Questionnaire: A new measure. *Psychopharmacology Bulletin, 29*, 321–326.

Engel, G.L. (1977). The need for a new medical model: A challenge to biomedicine. *Science*, *196*, 129–136.

Epstein, L., & Feiner, A.H. (1979) (Eds.). *Countertransference*. New York: Jason Aronson.

Ferenczi, S. (1932). *The clinical diary of Sandor Ferenzi*. J. Dupont, M. Baliant, & N.Z. Jackson (Eds.). Cambridge, MA: Harvard University Press.

First, M.B., Spitzer, R.L., Gibbon, M., & Williams, J.B.W. (1995). *Structured Clinical Interview for DSM-IV Axis I Disorders: Patient Edition* (SCID-P). New York: Biometrics Research Department, New York State Psychiatric Institute.

First, M.B., Spitzer, R.L., Gibbon, M., Williams, J.B.W., & Benjamin, L. (1994). Structured Clinical Interview for DSM-IV Axis II Personality Disorders (SCID-II). New York: Biometrics Research Department, New York State Psychiatric Institute.

Foa, E.B, Dancu, C, V., Hembree, E.A., Jaycox, L.H., Meadows, E.A., & Street, G.P. (1999). A comparison of exposure therapy, stress inoculation training, and their combination for reducing posttraumatic stress disorder in female assault victims. *Journal of Consulting and Clinical Psychology*, *67*, 194–200.

Foa, E.B., & Rothbaum, B.O. (1998). *Treating the trauma of rape: Cognitive–Behavioral therapy for PTSD*. New York: Guilford Press.

Folkman, S., & Lazarus, R.S. (1988). *Ways of Coping Questionnaire: Manual, test, booklet, scoring key*. Palo Alto, CA: Mind Garden.

Freire, P. (2000). *Pedagogy of the oppressed*. New York: Continuum International.

Freud, S. (1938). *The basic writings of Sigmund Freud* (A.A. Brill, Trans.). New York: Modern Library.

Freud, S. (1956). *The interpretation of dreams* (J. Strachey, Trans.). New York: Basic Books.

Freud, S. (1963). *Character and culture*. New York: Collier Books.

Garber, J., Quiggle, N., Panak, W., & Dodge, K. (1991). Aggression and depression in children: Comorbidity, specificity, and social cognitive processing. In D. Cicchetti & S.L. Toth (Eds.), *Rochester symposium on developmental psychopathology: Vol. 2. Internalizing and externalizing expressions of dysfunction* (pp. 225–264). Hillsdale, NJ: Erlbaum.

Gendlin, E.T. (1964). A theory of personality change. In P.Worchel & D. Byrne (Eds.), *Personality change* (pp. 102–148). New York: Wiley.

Gendlin, E.T. (1968). The experimental response. In E. Hammer (Ed.), *Use of interpretation in treatment* (pp. 208–228). New York: Grune & Stratton.

Gendlin, E.T. (1970). Research in psychotherapy with schizophrenic patients and the nature of that "illness." In J.T. Hart & T.M. Tomlinson (Eds.), *New directions in client-centered therapy* (p. 288). Boston: Houghton Mifflin.

Gendlin, E.T. (1974). Client-centered and experiential psychotherapy. In D. Wexler & L. Rice (Eds.), *Innovations in client-centered therapy* (pp. 211–216). New York: Wiley.

Gendlin, E.T. (1979). Experiential psychotherapy. In R. Corsini (Ed.), *Current psychotherapies*. (2nd ed., pp. 340–373). Itasca, Il: Peacock.

Gendlin, E.T., & Berlin, J. (1961). Galvanic skin response correlates: Differential modes of experiencing. *Journal of Clinical Psychology*, *17*, 73–77.

Gentry, W.D. (1984). Behavioral medicine: A new research paradigm. In W.D. Gentry (Ed.), *Handbook of behavior medicine* (pp. 1–12). New York: Guilford Press.

Ghent, E. (1989). Credo: The dialectics of one-person and two-person psychologies. *Contemporary Psychoanalysis*, *25*, 169–211.

Gilbert, P., & Bailey, K.G. (Eds) (2000). *Genes on the couch: Explorations in evolutionary psychotherapy*. Philadelphia: Taylor & Francis.

Goldfried, M., & Davison, G. (1974). *Clinical behavior therapy*. New York: Holt, Rinehart & Winston.

Goldfried, M., & Davison, G. (1994). *Clinical behavior therapy* (expanded ed.). New York: Wiley.

Gordon, D.E. (1988). Formal operations and interpersonal and affective disturbances in adolescents. In E.D. Nannis & P.A. Coward (Eds.), *Developmental psychopathology and its treatment* (pp. 51–73). San Francisco: Jossey-Bass.

Green, M.W. (Fall, 2004). From the editor. *Virginia Academy of Clinical Psychology Psychogram, 29*, 3.

Greenberg, J. (1995a). Psychoanalytic technique and the interactive matrix. *Psychoanalytic Quarterly, 64*, 1–22.

Greenberg, J. (1995b). Self-disclosure: Is it psychoanalytic? *Contemporary Psychoanalysis, 31*, 193–205.

Greenberg, L.S., Rice, L.N., & Elliott, R. (1993). *Facilitating emotional change: The moment-by-moment process*. New York: Guilford Press.

Greenson, R. (1967). *The technique and practice of psychoanalysis*. New York: International Universities Press.

Greenson, R. (1971). The real relationship between the patient and the psychoanalyst. In M. Kanzer (Ed.), *The unconscious today* (pp. 213–232). New York: International Universities Press.

Guidano, V.F., & Liotti, G. (1983). *Cognitive processes and emotional processes*. New York: Guilford Press.

Hamilton, M. (1967). Development of a rating scale of primary depressive illness. *British Journal of Social and Clinical Psychology, 6*, 278–296.

Hammen, C. (1988). Self-cognitions, stressful events, and the prediction of depression in children of depressed mothers. *Journal of Abnormal Child Psychology, 16*, 347–360.

Hammen, C. (1992). Cognitive, life stress, and interpersonal approaches to a developmental model of depression. *Development and Psychopathology, 4*, 189–206.

Hathaway, S.R., & McKinley, J.C. (1943). *Manual for the Minnesota Multiphasic Personality Inventory*. New York: Psychological Corporation.

Hembree, E.A., Rausch, S.A., & Foa, E.B. (2003). Beyond the manual: The insider's guide to prolonged exposure therapy for PTSD. *Cognitive and Behavioral Practice, 10*, 22–30.

Herson, M., & Barlow, D.H. (1976). *Single case experimental designs: Strategies for behavior change*. New York: Pergamon Press.

Hilgard, E.R., & Bower, G.H. (1966). *Theories of learning* (3rd ed.). New York: Appleton-Century-Crofts.

Hill, C.A., & Knox, S. (2002). Self-disclosure. In J.C. Norcross (Ed.), *Psychotherapy relationships that work: Therapist contributions and responsiveness to patients*. (pp. 255–265). Oxford, UK: Oxford University Press.

Hill, C.A., & O'Brien, K. (1999). *Helping skills: Facilitating exploration, insight, and action*. Washington, DC: American Psychological Association.

Hoffer, A. (2000). Neutrality and the therapeutic alliance: What does the analyst want? In S.T. Levy (Ed.), *The therapeutic alliance*. Madison, WS: International Universities Press.

Holahan, C.J., Moos, R.H., Holahan, C.K., & Cronkite, R.C. (2000). Long-term post treatment functioning among patients with unipolar depression: An integrative model. *Journal of Consulting and Clinical Psychology, 68*, 226–232.

Hollingshead, A.B. (1975). *Four-factor index of social status*. New Haven, CT: Yale University, Department of Sociology.

Horvath, A.O. (1994). Research on the alliance. In A.O. Horvath & L.S. Greenberg (Eds.), *The working alliance: Theory, research, and practice* (pp. 259–286). New York: Wiley.

Horvath, A.O. (1995). The therapeutic relationship: From transference to alliance. *Journal of Clinical Psychology/In Session, 1*, 7–17.

Horvath, A.O., & Greenberg, L.S. (1989). Development and validation of the Working Alliance Inventory. *Journal of Counseling Psychology, 36*, 223–233.

Horvath, A.O., & Greenberg, L.S. (Eds.) (1994). *The working alliance: Theory, research, and practice*. New York: Wiley.

Horvath, A.O., & Luborsky, L. (1993). The role of the therapeutic alliance in psychotherapy. *Journal of Consulting and Clinical Psychology, 61*, 561–573.

Horwitz, J.A. (2001). *Early-onset versus late-onset chronic depressive disorders: Comparison of retrospective reports of coping with adversity in the childhood home environment.* Unpublished master's thesis, Virginia Commonwealth University, Richmond, VA.

Hyman, S.E. (2000). The millennium of mind, brain, and behavior. *Archives of General Psychiatry, 57*, 88–89.

Izard, C.E. (1993). Four systems for emotional activation: Cognitive and non-cognitive processes. *Psychological Review, 100*, 68–90.

Jehle, P.J., & McCullough, J. P. Jr., (2002). Treatment of chronic major depression using the Cognitive Behavioral Analysis System of Psychotherapy. *Journal of Contemporary Psychology, 32*, 263–271.

Jones, E. (1953). *The life and work of Sigmund Freud* (Vol. I). New York: Basic Books.

Kagan, J., Snidman, N., Marcel, Z., & Peterson, F. (1999). Infant temperament and anxious symptoms in school age children. *Development and Psychopathology, 11*, 209–224.

Kazdin, A. (2001). Progression of therapy research and clinical application of treatment require better understanding of the change process. *Clinical Psychology: Science and Practice, 8*, 143–151.

Keller, M.B., Gelenberg, A.J., Hirschfeld, R.M.A., et al. (1998). The treatment of chronic depression, Part 2: A double-blind, randomized trial of sertraline and imipramine. *Journal of Clinical Psychiatry, 59*, 598–607.

Keller, M.B., & Hanks, D.L. (1994). The natural history and heterogeneity of depressive disorders. *Journal of Clinical Psychiatry, 56*, 22–29.

Keller, M.B., Lavori, P.W., Friedman, B., et al. (1987). The Longitudinal Follow-up Evaluation: A comprehensive method for assessing outcome in prospective longitudinal studies. *Archives of General Psychiatry, 44*, 540–548.

Keller, M.B., Lavori, P.W., Rice, J., Coryell, W., & Hirschfeld, R.M.A. (1986). The persistent risk of chronicity in recurrent episodes of nonbipolar major depressive disorder: A prospective follow-up. *American Journal of Psychiatry, 143*, 24–28.

Keller, M.B., McCullough, J.P., Klein, D.N., et al. (2000). A comparison of nefazodone, the Cognitive Behavioral Analysis System of Psychotherapy, and their combination for the treatment of chronic depression. *New England Journal of Medicine, 342*, 1462–1470.

Kendler, K.S., Walters, E.E., & Kessler, R.C. (1997). The prediction of length of major depressive episodes: Results from an epidemiological study of female twins. *Psychological Medicine, 27*, 107–117.

Kiesler, D.J. (1983). The 1982 interpersonal circle: A taxonomy for complementarity in human transactions. *Psychological Review, 90*, 185–214.

Kiesler, D.J. (1985). *The 1982 interpersonal circle. Acts version.* Unpublished manuscript, Virginia Commonwealth University, Richmond, VA.

Kiesler, D.J. (1986a). The 1982 interpersonal circle: An analysis of DSM-III personality disorders. In T. Millon & G. L. Klerman (Eds.), *Contemporary perspectives in psychopathology: Toward the DSM-IV*. New York: Guilford Press.

Kiesler, D.J. (1986b). Interpersonal methods of diagnosis and treatment. In J.O. Cavenoar (Ed.), *Psychiatry*. Philadelphia: Lippincott.

Kiesler, D.J. (1988). *Therapeutic metacommunication: Therapist impact disclosure as feedback in psychotherapy*. Palo Alto, CA: Consulting Psychologist Press.

Kiesler, D.J. (1996). *Contemporary interpersonal theory and research: Personality, psychopathology, and psychotherapy*. New York: Wiley.

Kiesler, D.J. (1999). *Beyond the disease model of mental disorders*. Westport, CT: Praeger.

Kiesler, D.J., & Schmidt, J.A. (1993). *The Impact Message Inventory: Form IIA Octant Scale Version*. Palo Alto, CA: Mind Garden.

Kiesler, D.J., Van Denburg, T.F., Sikes-Nova, V.E., Larus, J.P., & Goldston, C.S. (1990). Interpersonal behavior profiles of eight cases of DSM-III personality disorder. *Journal of Clinical Psychology, 46*, 440–453.

Kiesler, D.J., & Watkins, L.M. (1989). Interpersonal complementarity and the therapeutic alliance: A study of relationship in psychotherapy. *Psychotherapy, 26*, 183–194.

Klein, D.N., Schwartz, J.E., Santiago, N.J., et al. (2003). Therapeutic alliance in depression treatment: Controlling for prior change and patient characteristics. *Journal of Consulting and Clinical Psychology, 71*, 997–1006.

Klerman, G.L., Weissman, M.M., Rounsaville, B.J., & Chevron, E.S. (1984). *Interpersonal psychotherapy of depression*. New York: Basic Books.

Knox, S., Hess, S.A., Petersen, D.A., & Hill, C.E. (1997). A qualitative analysis of client perceptions of the effects of helpful therapist self-disclosure in long-term therapy. *Journal of Counseling Psychotherapy, 44*, 274–283.

Kocsis, J.H. (2002). CBASP augmentation in the treatment of chronic depression. NIMH Treatment Application: Revamp—research to evaluate validation of augmenting medication and psychotherapy. In progress.

Kraemer, H.C., Wilson, G.T., Fairburn, C.G., & Agras, W.S. (2002). Mediators and moderators of treatment effects in randomized clinical trials. *Archives of General Psychiatry, 59*, 877–883.

Lambert, M.J. (1992). Psychotherapy outcome research. In J.C. Norcross & M.R. Goldfried (Eds.), *Handbook of psychotherapy integration* (pp. 94–129). New York: Basic Books.

Lambert, M.J., & Bergin, A.E. (1994). The effectiveness of psychotherapy. In A.E. Bergin & S.L. Garfield (Eds.), *Handbook of psychotherapy and behavior change* (4th ed., pp. 143–189). New York: Wiley.

Lazarus, R.H. (1966). *Psychological stress and the coping process*. New York: McGraw-Hill.

Lazarus, R.H. (1984). On the primacy of cognition. *American Psychologist, 39*, 124–129.

Lazarus, R.H. (1990). Theory-based stress management. *Psychological Inquiry, 1*, 3–13.

Lazarus, R.H., & Alfert, E. (1964). Short-circuiting of threat by experimentally altering cognitive appraisal. *Journal of Abnormal and Social Psychology, 69*, 195–205.

Lazarus, R.H., Opton, E.M., Markellos, S., Nomikos, M.S. & Rankin, N.O. (1965). The principle of short-circuiting of threat: Further evidence. *Journal of Personality, 33*, 622–635.

Leary, T. (1957). *Interpersonal diagnosis of personality*. New York: Ronald.

Levy, S.T. (2000). (Ed.) *The therapeutic alliance*. Madison, WS: International Universities Press.

Linehan, M.M. (1993). *Cognitive–behavioral treatment of borderline personality disorder*. New York: Guilford Press.

Lizardi, H., Klein, D.N., Ouimette, P.C., Riso, L.P., Anderson, R.L., and Donaldson, S.K. (1995). Reports of the childhood home environment in early-onset dysthymia and episodic major depression. *Journal of Abnormal Psychology, 104*, 132–139.

Luborsky, L., McLellan, A.T., & Woody, G.E. (1985). Therapist success and its determinants. *Archives of General Psychiatry, 42*, 602–611.

Luborsky, L., Rosenthal, R., Diguer, L., et al. (2002). The dodo bird verdict is alive and well—mostly. *Clinical Psychology: Science and Practice, 9*, 2–12.

Luborsky, L., Singer, B., & Luborsky, L. (1975). Comparative studies of psychotherapy: Is it true that "Everyone has won and all must have prizes"? *Archives of General Psychiatry, 32*, 995–1008.

Mahoney, M.J. & Mahoney, K. (1976). *Permanent weight control*. New York: Norton.

Manber, R.M., Arnow, B.A., Blasey, C., et al. (2003). Patient's therapeutic skill acquisition and response to psychotherapy, alone or in combination with medication. *Journal of Psychological Medicine, 33*, 693–702.

Manber, R.M., & McCullough, J.P., Jr. (2000, November). *Patient Performance Rating Scale: PPRS*. Paper presented at the 34th annual meeting of the American Association of Behavior Therapists, New Orleans, LA.

Manning, E.A. (2005). Wrestling with vulnerability: Countertransference disclosure and the training therapist. *Psychotherapy Bulletin, 40*, 5–11.

Markowitz, J.C. (2002). *Manual for the administration of brief supportive psychotherapy*. Unpublished manuscript, Cornell University, New York.

Maroda, K. (1999a). *Seduction, surrender, and transformation: Emotional engagement in the analytic process*. Hillsdale, NJ: Analytic Press.

Maroda, K. (1999b). Creating an intersubject context for self-disclosure. *Smith College Studies in Social Work, 69*, 475–489.

Martin, D.J., Garske, J.P., & Davis, M.K. (2000). Relation of the therapeutic alliance with outcome and other variables: A meta-analytic review. *Journal of Consulting and Clinical Psychology, 68*, 438–450.

May, R. (1958). Contributions of existential psychotherapy. In R. May, E. Angel, & H.F. Ellenberger (Eds.), *Existence: A new dimension in psychiatry and psychology*. (p. 079). New York: Basic Books.

McCullough, J.P., Jr. (1984a). Cognitive Behavioral Analysis System of Psychotherapy: An interactional treatment approach for dysthymic disorder. *Psychiatry, 47*, 234–250.

McCullough, J.P., Jr. (1984b). The need for new single-case design structure in applied cognitive psychology. *Psychotherapy: Theory, Research, and Practice, 21*, 389–400.

McCullough, J.P., Jr. (1984c). Single-case investigative research and its relevance for the nonoperant clinician. *Psychotherapy: Theory, Research, and Practice, 21*, 382–388.

McCullough, J.P., Jr. (1996). Global Assessment of Functioning Scale—Revised (GAF-R). Unpublished scale, Virginia Commonwealth University, Richmond, VA.

McCullough, J.P., Jr. (1991). Psychotherapy for dysthymia: Naturalistic study of ten cases. *Journal of Nervous and Mental Disease, 179*, 734–740.

McCullough, J.P., Jr. (2000). *Treatment for chronic depression: Cognitive Behavioral Analysis System of Psychotherapy* (CBASP). New York: Guilford Press.

McCullough, J.P., Jr. (2001). *Skills training manual for diagnosing and treating chronic depression: Cognitive Behavioral Analysis System of Psychotherapy*. New York: Guilford Press.

McCullough, J.P., Jr. (2003a). *Patient's manual for CBASP*. New York: Guilford Press.

McCullough, J.P., Jr. (2003b). Treatment for chronic depression using Cognitive Behavioral Analysis System of Psychotherapy (CBASP). *Journal of Clinical Psychology: In Session, 59*, 833–846.

McCullough, J.P., Jr. (2003c). Treatment for chronic depression using Cognitive Behavioral Analysis System of Psychotherapy (CBASP). *Journal of Psychotherapy Integration, 13*, 241–263.

McCullough, J.P., Jr. & Carr, K.F. (1987). Stage process design: A predictive confirmation structure for the single case. *Psychotherapy: Theory, Research, and Practice, 24*, 759–768.

McCullough, J.P., Jr. Cornell, J.E., McDaniel, M.H., & Mueller, R.K. (1974). Utilization of the simultaneous treatment design to improve student behavior in a first-grade classroom. *Journal of Consulting and Clinical Psychology, 42*, 288–292.

McCullough, J.P., & Kasnetz, M.D. (1982). *Manual for the construction and scoring of the personal questionnaire*. Unpublished manuscript, Virginia Commonwealth University, Richmond, VA.

McCullough, J.P., Jr. Kasnetz, M.D., Braith, J.A., et al. (1988). A longitudinal study of an untreated sample of predominantly late-onset characterological dysthymia. *Journal of Nervous and Mental Disease, 176*, 658–667.

McCullough, J.P., Jr. & Kaye, A.L. (1993, May). *Differential diagnosis of chronic depressive disorders*. Paper presented at the 146th annual meeting of the American Psychiatric Association, San Francisco.

McCullough, J.P., Jr. Kornstein, S.G., Belyea-Caldwell, S., et al. (1996). Differential diagnosis of chronic depressive disorders. *Psychiatric Clinics of North American, 19*, 55–71.

McCullough, J.P., Jr. McCune, K.J., Kaye, A.L., et al. (1994a). Comparison of a community dysthymia sample at screening with a matched group of nondepressed community controls. *Journal of Nervous and Mental Disease, 182*, 402–407.

McCullough, J.P., Jr. McCune, K.J., Kaye, A.L., et al. (1994b). One-year prospective replication study of an untreated sample of community dysthymic subjects. *Journal of Nervous and Mental Disease, 182*, 396-401.

McCullough, J.P., Jr. Roberts, W.C., McCune, K.J., et al. (1994). Social adjustment, coping style, and clinical course among DSM-III-R community unipolar depressives. *Depression, 2*, 36–42.

McCullough, J.P., Jr. & Southard, L.D. (1972). A study hall program within a county foster home setting. *Journal of Counseling Psychology, 19*, 112–116.

Meichenbaum, D. (1971). Examination of model characteristics in reducing avoidance behavior. *Journal of Personality and Social Psychology, 17*, 298–307.

Messer, S.B., & Wampold, B.E. (2002). Let's face facts: Common factors are more potent than specific therapy ingredients. *Clinical Psychology: Science and Practice, 9*, 21–25.

Mischel, W. (1973). Toward a cognitive social learning reconceptualization of personality. *Psychological Review, 80*, 252–283.

Mitchell, S.A. (1988). *Relational concepts in psychoanalysis*. Cambridge, MA: Harvard University Press.

Money, J. (1992). *The Kaspar Hauser syndrome of "psychosocial dwarfism": Deficient structural, intellectual, and social growth induced by child abuse*. Buffalo, NY: Prometheus Books.

Money, J., Annecillo, C., & Hutchinson, J.W. (1985). Forensic and family psychiatry in abuse dwarfism: Munchausen's syndrome by proxy, atonement, and addiction to abuse. *Journal of Sex and Marital Therapy, 11*, 30–40.

Nannis, E.D. (1988). Cognitive-developmental differences in emotional understanding. In E.D. Nannis & P.A. Cowan (Eds.), *Developmental psychopathology and its treatment* (pp. 31–49). San Francisco: Jossey-Bass.

Nay, W.R. (2004). *Taking charge of anger.* New York: Guilford Press.

Nemeroff, C.B., Heim, C.M., Thase, M.E., et al. (2003). Differential responses to psychotherapy versus pharmacotherapy in patients with chronic forms of major depression and childhood trauma. *Proceedings of the National Academy of Sciences, 100*, 14293–14296.

Nisbett, R.E., & Wilson, T.D. (1977). Telling more than we can know: Verbal reports on mental processes. *Psychological Review, 84*, 231–259.

Norcross, J.C. (Ed.) (2002). *Psychotherapy relationships that work: therapist contributions and responsiveness to patients.* Oxford, UK: Oxford University Press.

Norcross, J.D. (2001). Purposes, processes, and products of the task force on empirically supported therapy relationships. *Psychotherapy: Theory, Research, Practice, Training, 38*, 345–356.

Orlinsky, D.E., & Howard, K.I. (1986). The psychological interior of psychotherapy: Explorations with the therapy sessions reports. In L.S.

Paul, G.L. (1967). Outcome research in psychotherapy. *Journal of Consulting Psychology, 31*, 109–118.

Piaget, J. (1981). Intelligence and affectivity: Their relationship during child development. Palo Alto, CA: Annual Reviews. (Original work published 1954)

Piaget, J. (1967). Six psychological studies (D. Elkind, Ed.). New York: Random House. (Original work published 1964)

Piaget, J. (1926). The language and thought of the child. New York: Harcourt, Brace. (Original work published 1923)

Polanyi, M. (1968). Logic and psychology. *American Psychologist, 23*, 27–43.

Polanyi, M. (1976). Tacit knowing. In M.H. Marx & F.E. Goodson (Eds.), *Theories in contemporary psychology* (2nd ed., pp. 330–434). New York: Macmillan.

Prouty, G. (1994). *Theoretical evolutions in person-centered/experiential therapy: Applications to schizophrenic and retarded psychoses.* Westport CT: Praeger.

Reichard, G.A. (1938). Social life. In F. Boas (Ed.), *General anthropology* (pp. 409–486). Boston: Health.

Riso, L.P., Miyatake, R.K., & Thase, M.E. (2002). The search for determinants of chronic depression: A review of six factors. *Journal of Affective Disorders, 70*, 103–115.

Robitschek, C.G., & McCarthy, P.R. (1991). Prevalence of counselor self-reference in the therapeutic dyad. *Journal of Counseling and Development, 69*, 218–221.

Rogers, C.R. (1940, December). *Newer concepts of psychotherapy.* Paper presented at the Minnesota Chapter of Psi Chi, Department of Psychology, University of Minnesota, Minneapolis–St. Paul.

Rogers, C.R. (1942). *Counseling and psychotherapy: Newer concepts in practice.* Boston: Houghton Mifflin.

Rogers, C.R. (1951). *Client-centered therapy: Its current practice implications, and theory.* Boston: Houghton Mifflin.

Rogers, C.R. (1959). A theory of therapy, personality, and interpersonal relationships as developed in the client-centered framework. In E. Koch (Ed.), *Psychology: A study of a science* (Vol. 3, p. 251). New York: McGraw-Hill.

Rogers, C.R. (1978). The formative tendency. *Journal of Humanistic Psychology, 18,* 23–26.

Rogers, C.R., Gendlin, E.T., Kiesler, D.N., & Truax, C.B. (1967). The findings in brief. In C.R. Rogers (Ed.), *The therapeutic relationship and its impact: A study of psychotherapy with schizophrenics* (pp. 73–93). Madison, WI: University of Wisconsin Press.

Rosenzweig, S. (1936). Some implicit common factors in diverse methods of psychotherapy: "At last the dodo said, 'Everybody has won and all must have prizes.' " *American Journal of Orthopsychiatry, 6,* 412–415.

Rounsaville, B.J., Carroll, K.M., & Onken, L.S. (2001). A stage model of behavioral therapies research: Getting started and moving from Stage I. *Clinical Psychology: Science and Practice, 8,* 133–142.

Safran, J.D. (1993a). Breaches in the therapeutic alliance: An arena for negotiating authentic relatedness. *Psychotherapy: Theory, Research, and Practice, 30,* 11–24.

Safran, J.D. (1993b). The therapeutic alliance as a transtheoretical phenomenon: Definitional and conceptual issues. *Journal of Psychotherapy Integration, 3,* 33–49.

Safran, J.D. (1998). *Widening the scope of cognitive therapy.* Northvale, NJ: Jason Aronson.

Safran, J.D., & Muran, J.C. (1995). Resolving therapeutic alliance ruptures: Diversity and integration. *In Session: Psychotherapy in Practice, 1,* 81–82.

Safran, J.D., & Muran, J.C. (1996). The resolution of ruptures in the therapeutic alliance. *Journal of Consulting and Clinical Psychology, 64,* 447–458.

Safran, J.D., & Muran, J.C. (2000). *Negotiating the therapeutic alliance: A relational treatment guide.* New York: Guilford Press.

Safran, J.D., Muran, J.C., & Samstag, L.W. (1994). Resolving therapeutic alliance ruptures: A task analytic investigation. In A.O. Horvath & L.S. Greenberg (Eds.), *The Working Alliance: Theory, Research, and Practice* (pp. 225–255). New York: Wiley.

Safran, J.D., & Segal, Z.V. (1996). *Interpersonal process in cognitive therapy* (2nd ed.). New York: Basic Books. Northvale, NJ: Jason Aronson.

Sartre, J.P. (1961). *No exit and three other plays.* New York: Vintage Books.

Schachter, S. (1978). The interaction of cognitive and physiological determinants of emotional state. In L. Berkowitz (Ed.), *Cognitive theories in social psychology* (pp. 401–432). New York: Academic Press.

Schachter, S., & Singer, J.E. (1962). Cognitive, social, and physiological determinants of emotional state. *Psychological Review, 69,* 379–399.

Schaefer, K.L. (2004). *Adult attachment as a developmental mediator for chronic depression.* Master's thesis, Virginia Commonwealth University, Richmond, VA.

Schore, A.N. (1996). The experience-dependent maturation of a regulatory system in the orbital prefrontal cortex and the origin of developmental psychopathology. *Development and Psychopathology, 8,* 59–87.

Seligman, M.E.P. (1995). The effectiveness of psychotherapy: The *Consumer Reports* study. *American Psychologist, 50,* 965–974.

Shapiro, M.B. (1961). A method of measuring psychological changes specific to the individual psychiatric patient. *British Journal of Medical Psychology, 34,* 151–155.

Shapiro, M.B. (1964). The measurement of clinically relevant variables. *Journal of Psychosomatic Research, 8,* 245–254.

Shapiro, M.B., Litman, G.K., Nias, D.K.B., & Hendry, E.R. (1973). A clinician's approach to experimental research. *Journal of Clinical Psychology,* April, 165–169.

Skinner, B.F. (1948). *Walden II.* New York: Macmillan.

Skinner, B.F. (1953). *Science and human behavior.* New York: Macmillan.

Skinner, B.F. (1968). *The technology of teaching.* New York: Appleton-Century-Crofts.

Smith, M., & Glass, G.V. (1977). Meta-analyses of psychotherapy outcome studies. *American Psychologist*, *32*, 752–760.

Spanier, G.B. (1976). Measuring marital adjustment: New scales for assessing the quality of marriage and similar dyads. *Journal of Marriage and the Family*, *38*, 15–28.

Spitz, R. (1946). Hospitalism: A follow-up report on investigation described in Volume I, 1945. *Psychoanalytic Study of the Child*, *2*, 113–117.

Spotnitz, H. (1969). *Modern psychoanalysis of the schizophrenic patient*. New York: Grune & Stratton.

Sterba, R. (1934). The fate of the ego in analytic therapy. *International Journal of Psycho-Analysis*, *15*, 117–126.

Sterba, R. (1940). The dynamics of the dissolution of the transference resistance. *Psychoanalytic Quarterly*, *9*, 363–379.

Sullivan, H.S. (1953). *The interpersonal theory of psychiatry*. New York: Norton.

Sullivan, H.S. (1954). *The psychiatric interview*. New York: Norton.

Tansey, M., & Burke, W. (1991). *Understanding countertransference: From projective identification to empathy*. Hillsdale, NJ: Analytic Press.

Teyber, E. (1992). *Interpersonal process in psychotherapy: A guide for clinical training* (2nd ed.). Pacific Grove, CA: Brooks-Cole.

Todd, J., & Bohart, A.C. (1999). *Foundations of clinical and counseling psychology* (3rd ed.). New York: Longman.

Tracey, T.J., & Kokotovic, A.M. (1989). Factor structure of the Working Alliance Inventory. *Psychological Assessment*, *1*, 207–210.

Ullmann, L.P., & Krasner, L. (1965). *Case studies in behavior modification*. New York: Holt, Rinehart & Winston.

Van Balen, R. (1991). *On Rogers' and Gendlin's theory of personality change*. Private circulation. Paper presented at 2nd international conference on Person-Centered/Experimental Psychotherapy, Stirling, Scotland (pp. 8–17).

Wachtel, P.L. (1977). *Psychoanalysis and behavior therapy*. New York: Basic Books.

Wachtel, P.L. (1993). *Therapeutic Communication: Principles and Effective Practice*. New York: Guilford Press.

Ware, J.E., & Sherbourne, C.D. (1992). The MOS 36-Item Short Form Health Survey (SF-36): I. Conceptual framework and item selection. *Medical Care*, *30*, 473–483.

Winnicott, D.W. (1949). Hate in the countertransference. *International Journal of Psycho-Analysis*, *30*, 69–75.

Yalom, I.D. (1975). *Theory and practice of group psychotherapy* (2nd ed.). New York: Basic Books.

Zetzel, E. (1956). Current concepts of transference. *International Journal of Psycho-Analysis*, *37*, 369–376.

Zetzel, E. (1966). The analytic situation. In R.E. Litman (Ed.), *Psychoanalysis in America* (pp. 86–106). New York: International Universities Press.

Index

abandonment, 155, 156, 158
abstinence, 13
abuse, 112–15, 172–73
acceptance, Rogerian principle of, 15, 16, 17,
   18, 63, 81
acquisition learning
   CBASP model of, 145, 161
   of formal operational functioning, 58
   Interpersonal Discrimination Exercise
     provides, 133, 139
   to penetrate closed perceptual system, 118
   performance measures reflecting, 163–173
   in therapy, 18–19
action tendency, 25, 26, 85, 88, 102, 110 (see
   also "pull[s]")
affective constriction, 63 (see also emotion)
affiliation dimension, 26
alliance, see therapeutic alliance
American Psychological Association, 1
anger, 99–100, 118, 119 (see also patient,
   hostile)
anonymity, 13, 30
anxiety
   in patient, 142
   in therapist, 111
attachment bonds, 45, 46, 47, 131, 148,
   163
asocial response, 29
assessment data, 29, 47, 166,
   172
authenticity versus manipulation, 105

Bailey, Kent G., 33–36, 47
Bandura, Albert, 3–4, 7, 57, 58
Barret, M. S., 7
Beck, A. T., 61, 65
Beck Depression Inventory–II (BDI-II), 112,
   147, 161

behavior(al)
   adaptive, teaching, 4, 7 (see also formal
     operational functioning)
   consequences of, 42, 46, 50, 53, 57, 58, 65,
     74, 81, 92, 96, 103–4, 115, 163, 164, 166
     (see also "consequating"; contingent
     personal responsivity)
   maladaptive, types of patient in-session,
     167–68
   modifying/modification strategies, 23–24, 59,
     61, 63, 72–73, 82
   rigidity, 82
   therapy movement, 5, 36
   target, 145, 168, 170, 171
"beneficial uncertainty," 29
biopsychosocial model, 5–6
blank screen
   in Kieslerian approach, 30, 61
   in psychoanalysis, 12, 24, 61
   in Rogerian psychotherapy, 16,
     61
Bleuler, Eugene, 31
Bloom, Rube, 85
borderline personality disorder, 34
Borys, D., 61
boundaries, personal/interpersonal, 62–63, 76,
   77
Bowlby, J., 131
brief supportive psychotherapy (BSP)
Bridges, N. A., 7
Brown, G. W., 43

case examples
   of abuse, 112–15
   of contingent feedback to patient, 63–66, 68,
     86–90
   of creating dissonance, 90–94
   of defensive humor, 100–104

case examples (*Cont.*)
    of disciplined personal involvement, 47–53,
      83–85
    of extreme perceptual disconnection, 119–122
    of grieving cancer patient, 108–111
    of Interpersonal Discrimination Exercise,
      134–158
    of kinship psychotherapy, 34–36
    of seductive behavior, 104–8
    of self-monitoring, 66–68
    of success, 115–19
    of therapist becoming problem for patient,
      94–96, 103
Cashdan, Sheldon, 22
causal theory conclusions (CTC), 130, 134,
    135–36, 141–42, 147–48, 153–55, 171,
    173
CBASP
    acquisition model of therapy, 145, 161
    agenda of, 40
    instructed in/prepared for methodology of, 72,
      73, 82
    pedagogy of, 58–60, 111, 122
    rationale of, 58–60, 70, 122
    Stage II research, 162–63, 173–74
    unidirectional contingencies of, 61, 62
censure, professional, 62
change task/variable/effect, 13, 30, 31, 53, 59,
    100
childhood adversity, 42–44
choice point, 107–8
chronically depressed patient
    challenges of treating, 40–41
    depression of, *see* separate entry
    goals of treating, 46–47, 74
    isolation of, 45–47
    limitations of, 38, 45, 46, 58, 118, 152
    psychopathology of, 40–45
Cicchetti, D., 42, 43, 124
circumplex (Kiesler's), 25
client-centered model, 14 (*see also*
    person–centered psychotherapy)
Clinical Psychology: Science and Practice, 21
code of conduct, 1
cognitive
    –emotional limitations of patients, 38, 45, 46,
      58, 118
    –emotional model of functioning, 124–29
    restructuring, 124
Cognitive Behavioral Analysis System of
    Psychotherapy, *see* CBASP
complementarity, 25–27, 85 (*see also* "pull[s]")
conditioning, 13

conduct disorder, 129
congruence, 17, 30
"consequating"
    in-session behavior, 4, 5, 48, 57, 67, 68, 71,
      75, 81, 94–95, 103, 118–19, 122, 161
    see also behavior, consequences of;
      contingent personal responsivity
consequence recognition, measuring, 164–67
contact functions, 31, 32
contingencies
    disciplined personal involvement as, 58,
      63–66
    interaction methodology of, 71
    personal responses as, 3, 7
    unidirectional, of CBASP, 61, 62
contingent personal responsivity (CPR)
    assessing, 161, 167–171, 175
    core CBASP technique, 81
    see also "consequating"; Interpersonal
      Discrimination Exercise
control
    dimension, 26
    social, bidirectional view of, 58
coping patterns, 130
Coping Survey Questionnaire, 66, 94
countertransference
    avoiding, 65
    as learned expectancy, 24
    in metacommunication, 27–28
    objective versus subjective, 4, 29, 62–63

decoders, 25, 26
denial, 15
depression, chronic
    "double," 47–53, 86, 97, 104, 135, 140
    early-onset, 42–43, 86, 91, 97, 104, 119, 128,
      129, 134, 146, 152
    late-onset, 44–45, 100, 108, 111, 115
    refractory nature of the disorder, 122, 127
deprivation (emotional), 148
Dewey, John, 14
diagnosis, eclipsed in Rogerian and alliance
    traditions, 22
directive therapy model, 15–16
disciplined personal involvement
    assessing the efficacy of, 160–175
    case example of, 47–53
    as change vehicle, 18, 53
    to differentiate therapist from significant
      others, 50–52, 75 (*see also* Interpersonal
      Discrimination Exercise)
    distinguished from therapeutic
      self–disclosure, 7–8

goals of, 4, 7, 57–59, 73
    limited to chronically depressed patients, 5, 77
    mediating effects of, researching, 173–74
    to modify/"consequate" behavior, *see*
        "consequating"
    patient change, researching, 162–63
    population suited for, 5, 77
    requirements of, 4
    scenarios describing, 1–3
    trainees' issues and questions regarding, 59,
        61–68, 69–70
    training in, 68–76 (*see also* separate entry)
discomfort
    of disciplined personal involvement for
        therapist, 73, 74–75, 99
    in patient, 139, 143, 145
discrimination, *see* Interpersonal Discrimination
    Exercise
dismantling design, 175
dissonance, 93, 94
Durbin, C. E., 43
Dyadic Adjustment Scale (DAS), 161
dysthymic disorder, 43, 86, 88, 91, 97, 104, 119,
    135, 140

egocentricity, 41–42, 58, 128, 152
emotion(al)
    constricted, 127
    discriminating positive from negative, 133–34
    dysfunctional control of, 42
    negative, and significant others, 132
    regulation, 126–27
empathy/empathic behavior
    inability to generate, 42
    modeling, 4, 5, 7, 17, 30
empowerment, of patient, 115, 119
encoder, 25, 26
encoding strategies, 25
environment
    connect patient to, 7
    contingency, creating, 85
    eliminated in psychoanalysis, 13
    perceptual (dis)connection (from) to, 46, 50,
        58, 81, 113, 119–122, 125, 128, 129, 145,
        151, 159, 164
    Person x Environment connection, 50, 58, 63,
        66, 72, 113, 125
ethical principles/ethicality, 1, 73
exhibitionism, sexual, 104–8
expectancies
    learned, 24, 131
    transference, 26
"experiencing gap," 30

exposure
    non-CBASP types of, 151–52
    of patients to contingency responses, 90, 159

failure to thrive, 124
flooding, 74
forgetting, 19
formal operational functioning/behavior, 42, 53,
    58, 60, 126, 127, 139
Frank and Ernest, 82
Freire, Paulo, 60, 111
Freud, Sigmund, 12–13

Gendlin, Eugene, 30, 31
generalization, 13, 118 (*see also* learning,
    transfer of)
generalized treatment effects (GTEs; variables),
    19, 31, 161, 173–74
Global Assessment of Functioning (GAF), 45
Green, Meredith W., 81
Greenberg, J., 24
grief, unacknowledged, 108–111
growth
    as autonomous, 16, 17
    of therapist–patient relationship, 133–34
Guidano, V. F., 131

habits, 19
helplessness/hopelessness
    in case examples, 94–96, 109, 111, 116
    consequences of, 122
    hallmark of chronic depression, 42–43, 44, 45
    hopelessness-to-hope moment, 92, 158
    victory over, 46, 118, 119
Hill, C. A., 6, 7
histrionic personality disorder, 104
Hoffer, A., 11–12, 18, 23, 24
Holahan, C. J., 44
Horwitz, J. A., 44
hostility
    measuring, 170
    patient, 71–72, 96–100, 116
hot spots/seat, 48, 50, 95, 131, 132, 136, 142,
    149, 152, 155, 173
Hyman, S. E., 160

Impact Message Inventory (IMI), 25, 66, 85, 91,
    97, 101, 105, 109, 113, 116
information, overload/preemptory provision of,
    39
insight, 124
interactional psychotherapy model, 22
"interactive matrix," 24

internal consistency/inconsistency of rating
    patterns, 165, 166, 172
interpersonal
    act (Kieslerian), 24–25
    action–counteraction pattern, 57
    impact, 27–28 (*see also* Impact Message
        Inventory)
    psychology research, 23–30
    rejection, in Rogerian model, 15, 16–17
    theme, 130, 136, 142, 148, 155
Interpersonal Discrimination Exercise (IDE)
    applying, 50–52, 53
    demonstration of the method, 135–158
    described, 128–29, 161, 172
    goals of, 159, 171
    healing and, 132
    measuring, 171–73
    performance goals of, 123–24
    predict treatment outcome, 175
    therapist responses, 75
interpretations, 5, 13, 126
intimacy
    between patient and significant other, 132,
        148, 155
    between patient and therapist, 45–46
introjection, 15

"jumping the gun," 39

Kendler, K. S., 43
Kiesler, Donald J., 23–30, 36, 66
kinship psychotherapy, 33–36
Klerman, G. L., 61, 65, 66
Knox, S., 6, 7
Kraemer, H. C., 161, 162

Lazarus, Richard S., 126
learning (principles)
    absent in psychoanalysis, 13
    absent in therapeutic alliance tradition, 23
    acquisition, *see* separate entry
    agenda of CBASP, 40
    basis of disciplined personal involvement, 7
    discrimination, *see* Interpersonal
        Discrimination Exercise
    disengaged from psychotherapy, 5
    environment, creating, 60, 82
    imitation, 3
    inhibited by overload, 39–40
    measuring, 19
    operationalize goals of, 19
    outcome related to, 19
    patient, *see* patient learning

performance data and, 19
    in therapeutic alliance tradition, 22
    transfer of, 13, 19, 53, 59, 62, 76, 82, 124,
        131, 146, 159, 163
Leary, T., 24
limit setting, 62
literality, usefulness of, 99–100
Lizardi, H., 43
loneliness, 146

mainstream, out of, 69
Manning, E. A., 7, 77
mastery, interpersonal, 118
matching functional capability, 47
maturity, 4, 63
May, Rollo, 123, 124
medication, in case examples, 112, 115–16, 119,
        146, 163
memories
    of abuse/trauma, 128, 151
    interpersonal responsivity and, 127
    in Significant Other History, 129, 133
Mercer, Johnny, 85
metacommunication
    overview of, 24–25
    technique/goal of, 27–30
mind reading, 119
mind–set, novel, 122
Minnesota Multiphasic Personality Inventory
        (MMPI), 161
minority groups, 34
"mismatching" exercise, 130, 138–39, 143, 151
        (*see also* Significant Other History)
mistakes, 123, 128, 132, 135, 136, 139,
        172
modeling
    effect of self-disclosure, 7
    learning principle of, 3, 7
    skills, 70
motivation, 52–53, 122, 145

National Institute of Mental Health, 162
needs
    patient needs determining therapeutic
        approach, 7
    in Prouty's pretherapy approach, 33
    therapists', 62–63
neutrality
    absent from disciplined personal involvement,
        4, 60, 84
    consequences of, 61, 77
    differing amounts of, 36
    as impossible, 23

in psychoanalysis, 13, 24
in Rogerian and alliance traditions, 22, 23
nondirective psychotherapy model, 14, 15–16
    (*see also* person-centered psychotherapy)
nonresponders, 163, 173, 174
Norcross, J. C., 6–7, 22
normalize, patient behavior, 7, 111

obsessive–compulsive personality disorder, 119
one-person psychology, 23
operant design, 10, 160
operationalization
    of goals, 19
    of patient pathological behavior, 168–69
    of therapist consequating responses, 169
outcome (goals)
    assessing, 174
    desired, 142, 148
    kinship, degree of, in relation to, 36
    learning and, 19
    patient–therapist relationship related to, 23
overestimation errors, 38–40, 47, 53

pacing the patient, 40, 47, 60, 85, 90, 122, 139
paired comparison procedure, 164–65, 172
paleopsychology, 33
"parallel talk," 121
patient(s)
    chronically depressed, *see* chronically
        depressed patient
    compliant, 113–15, 140, 142
    effects of self-isclosure on, 7
    hostile/angry, dealing with, 71–72, 96–100,
        116
    instructed in/prepared for CBASP
        methodology, 72, 73, 82
    interpersonal style of, 26, 107
    kinship, need for, 34, 36
    label, 5–6
    language of, using, 122
    learning, *see* patient learning
    needs, *see* separate entry
    noncompliant, 65
    nonresponders, characteristics of, 163, 173,
        174
    overwhelmed, by therapist responses, 65–68
    responsibility, 59, 60, 111
    retarded psychotic, 31
    role inequality of, 18
    role in psychoanalysis, 12, 24
    schizophrenic, 31
    –therapist relationship, *see* patient–therapist
        relationship

patient learning
    concept of, 5
    goals, 40
    ignored in Rogerian psychotherapy, 17–20
    in Prouty's pretherapy approach, 31, 47
Patient Performance Rating Scale (PPRF), 167,
    175
patient–therapist relationship
    abusing, 159
    attachment bonds in, 46–47, 52
    as cocreators (Kieslerian), 24
    experiential dimension of, 21, 30–31
    goals of, rethinking, 70, 76
    in kinship psychotherapy, 34–36, 47
    outcome related to, 23
    power differential in, 18
    reciprocal interactive process of, 25, 47, 57,
        69, 96
    self-disclosure affects quality of, 6–7
    separatist model of, 13
    status of, in Rogerian psychotherapy, 18, 22
    in therapeutic alliance tradition, 20–23
Paul, G. L., 160
pedagogy of CBASP, 58–60, 111, 122
Pedagogy of the Oppressed, 60
perceived functionality, 42, 46, 81, 115, 164,
    167
perceptual patterns
    modifying refractory, 8
    Person x Environment, *see* environment
personal involvement
    contingent, 85–122
    decision to employ, 36
    in kinship psychotherapy, 33, 36
    pioneers of, 30–36
    in Prouty's pretherapy approach, 31
    rethinking the issue, 3–5, 70, 73
    taboo of/proscriptions against, 5, 6, 8, 11, 22,
        33, 36, 53, 59, 61
    unconditional positive regard versus, 14
    see also disciplined personal involvement
Personal Questionnaire (PQ), 164–67, 171
personal responsivity, *see* contingent personal
        responsivity; disciplined personal
        involvement; personal involvement
person-centered (Rogerian) psychotherapy,
    14–20
Piaget, J., 41, 42, 124, 129
PQ Patient Scoring Worksheet, 164, 165, 172
PQ Summary Data Sheet, 166, 172
preoperational functioning, 41–42, 45, 58, 121,
    123, 124–26, 128, 143, 145, 146
pretherapy method of Prouty, 30–33

Prouty, Garry, 30–33, 36, 47
psychoanalysis, overview of, 12–13
psychosocial impairment, 45
Psychotherapy, 22
Psychotherapy Bulletin, 76
Psychotherapy:
    Theory/Recearch/Practice/Training, 22
"pull(s)," for complementarity
    in case examples, 91–92, 94, 101, 115
    figure of, 28
    inferred from Impact Message Inventory,
        85–86, 100
    observing covert, 26, 71
    for therapist to take charge, 39, 109
    therapist responses to, 76, 109

randomized clinical trials (RCTs), 162
rationale of CBASP, 58–60, 70, 122
reinforcement, negative, 52, 68, 133, 143
reliability
    estimate (grand), 166, 167, 172
    test, of transference hypothesis construction,
        75
research(ing)
    interpersonal psychology, 23–30
    mediating effects, 173–74
    self-disclosure, 6–8
    single–case, 31, 160
    Stage II CBASP, 162–63, 173–74
    Stage III, 162
    therapeutic alliance, 7, 20–23, 61
"resource deterioration" model, 44
response versus reaction, 4
Riso, L. P., 44
Rogerian psychotherapy, *see* person–centered
Rogers, Carl R., 13–20, 22, 23, 30, 31, 36, 61, 63
role
    observer, 96
    participant, 103
    therapist, *see* therapist role
Rounsaville, B. J., 162

Safran, J. D., 7, 21, 22, 23
Schachter, Stanley, 126
Schaefer, Katherine L., 38
self-actualization, 14, 17
self-disclosure
    distinguished from therapeutic
        self–disclosure, 7–8
    modeling effect of, 7
    reactions to, 46, 61
    research, 6–8
    and significant others, 132, 142

self-monitoring, 38, 39, 66–68
self-report methodology, 164
self-structure, 15–16
self-talk, 126
self-worth, 44
shaping, 13
Shapiro, M. B., 164
Significant Other History, 48, 50, 129–130, 131,
    141–42, 147–48, 153–55, 171
significant others, 129 (*see also* Interpersonal
    Discrimination Exercise; Significant Other
    History)
Situational Analysis
    in case examples, 63, 66, 94, 102, 118, 142,
        148
    core CBASP technique, 57, 81
    performance measures of, 161, 163–67
    self-administering, 163, 167
single–case research, 31, 160
Skinner, B. F., 3, 7, 111, 123
"snapshot" view of reality, 41, 45, 127, 128
social-philosophical optimism, 14
Spitz, R., 42, 124
Spotnitz, H., 62
stimulus value, 4, 26, 66, 71, 73, 85, 164
Sullivan, Harry Stack, 23, 24
supervision, 70, 72, 75

tacit knowledge, 25
task-focused stance, 29
"talking cure," 12
therapeutic alliance
    preceding disciplined personal involvement,
        73
    research tradition, 7, 20–23, 61
therapeutic rupture, in the alliance tradition,
    22–23
therapist
    as comrade, 47, 60
    dependence on, 62
    differentiating from significant others, 4,
        50–52, 53, 70, 72, 159, 171 (*see also*
        Interpersonal Discrimination Exercise)
    emotional responses to patients, taking
        seriously, 70–71, 73, 76
    genuineness of, 17
    interpersonal "stimulus value" of, 4,
        73
    interpersonal (evoking) styles of, 11, 28,
        71
    in the line of fire, 72, 76
    kinship and, 33–34
    optimal IMI profile of, 86, 87

–patient relationship, *see* patient–therapist
relationship
reactions to disciplined personal involvement
training, 69–76
role, *see* therapist role
rules, 40
training, 68–76 (*see also* separate entry)
vulnerability, 69, 72, 77
"walking with" patient, 122
therapist role (enactment)
in CBASP, 3–4, 57, 82–85
characteristics of, 82–85
limited, 63
novel, 32–33, 75, 122
in psychoanalysis, 12–13
in Rogerian psychotherapy, 16–20
take-charge, 39
thinking
causal, 38, 122
errors (Beckian), 65
precausal/prelogical, 41
tracking, 66, 76 (*see also* self-monitoring)
training (CBASP)
personal issues with, 69–70
phases/stages of, 70–73
problems faced and resolved, 73–75

transference, 24, 26
avoiding, 65
CBASP view of, 131
hypothesis, 48, 50, 75, 130–32, 132, 136, 142,
148, 155, 171, 173
problem, 124–25
trauma
categories of, in CBASP, 132
early-onset depression and, 43–44
extent of, 38
healing via disciplined personal involvement,
4, 5, 7, 38, 46–47, 57, 73
two-person psychology, 23, 24, 61

unconditional positive regard, 14, 17, 18, 30, 63,
66, 81
universality, sense of, 7

variables
dependent, 19, 161–62
generalized treatment effects, *see* separate
entry
mediating, 158, 162, 173, 174, 175
moderator, 161, 162, 163, 174
patient, 162–63
psychopathology, 21, 23, 38, 40–45, 53, 86